Being Missional, *Becoming* Missional

Evangelical Missiological Society Monograph Series

Anthony Casey, Allen Yeh, Mark Kreitzer, and Edward L. Smither
SERIES EDITORS

———————————

A Project of the Evangelical Missiological Society
www.emsweb.org

Being Missional, *Becoming* Missional

A Biblical-Theological Study of the Missional Conversion of the Church

Banseok Cho

FOREWORD BY
Lalsangkima Pachuau

◆PICKWICK *Publications* • Eugene, Oregon

BEING MISSIONAL, BECOMING MISSIONAL
A Biblical-Theological Study of the Missional Conversion of the Church

Evangelical Missiological Society Monograph Series 11

Copyright © 2021 Banseok Cho. All rights reserved. Except for brief quotations in critical publications or reviews, no part of this book may be reproduced in any manner without prior written permission from the publisher. Write: Permissions, Wipf and Stock Publishers, 199 W. 8th Ave., Suite 3, Eugene, OR 97401.

Pickwick Publications
An Imprint of Wipf and Stock Publishers
199 W. 8th Ave., Suite 3
Eugene, OR 97401

www.wipfandstock.com

PAPERBACK ISBN: 978-1-7252-9293-2
HARDCOVER ISBN: 978-1-7252-9294-9
EBOOK ISBN: 978-1-7252-9295-6

Cataloguing-in-Publication data:

Names: Cho, Banseok, author. | Pachuau, Lalsangkima, foreword.

Title: Being missional, becoming missional : a biblical-theological study of the missional conversion of the church / by Banseok Cho ; foreword by Lalsangkima Pachuau.

Description: Eugene, OR: Pickwick Publications, 2021 | Evangelical Missiological Society Monograph Series 11 | Includes bibliographical references and index.

Identifiers: ISBN 978-1-7252-9293-2 (paperback) | ISBN 978-1-7252-9294-9 (hardcover) | ISBN 978-1-7252-9295-6 (ebook)

Subjects: LCSH: Mission of the church. | Holy Spirit. | Missions—History—Early church, ca. 30–600. | Missions—Biblical teaching. | Missions—Theory.

Classification: BV2073 C56 2021 (print) | BV2073 (ebook)

11/30/21

Dedicated to all who supported, inspired,
and guided me during my PhD studies

Contents

List of Figures | ix
Foreword by Lalsangkima Pachuau | xi
Acknowledgments | xiii

1. Introduction | 1
   A. Background to the Study 1
   B. Literary Background of the Study 3
   C. Statement of the Problem 7
   D. Research Claim and Significance of the Study 7
   E. Definition of Key Terms 8
   F. Hermeneutical Approach 13
   G. Theological Framework 14
   H. Research Questions 19
   I. Delimitations 19

2. Israel's Encounter with Yahweh and Her Missional Conversion | 21
   A. Yahweh Has a Missional Intention in His Liberation of Israel 22
   B. Yahweh Calls Israel to Participate in His Mission 25
   C. Yahweh Gives the Missional and Holistic Law to Israel 54
   D. Yahweh Dwells in the Midst of Israel 61
   E. Yahweh Wrestles with Israel 71
   F. Yahweh Encounters Israel through Prophets 75
   G. Summary and Conclusion of the Chapter 84

3. The Disciples' Encounter with Jesus and Their Missional Conversion | 88
   A. Jesus Continues the Father's Work of the Missional Conversion of Israel 89
   B. Jesus Focuses on Israel in His Earthly Ministry 95

C. Jesus Bridges Israel's Mission and the Disciples'
　　　　Gentile Mission   97
　　D. Jesus Shapes the Disciples as a *Radical* Contrast People   102
　　E. Jesus Shapes the Disciples as an *Inclusive* Contrast People   114
　　F. The Risen Jesus Rebuilds and Expands the Disciples'
　　　　Missionary Vocation   124
　　G. The Crucified Jesus Intensifies and Expands the Disciple's
　　　　Missionary Vocation   137
　　H. Summary and Conclusion of the Chapter   142

4. **The Earliest Church's Encounter with the Holy Spirit
and Its Missional Conversion | 147**
　　A. The Triune God Continues to Shape His People
　　　　for His Mission   148
　　B. The Holy Spirit Empowers and Transforms
　　　　the Earliest Church   155
　　C. The Holy Spirit Shapes the Earliest Church
　　　　in a *Crosscultural* Context   167
　　D. The Holy Spirit Shapes the Earliest Church
　　　　in an *Intercultural* Context   176
　　E. Summary and Conclusion of the Chapter   198

5. **Conclusion | 202**
　　A. Main Thesis   202
　　B. Four Foundational Components of the Church's
　　　　Missional Conversion   203
　　C. The Trinitarian Aspect of the Church's Missional Conversion   206
　　D. Other Aspects of the Church's Missional Conversion   211
　　E. Contributive Factors for the Church's Missional Conversion   215
　　F. Four Primary Resources for the Church's Missional Conversion   218

Bibliography | 223
Scripture Index | 239

Figures

Figure 1: Motif of the missionary conversion of God's people in biblical contexts | 14

Figure 2: The priestly formation of the nations through Israel's priesthood | 35

Figure 3: The overall contours of the church's missional conversion | 205

Foreword

IN MY YEARS OF supervising doctoral research works, I've been enamored by the variety of scholarly gifts and approaches students bring. Dr. Banseok Cho's analytical faculty, his gift of logical argumentation, and his precision in articulating his points made him stand out among his peers. That is clearly displayed in this comprehensive and well-argued work, which was originally submitted as his PhD dissertation that I was honored to supervise.

Framed within what has become a popular approach to the theology of mission in recent years, namely restoration theology, the book provides a biblical overview of how the call to God's mission is realized through the conversion process. God's covenantal call on Israel to be his people in the Old Testament is renewed in Jesus Christ and climaxed in his eschatological saving work at the cross and the resurrection. The eschatological saving work of Christ is for the restoration of wayward Israel to God's mission and for the inclusion of Gentiles in God's redemptive mission. Thus, in Christ, God claims the whole humanity and the entire creation to his kingdom. The book sought out how the Bible presents God's work of transforming his people to become his missionaries for the redemption of the world. It does this by constructing a biblical theology of "missional conversion." God's work of transforming his people and calling them to his mission is shown through three major episodic dealings in the Bible: Israel's encounter with Yahweh (God the Father), the disciples' encounter with Jesus (God the Son), and the earliest church's encounter with the Holy Spirit (God the Sprit). The triune work of the Triune God is carefully crafted as a theological model for the church to see and emulate.

Seeing God's dealings with Israel as both a precursor and an archetype for God's calling of the church, the book shows how the different aspects of God's mission meet in Jesus Christ and how that establishes the church in mission. God's mission with Israel before the incarnation of Christ portrays the mission of God the Father. which continues in Jesus the Son. In his ministry, Jesus Christ intensified that mission; in his death and resurrection, Jesus Christ fulfilled God's call of Israel to his mission and brought salvation for all. Through his ministry of discipleship, Jesus laid the foundation of the church as the disciples continued the missionary calling of Israel. The earliest church arose from Jesus' disciples, whose empowering experience of the Holy Spirit transformed them into a community of faith crossing the cultural, social, and territorial boundaries.

In the past few decades, we have seen some outstanding books on biblical theology of mission. Aside from other excellent theological works on mission, a line of biblical theology of mission has been building up starting with Johannes Blauw's survey of the biblical theology of mission in his *The Missionary Nature of the Church*. We've seen the full blossoming of the line of argument based on restoration theology in such books as Christopher Wright's *The Mission of God* and Michael Goheen's *A Light to the Nations*. Most of these have followed biblical-historical narration. What distinguished Cho's work here is the clear Trinitarian frame he skillfully employs to tell the conversion story of God's people. The focus on the transformative conversion of God's people for an active participation in his redemptive mission is particularly helpful at this time. This book deserves the attention of any serious student of the biblical theology of Christian mission in the twenty-first century.

LalsangkimaPachuau, PhD
J. W. Beeson Professor of Christian Mission and
Dean of Advanced Research Programs
Asbury Theological Seminary
Summer, 2021

Acknowledgments

I WISH TO EXPRESS my heartfelt gratitude to Pickwick Publications and Evangelical Missiological Society for the generous offer to publish my Ph.D. dissertation in the EMS Monographs Series. I am also deeply indebted to the following persons and institutions whom God has sent into my journey at Asbury Theological Seminary for the successful completion of my joyful but, at the same time, academically and spiritually challenging doctoral studies:

To Dr. Lalsangkima Pachuau, advisor and mentor, for his thoughtful and insightful guidance throughout my doctoral program;

To Dr. Howard A. Snyder and Dr. A. Sue Russell for their scholarly comments and suggestions in improving and finishing my Ph.D. dissertation;

To Rev. Dr. Andy Ponce, my dear friend and proofreader, for his dedicated service of proofreading my whole dissertation manuscript;

To Dr. Hyung Keun Choi for his recommendation letter for me when I applied to the Ph.D. program at Asbury Theological Seminary;

To my parents and parents-in-law for their constant prayer and support;

To Jungsoon Park and Kyuhaeng Huh, my aunt and uncle, and Sam's family and Philip's family, my cousins' families, for their generous financial support;

To Mrs. Jin S. Snowden, Mrs. Mrs. Dokhui Choi, Rev. Joungsik Park, Sunhee Lee, Kihyun Kim, Okhee Lee, and Youngkee Hong for their generous financial support;

To Myunghee Lee, my wife, for her self-sacrificing support during my whole doctoral studies at Asbury Theological Seminary;

To Lord Glory Church for the scholarship granted through the Korea Evangelical Holiness Church's Education Department;

To Youngnak Church of Los Angeles for their gracious scholarship;

To the Office of Advanced Research Programs at Asbury Theological Seminary for the thoughtful provision of academic facility, and scholarship helpful for the successful completion of my doctoral studies.

Had it not been for the grace and guidance of God, my doctoral study would have failed. It is God who truly deserves my highest appreciation for the successful completion of my doctoral studies at Asbury Theological Seminary.

Glory to God!

1

Introduction

A. Background to the Study

THE REDISCOVERY OF THE missionary nature of the church, which led to the birth of so-called missional (or missionary) ecclesiology, represents one of the major missiological breakthroughs of the twentieth century.[1] The conceptual crystallization of missional ecclesiology began to develop in the West, particularly with recognition of the post-Christian North American context as a mission field, with the term *missional church*.[2] The publication of *Missional Church* in 1998 introduced missional ecclesiology to the public, particularly in the West.[3] This book critically analyzes the North American Church and argues that the North American Church was driven by a Christendom mindset in post-Christian North America. The term "missional" was a key corrective to the North American Church, which understands its mission mainly as sending or supporting individual long-term missionaries for foreign missions. Based on two major theological concepts, *missio Dei* and the reign of God, the book proposed that the church itself is called to participate

---

1. For the historical development of a missional ecclesiology or the concept of missional church, see Laing, "Recovering Missional Ecclesiology," 17–21; Van Gelder and Zscheile, *Missional Church in Perspective*, 15–40; Nikolajsen, "Missional Church." While the analysis by Nikolajsen and Laing focus on historical events, Gelder's historical analysis is based more on major theological concepts defining the missional church. Literature on the historical analysis of a missional ecclesiology identify three major historical and theological factors that contributed to the conceptualization of a missional ecclesiology: the ecumenical movement, Lesslie Newbigin's theological contribution, and the Gospel and Our Culture Network (particularly its publication of *Missional Church*).

2. The authors of *Missional Church* address the radical change of North American culture and the decline and marginalization of the North American Church as the religious context of North America profoundly shifted from what is called Christendom, "becoming more pluralistic, more individualistic and more private." Guder, *Missional Church*, 1. This radical change of Western culture is already recognized by Lesslie Newbigin. See Newbigin, *Other Side of 1984*.

3. Guder, *Missional Church*.

in the mission of God. The authors of *Missional Church* argue that while the North American Church customarily views North America as largely Christianized, North America is culturally post-Christian and thus is also a mission field. The term *missional church* was a missiological proposal for mission in post-Christian North America.

While a missional ecclesiology decisively developed as a missiological proposal for the North American Church's mission in North America, the significance of missional ecclesiology is not limited to the Western post-Christian context since the foundational theological concepts for missional ecclesiology—particularly *missio Dei* and the kingdom of God—developed throughout the twentieth century in a global context by the global Church and not only in the Western context. First, the 1952 conference of the International Missionary Council, held in Willingen, Germany, initially proposed and accepted the concept of *missio Dei*, the theological foundation of missional ecclesiology.[4] This concept theologically anchored the integration of the church and mission, that the church is missionary by nature, called to participate in the mission of God.[5] The concept of missional ecclesiology emerged as a new understanding of the nature and vocation of the church in light of the concept of *missio Dei*. Second, the biblical motif of the kingdom of God was brought to the fore in discussions on the missiological issues at world mission conferences, particularly by delegates from the Majority World.[6] The biblical concept of the Kingdom of God served as the theological foundation for a holistic or comprehensive understanding of (the church's) mission by incorporating evangelism and social justice

---

4. The idea of mission as a divine initiative in the Willingen Conference is generally credited to Karl Barth who was known as one of the first to write of mission as an activity of God in 1932; John Flett challenges this historical connection. For Karl Barth's contribution to the Willingen Conference, see Bosch, *Transforming Mission*, 389–90; Snyder, *Yes in Christ*, 295–96. For Flett's antithetical argument concerning the historical connection between the Willingen Conference and Karl Barth, see Flett, *Witness of God*, 11–17.

5. While John Flett challenges the historical connection between Karl Barth and the Willengen Conference, Barth was the first, or nearly the first, to advocate the view of the church's mission as participation in God's mission. See Snyder, *Yes in Christ*, 295–320.

6. Van Gelder and Zscheile, *Missional Church in Perspective*, 27–29. The theme of the kingdom of God has actively been studied by biblical scholars since the late nineteenth century. However, missiological implications of the motif began to be suggested and recognized in mission theology only since the 1970s. Particularly, two world mission conferences stimulated missiological reflection on the kingdom of God: The International Congress on World Evangelization (1974) and the CWME (Commission on World Mission and Evangelism) meeting of the World Council of Churches (1980). For a survey of this historical development, see Tizon, *Transformation After Lausanne*, 37–50; Van Gelder and Zscheile, *Missional Church in Perspective*, 27–29.

together as essential parts of mission within the broader context of God's reign. The concept of missional ecclesiology views the church's nature and vocation in relation to the kingdom of God. For example, the authors of *Missional Church* regard the church as being called to represent the reign of God. Thus, in this sense, a missional ecclesiology has been developed by the global Church in the global context.

As the concept of missional ecclesiology or missional church began to be popularized, one critique about the concept was that the concept of missional ecclesiology is not practical but too academic. Naturally, those who were captured by this new concept of missional ecclesiology began to ask practical questions.[7] One particular question concerned the church's "missional conversion,"[8] namely, how a traditional church can become a missional church. Responding to the practical questions about the concept of missional ecclesiology, literature on this practical interest began to emerge and grow through academic studies and practical publications, as reviewed in the literature review section below.

B. Literary Background of the Study

As the concept of missional ecclesiology became popular among some church and denominational leaders in the West, those who took the idea of missional church seriously began to search for practical implications of missional ecclesiology. This practical interest falls into two categories. The first deals with how to *practice* being a missional church;[9] this, however, is not the major concern of this research. The second, which is the focus of this study, is concerned with how the church can become missional. It is about the transformation of the church into a missional church. There have been attempts made to find theoretical and practical solutions to this practical concern, and the dominant approaches to it are categorized into two approaches.

The first approach to the church's missional transformation is primarily *sociological*, drawing on *theoretical* sources (such as leadership principles, congregational change theories, or social movement theories) or *empirical* findings (through field research on existing local churches). One representative example is *The Missional Leader* by Alan Roxburgh and

---

7. Roxburgh and Romanuk, *Missional Leader*, xi–xiv, 3–4; Rouse and Van Gelder, *Field Guide*, 13–14.

8. For the definition of the phrase *missional conversion*, see the Definition of Key Terms in this chapter.

9. For example, see Minatrea, *Shaped by God's Heart*.

Fred Romanuk.[10] For the authors, the key to the church's missional change is leadership. They propose a leadership model they call "the Missional Change Model" for the church's missional conversion. In *A Field Guide for the Missional Congregation,* Rick Rouse and Craig Van Gelder propose what they call *"Seven Transformational Keys"* as a practical guide for the missional transformation of a congregation. The authors give seven suggestions as keys that serve as check points for a congregational change toward the missional church.[11] While some of the keys pay attention to theological topics such as the mission of God and discipleship, most of them draw upon leadership theories or congregational change theories. In *Leading Missional Change*, Paul J. Dunbar and Anthony L. Blair provide practical suggestions for the church's missional change.[12] The authors focus on one particular aspect of leadership that can stimulate the church's missional change: "a matter of trust."[13] The authors researched "the impact of trust on congregational resistance to or readiness for missional change."[14] The primary source for their research is quantitative and qualitative research on local churches, although the authors briefly touch on the early church in the book of Acts and Paul's writings. Randolph C. Ferebee's *Cultivating the Missional Church* suggests ten practical tools that Christian leaders can use for their congregations' missional change.[15] The ten tools cover areas of administration, leadership, relationship, discipleship, and mission.

Along with the published monographies mentioned above, several doctoral studies have been done on this subject by using sociological or empirical approaches. One particular case that uses congregational change theories for doctoral research is Gil Pyo Lee's dissertation, "From Traditional to Missional Church: Describing a Contextual Model of Change for Ingrown Korean Diaspora Church in North America."[16] Lee uses four congregational change theories to interpret the data of his qualitative research on selected Korean immigrant churches in North America, and then makes missiological suggestions for the church's missional change. These examples

---

10. Roxburgh and Romanuk, *Missional Leader*.

11. The seven transformational keys are: (1) develop a vision for God's mission, (2) focus on God's mission and discipleship, (3) cultivate a healthy climate, (4) build a supportive team of staff and lay leadership, (5) stay the course when facing conflict, (6) practice stewardship to build financial viability, and (7) celebrate successes and the contributions of all.

12. Dunbar and Blair, *Leading Missional Change*.

13. Dunbar and Blair, *Leading Missional Change*, 6.

14. Dunbar and Blair, *Leading Missional Change*, 46.

15. Ferebee, *Cultivating the Missional Church*.

16. Lee, "From Traditional to Missional Church."

use existing congregational change theories or leadership principles or propose new ones for the church's missional transformation. Their approaches are more sociological or empirical in nature. The biblical resources they engage are limited mostly to leadership or organizational change. Another similar doctoral research is Sinyil Kim's dissertation, "Korean Immigrants and Their Mission: Exploring the Missional Identity of Korean Immigrant Churches in North America."[17] The author focuses on discovering Korean immigrant Christians' identity and its implication for fostering their missional potential. In his qualitative field research on six Korean immigrant churches in North America, he analyzes how the churches and their members understand Scripture, self-identity (in their immigrant context), and mission. Based on his empirical research findings, he suggests theoretical and practical implications for Korean immigrant Christians' identity transformation which can stimulate their missional identity.

Different from the doctoral studies addressed above, Gregory Paul Leffel's doctoral dissertation, "Faith Seeking Action: Missio-Ecclesiology, Social Movements, and the Church as a movement of the People of God,"[18] draws from two different sources: (1) theological discourse on the church's mission as participating in *missio Dei* and (2) social movements. While he draws from theological literature, his primary research focus is sociological, guided by a research question, "How can contemporary social movements inform the theology and action of the church . . . ?"[19] Out of the dialogue between a theological description of the church and three social movements, he proposes what he calls "missio-ecclesiology" as "a conceptual framework for understanding, strategizing, and organizing the actions of Christian communities that are truly missionary in their self-understanding."[20]

Another approach to the missional conversion of the church is biblical, theological, or historical. In *The Continuing Conversion of the Church*, Darrell L. Guder takes a different approach to the church's missional change.[21] The author traces theologically and historically how the historical process of the translation of the gospel resulted in reductionism of the gospel and concludes that the key factor for the church's missional change is not a new leadership nor a new congregational change model, but has to do with the church's understanding of the gospel. The author argues that the church should be continuously converted by encountering the gospel afresh in order to become

17. Kim, "Korean Immigrants and Their Mission."
18. Leffel, "Faith Seeking Action."
19. Leffel, "Faith Seeking Action," 11.
20. Leffel, "Faith Seeking Action," 280.
21. Guder, *Continuing Conversion*.

missional. As implications for the church, the author makes some practical suggestions for the church to encounter the gospel afresh.

Kurt Norman Fredrickson's dissertation, "An Ecclesial Ecology for Denominational Futures: Nurturing Organic Structures for Missional Engagement," epitomizes another case that employs a theological approach to the church's missional change.[22] While his approach is interdisciplinary, the author draws some practical and theoretical implications from three metaphors for the church—the people of God, the body of Christ, and the Temple of the Spirit. As a research outcome, the author proposes practical suggestions that can stimulate the creation of a missional environment for a denomination, and hopes that missional local churches emerge ecologically within that missional environment. However, the focus of his dissertation is not the church but structural change of a denomination.

One book which is popularly used for training pastors who want to change their existing churches to missional ones or who want to initiate missional churches, is Alan Hirsch's *The Forgotten Ways*.[23] Its approach is biblical and historical by using as two key resources the early church (an ancient case)[24] and the underground church in China (a contemporary case). The author identifies theoretical and practical factors that lead to the emergence and growth of missional churches in the West. For that purpose, the author uses two key terms. The first is *Apostolic Genius*, which refers to an ancient, radical Christian movement. The second term is *missional DNA* (mDNA) which consists of six elements: (1) Jesus is Lord, (2) disciple making, (3) missional-incarnational impulse, (4) apostolic environment (which deals with the significance of missional leadership), (5) organic system, and (6) *communitas* (outward-focused group), not community (inward-focused group). According to the author, Apostolic Genius emerges out of an interrelated operation of the six elements of mDNA. The author identifies the six elements of mDNA out of the two key examples of Apostolic Genius: the early church and the underground church in China. While the author proposes mDNA as a transformative force that would lead to the birth or growth of missional churches, the six elements of mDNA are six major characteristics of the missional church, rather than six transformative factors that lead to the missional transformation of the church.

This survey of the literary background shows that there has been a growing body of literature on the church's missional transformation, indicating a

---

22. Fredrickson, "Ecclesial Ecology."
23. Hirsch, *Forgotten Ways*.
24. By the early church, Alan Hirsh means the church in the apostolic period. He draws implications and insights from writings in the New Testament.

growing interest in this practical, missiological topic. As this literary survey shows, various approaches have been attempted to provide practical and theoretical suggestions for the transformation of the church toward being a missional church. However, the dominant approach to the topic has been sociological and empirical, when compared with other approaches.

C. Statement of the Problem

The research problem that this study deals with is the insufficiency of biblical-theological studies on the topic of how the church becomes missional. Studies on the missional transformation of the church have been done, drawing on practical and theoretical insights from various perspectives—sociological, historical, empirical, theological, and biblical. The dominant approach to the missional transformation of the church has drawn on sociological or empirical resources. This approach attempted to draw implications from leadership models, organizational change theories, or social movements, or find implications from field research on several selected local churches. While this approach did not neglect biblical and theological resources, the biblical-theological resources they drew from were insufficient and limited, primarily to discussions on leadership or organizational change. A few other studies have attempted to draw practical and theoretical implications through considerable engagement with biblical and theological resources. However, while there have been a number of in-depth biblical-theological studies on a missional ecclesiology or the practice of a missional ecclesiology,[25] no major research on the topic of the missional conversion of the church has been done through an in-depth biblical-theological approach.

D. Research Claim and Significance of the Study

The purpose of this study is to construct a biblical theology of the missional conversion of the church by examining relevant biblical cases or themes from a missional perspective in order to find theoretical and practical implications which are biblically grounded and which can help the church today to continuously be transformed toward its missionary vocation.

The missiological significance and contribution of this study are twofold. The first contribution of this study is the approach this study takes.

---

25. For examples, see Wright, *Mission of God*; Wright, *Mission of God's People*; Goheen, *Light to the Nations*.

As noted earlier, major biblical-theological studies of missional church (or missional ecclesiology) have focused on what the church *should be* for God's mission, not the *transformation* of the church toward its missionary vocation. Thus, this study's biblical-theological approach to the theme of the church's missional conversion is a unique missiological contribution to biblical theology of mission in general, and the study of the missional conversion of the church in particular. Second, derived from the foregoing contribution, this study constitutes an academic contribution by providing a better theological and theoretical understanding of the nature of the church's missional conversion. Integrating research findings, this study identifies biblically grounded, theologically sound, and practically applicable implications for the church's missional transformation.

E. Definition of Key Terms

The People of God, the Church

Biblical scholars use the phrase "the people of God" from a perspective which views the church as having its origin in God's initiation of the covenant with the people of Israel.[26] Paul S. Minear states, "the galaxy of images that oscillate around this conception [of the people of God] serves in a distinctive way to place the New Testament church in the meeting of the long story of God's dealings with his chosen people."[27] In the same manner, Christopher J. H. Wright used "the mission of God's people" as the title of his book on theology of the church's mission. Wright argues that the New Testament church and its mission are rooted in the identity and vocation of the people of Israel in the Old Testament. Wright states, "After all, the New Testament church did not actually have a New Testament when they set out on the task of world mission. It was the Scriptures of the Old Testament that provided the motivation and justification for their missional practice, as well as the underlying theological assumptions and expectations that reassured them that what they were doing was 'biblical.'"[28]

Drawing on biblical scholars' use of the phrase, "the people of God" (or "God's people") to refer to the church, this study affirms that the biblical origin of the church goes back to the people of Israel in the Old Testament. In this sense, this study uses the term "the people of God" as a way of referring to a particular people (whose biblical origin is in continuation of the

---

26. For example, see Minear, *Images*, 67–71.
27. Minear, *Images*, 71.
28. Wright, *Mission of God's People*, 29.

people of Israel) such as the disciples of Jesus and the earliest church in the New Testament, and the church today.

Missio Dei, Mission of God

Missio Dei is a Latin term literally meaning "the sending of God." According to Lalsangkima Pachuau, this term has been "a reference to the Christian theological understanding of mission, which seeks to ground Christian missionary theory and practice in the missionary activity of the Triune God."[29] Influenced by two German theologians, Karl Barth and Karl Hartenstein,[30] the theocentric conceptualization of mission was proposed at and was accepted by the International Missionary Council, at a conference held in Willingen, Germany in 1952, although the term itself was not used at the conference. The conference did not define mission in light of soteriology, but grounded mission in the doctrine of the Trinity.[31] The term *missio Dei* became popular through Georg F. Vicedom's *The Mission of God: An Introduction to a Theology of Mission*.[32]

While the term *missio Dei* has been interpreted differently in the history of mission theology, the concept of *missio Dei* brought out a new understanding of the mission of the church in at least two ways. First, the term *missio Dei* laid a theological foundation for the holistic nature of mission. Since mission is grounded in the nature of God, any attempt at defining mission in a narrow way is theologically untenable. Rather, the scope of mission includes God's ultimate intention for every dimension—spiritual, social, economic, political, and environmental—of the whole creation. As Timothy C. Tennent states, the church's mission in light of the *missio Dei* includes both "evangelism and social action,"[33] and, as Wright notes, the church is called to participate in the mission of God "for the redemption of *God's creation*."[34] Second, the concept of *missio Dei* theologically established the missionary nature of the church in such a way that, as Johannes Blauw states, "There is no other Church than the Church sent into the world, and there is no other mission than that of the Church of Christ."[35] In light of *missio Dei*, mission is no longer merely one of the ministries that the church does, but the church

29. Pachuau, "*Missio Dei*," 232.
30. Bosch, *Transforming Mission*, 389–90.
31. Bosch, *Transforming Mission*, 390.
32. Vicedom, *Mission of God*.
33. Tennent, *Invitation to World Missions*, 405.
34. Wright, *Mission of God*, 23. Emphasis added.
35. Blauw, *Missionary Nature of the Church*, 121.

is missionary by its nature, being called to participate in the redemptive mission of God. This rediscovery of the integration of the church and mission led to the birth of the term *missional (or missionary) ecclesiology* or *missional (or missionary) church* in the late twentieth century.

In this study, the term *the mission of God* is intended to generally reaffirm the theocentric understanding of mission, which is what the term *missio Dei* theologically established. Since the term *missio Dei* has been the theological reference to the view of mission as the sending activity of the triune God, this study views the term *missio Dei* and the phrase *the mission of God* as fundamentally synonymous.

Missionary, Missional

When the term *missional* was introduced to the North American Church in the 1990s through the publication of the book *Missional Church*, this term was used particularly as an adjective with the word "church" to describe the identity, nature, or vocation of the church in light of the concept of *missio Dei*. In defining the meaning and practice of missional church or missional ecclesiology, *Missional Church* uses the term *missional* to define the nature and vocation of the church, accentuating "the sent-ness of the church," as a concept opposite to "the church sending." The authors state, "With the term *missional* we emphasize the essential nature and vocation of the church as God's called and sent people."[36] Differently, Wright in *The Mission of God* defines the term more broadly: "*Missional* is simply an adjective denoting something that is related to or characterized by mission, or has the qualities, attributes or dynamics of mission."[37] For Wright, the use of the term missional is not limited to the church, but can be used more broadly. However, when the term *missional* was introduced among pastors and mission theologians in the 1990s, its meaning was not a new concept. While the term *missionary* is more commonly used as a noun, the term *missionary* had been already used with the same meaning as the term *missional* (that is, as an adjective modifying "church") since the 1950s in Catholic and ecumenical circles.[38]

---

36. Guder, *Missional Church*, 11. Also see Van Gelder and Zscheile, *Missional Church in Perspective*, 1.

37. Wright, *Mission of God*, 24.

38. For the earliest use of the term *missionary* as an adjective in Catholic and ecumenical circles, see International Missionary Council, *Missionary Obligation of the Church*; Paul VI, *Decree on the Mission Activity of the Church: Ad Gentes*.

As this survey shows, the two terms *missional* and *missionary*, when used as adjectives, share the same meaning. In this sense, they can be used interchangeably, but this study will use these terms selectively in two ways. First, this study will prefer the term *missionary* as an adjective to refer to the identity, nature, or vocation of the church (or the people of God). Second, when this study generally addresses something that is related to mission, the term *missional* will be chosen instead of the term *missionary*, following Wright's general definition of the term.

Missional Conversion, Conversion

While the phrase was already used before him, Guder was the first to use the phrase *conversion of the church* in order to refer to the missional transformation of the church.[39] He in his 1998 article, "Missional Theology for a Missionary Church," used the word *conversion* for the first time in order to describe the transformation of the North American Church toward its missionary vocation: "The paradigm shift we are going through requires the missional re-orientation of the church, especially in the North American context. More bluntly, it calls for the conversion of the church to its missionary vocation."[40] He then used the term in his book, *The Continuous Conversion of the Church*, calling the church to continuously encounter the gospel afresh to restore its missionary vocation. In his article, "*Missio Dei*: Integrating Theological Formation for Apostolic Vocation," he used the term *conversion* as the work of God to restore the church's missionary vocation. He states, "I find more and more reasons to insist that the challenge before us is not one merely of renewal, or re-tooling, but of conversion—the conversion of the church to its radically simple missional vocation. Since conversion is a work of God's Spirit and is not under our control, our theological formation for apostolic vocation must be done in a posture of patient and confident prayer."[41]

Adapting Guder's use of the term *conversion* for the church's missional transformation, Hyung Keun Choi used the term *missional conversion* as a guiding term in his article, "Missional Conversion and Transformation in the Context of the Korean Protestant Church," in which he suggests that the Korean Protestant Church be transformed toward *missio Dei*.[42]

---

39. For the earlier use of the phrase, see Shoemaker, *Conversion of the Church*; Shaull, "Toward the Conversion of the Church."

40. Guder, "Missional Theology for a Missionary Church," 9.

41. Guder, "*Missio Dei*," 74.

42. Choi, "Missional Conversion and Transformation."

In Catholicism, a similar term—*missionary conversion* of the church—was recently used in Pope Francis's apostolic exhortation, *The Joy of the Gospel* (*Evangelii Gaudium*), particularly in its first chapter in which the pope calls for the missionary transformation of the church.[43] The pope states, "Each particular Church, as a portion of the Catholic Church under the leadership of its bishop, is likewise called to *missionary conversion*."[44]

Adapting Guder's use of the term *conversion*, this study uses the phrase *missional conversion* as a guiding key term in the way that Choi and Pope Francis used it. However, unlike Choi who differentiates conversion from transformation (as indicated in the title of his article), this study views transformation as part of conversion. Thus, missional conversion and missional transformation are interchangeable, but the former is viewed as a broader concept which the latter is part of. This broad understanding of conversion is congruent with Beverly Roberts Gaventa's suggested three types of conversion — *alternation, pendulum-like conversion,* and *transformation*—which she identifies in her study of typology of conversion in the New Testament. Gaventa explains:

> *Alternation* occurs when change grows out of an individual's past behavior. It is the logical consequence of previous choices. *Pendulum conversion* involves the rejection of past convictions and affiliations for an affirmed present and future. *Transformation* applies to conversion in which a new way of perception forces the radical reinterpretation of the past. Here the past is not rejected but reconstrued as part of a new understanding of God and world.[45]

When we compare the meaning of *missional conversion* with the traditional Christian meaning of conversion, the term *missional conversion* helps us understand better the nature and process of the church's missional transformation in two ways.[46] First, conversion is about "turning to God." Likewise, the term *missional conversion* embodies the meaning of turning to God. However, it implies the church's turning to not just God, but to God in his full missionary character. Second, conversion is not the work of human beings, but of God. Thus, the term *missional conversion* implies that transformation toward faithful participation in God's mission is not primarily a consequence of human strategic efforts. Rather, the phrase

---

43. Francis, *Joy of the Gospel*. For an analysis of the pope's call for the conversion of the church, see Clifford, "Pope Francis' Call."

44. Francis, *Joy of the Gospel*, 16.

45. Gaventa, *From Darkness to Light*, 148.

46. See Choi, "Missional Conversion and Transformation," 60–61.

missional conversion highlights that such transformation is, first and foremost, the work of God.

The phrase *missional conversion* is chosen precisely as a phrase that describes a central key concept of this research. When this study mentions the missional conversion of the church, it reflects the process of its transformation toward what the church is called to be in order to participate in God's mission. By the missional conversion of the church, this study not only means its theological transformation but also addresses change in its inward life and outward ministry. However, the term *the missional conversion of the church* is not so much about how to *practice* a missional ecclesiology as it is on how to *transform* the church toward its missionary vocation. In other words, the missional conversion of the church focuses not on identifying mission activities the church should do as a missionary community, but on *the nature of change* toward being a missionary community that fully understands and fulfills its missionary vocation as God intended the church to be for his mission.

F. Hermeneutical Approach

This research approaches biblical narratives from a missional perspective. This means that this research explores biblical narratives based on the claim that, in Wright's words, "mission is what the Bible is all about."[47] More specifically, mission in the Bible is, first and foremost, God's mission; the people of God in the Bible are called to participate in God's mission.

Within this general missional perspective, Charles Van Engen's thematic hermeneutics provides a more specific hermeneutical principle for this study. Van Engen views the Bible as a "Tapestry of Missional Themes and Motifs in Context."[48] Building on David Bosch's "critical hermeneutics,"[49] Van Engen proposes a hermeneutic in which Scripture is to be examined from "the perspective of a number of themes and sub-themes (or motifs) of God's action in the world."[50] In this approach, the Bible is viewed as "a tapestry, with the woof (horizontal) threads of various themes and motifs interwoven in the warp (vertical) of each context's historical situation."[51]

The interpretive key in Van Engen's missional hermeneutics is "an intimate interrelationship of text and new contexts through the vehicle of

---

47. Wright, *Mission of God*, 29.
48. See Van Engen, "Relation of Bible and Mission."
49. See Bosch, *Transforming Mission*, 23–24.
50. Van Engen, "Relation of Bible and Mission," 32.
51. Van Engen, "Relation of Bible and Mission," 32.

particular themes or motifs that bridge the text's initial context with today's contexts of mission."[52] Approaching Scripture in this way, Van Engen observes "a creative interaction of word and deed throughout the history of God's missionary activity."[53] In this way, this method "involves a critical hermeneutic that attempts to discover the particular 'self-definition'... of God's people in a particular time and place—and then challenges all subsequent self-definitions, including our own."[54] Based on Van Engen's thematic hermeneutical approach, this research chooses one particular theme, "the missional conversion of God's people," and explores the theme in biblical contexts, as in Figure 1 below.

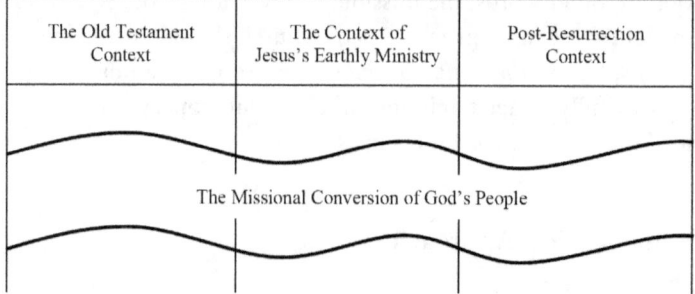

Figure 1. Motif of the missional conversion of God's people in biblical contexts.

G. Theological Framework

The concept of *missio Dei* has served as *the* theological anchor on which the missionary nature of the church is claimed, justified, and reinforced since the 1950s, while the concept can be and has been misconstrued.[55] When authentically understood and practiced, "The *missio Dei* purifies the church," as David Bosch remarks in *Transforming Mission*.[56] The church, called to be God's missionary people, needs to be continuously purified, renewed, and transformed in light of God's missional intent for it. From this perspective, this research takes *missio Dei* as a biblical-theological concept that guides

---

52. Van Engen, "Relation of Bible and Mission," 33.

53. Van Engen, "Relation of Bible and Mission," 33.

54. Van Engen, "Relation of Bible and Mission," 34.

55. For a historical survey of different interpretations of *missio Dei*, see Jung, "Toward a Theology of *Pareo Dei*."

56. Bosch, *Transforming Mission*, 519.

this study of missional conversion of the church. The theological rationale behind this relationship between *missio Dei* and the missional conversion of the church is that it is the missionary triune God (as the origin and source of mission) who calls, shapes, renews, and transforms the church toward truly being his missionary people for his mission in and for the world. In this regard, the church's missional conversion is not something that can be done purely by strategic human efforts, but is, first and foremost, the transformation of the church by God.

This relationship between *missio Dei* and the church's missional conversion is theologically and biblically established in light of *twofold* commitment of the missionary God in his mission. By the *twofold* missionary commitment of God is meant two major directions in God's mission: to the church and to the world.[57] In other words, the church as well as the world is an object of *missio Dei*. On the one hand, God in his mission constantly focuses on his chosen, particular people in shaping them toward their missionary vocation. On the other hand, God in his mission constantly aims at redeeming the whole world. According to Stephen B. Bevans and Roger Schroeder, God's mission has "two directions—to the church itself (*ad intra*) and to the world (*ad extra*)."[58] Bevans and Schroeder explain how these two dimensions are related to each other:

> Mission to the church itself is necessary so that the church can shine forth in the world for what it is, a community that *shares* the identity of Christ as his body. . . . Mission to the world points to the fact that the church is only the church as it is called to *continue* Jesus' mission of preaching, serving and witnessing to God's reign in *new* times and places.[59]

God's twofold commitment in *missio Dei* is indicated by biblical covenants. Wright contends, "The mission of God is as integral to the sequence of the covenants as they are to the overarching grand narrative of the whole Bible."[60] Biblical covenants show the particular-universal relationship in the biblical story of God's mission. On the one hand, biblical covenants present the *particular* dimension of the relationship between God and the

---

57. By the word "twofold" is not meant some sort of dualism in God's mission. The primary purpose of the choice of the word is to conceptually explain the relationship between *missio Dei* and the missional conversion of the church. As discussed throughout this study, this relationship is *not* merely God's election of a particular people for his mission, but is manifested as God's continuous "commitment" or "faithfulness" in shaping them into his missionary people.

58. Bevans and Schroeder, *Constants in Context*, 394.

59. Bevans and Schroeder, *Constants in Context*, 394. Italics in original.

60. Wright, *Mission of God*, 356.

people of God. On the other hand, as Walter Vogels states, "The whole historical covenant between Yahweh and Israel has from the beginning a universal dimension."[61] Richard J. Bauckham views three biblical covenants—Abrahamic, Sinaitic, and Davidic—as "the most important forms" showing that mission in the Bible is carried out by the movement from the particular to the universal.[62] In this regard, as Wright points out, "The covenants proclaim the mission of God as his committed promise to the nations and the whole of creation. The book of Revelation is the covenantal declaration 'Mission accomplished.'"[63]

The scope and nature of God's redemptive mission is *foreshadowed* in the Noahic Covenant in Genesis 9:8–17. Howard A. Snyder states, "The story of redemption begins here, not with Abraham's call."[64] It is not merely a covenant of "preservation," but also of "preparation" for the next step of God's mission.[65] This covenant indicates the comprehensive scope of God's mission as the covenant includes both humanity and the rest of creation as covenantal partners. God makes a covenant not only with Noah but also with the rest of creation (the earth and all creatures on it): "As for me, I am establishing my covenant with *you* and *your descendants* after you, and with *every living creature* that is with you, the birds, the domestic animals, and every animal of the earth with you, as many as came out of the ark" (Gen 9:9–10). Through the Noahic Covenant, God establishes a covenant not only between him and humanity but also between him and "all flesh that is on the earth" (Gen 9:17). It is "a covenant between God, all people, and all the earth, with all its creatures."[66] One aspect of God's mission, drawn from the Noahic Covenant, is that God's mission has an ecological (or environmental) dimension.[67] In this sense, God's mission, adumbrated in the Noahic

---

61. Vogels, *God's Universal Covenant*, 69. For Vogels, the covenant has a universal purpose because of the public dimension of God's dealing with the people of Israel. He says, "The nations are real witnesses. Yahweh's saving actions, the punishment, and the restoration which he imposed upon Israel were at the same time a preaching to the nations." Vogels, *God's Universal Covenant*, 69.

62. Bauckham, *Bible and Mission*, 27. Bauckham selects four different biblical cases of the biblical narrative of a movement from the particular to the universal. The first three are covenants—with Abraham, with Israel and with David—in the Old Testament. The fourth case is that "God singled out the poor and the powerless" for the movement. For Bauckham's argument on the fourth case, see Bauckham, *Bible and Mission*, 49–54.

63. Wright, *Mission of God*, 356.

64. Snyder, "Mission in the Context of Covenant," 6.

65. Snyder, "Mission in the Context of Covenant," 6.

66. Snyder, "Mission in the Context of Covenant," 6.

67. The ecological dimension of God's mission is already indicated in the fact that the first vocation God gave to the first human being, Adam, was "to till [the garden of

Covenant, is so much comprehensive as redeeming both humanity and the rest of creation. Thus, the scope of redemption and mission in the Bible is not limited to humanity, but includes the whole created world.[68]

Among biblical covenants, the Abrahamic Covenant of Genesis 12:1–3 is particularly important for understanding how God framed his mission for the rest of the Bible. Wright states, "the story of how that blessing for all nations [through Abraham and his descendants] has come about occupies the rest of the Bible, with Christ as the central focus."[69] Thus, as Dean Flemming comments, "It is hard to overstate the importance of God's covenant promise to Abraham in Genesis 12:1–3 for a biblical understanding of mission. . . . This promise, like a recurring musical theme, plays out through the entire symphony of Scripture."[70]

In the Abrahamic Covenant, the most explicit expression of God's twofold commitment in his mission is found, since it is this covenant that clearly reveals the particular-to-universal pattern of God's mission in the unfolding biblical narrative. On the one hand, the covenantal promise God makes with Abram in Genesis 12:1–3 has a universal purpose. The universal backdrop of the covenant implies the universal dimension and missional intent of the covenant. In Genesis 1–11, the focus in the biblical narrative is quite *universal* in scope, comprising the creation and fall of *the whole world* (Gen 1–3), the judgment of *all humanity* through the flood (Gen 6–8), the covenant with *the whole creation* (Gen 9), and the table of *nations* (Gen 10), then ending with God's judgment of *all humanity* gathered at the Babel Tower (Gen 11). As God's redemptive initiative for the whole creation, God calls one particular person, Abram, in Genesis 12.[71] The universal dimension and the missional purpose of the covenant is made explicit in Genesis 12:3 (NIV): "all peoples on earth will be blessed." When God called Abraham, he had all the nations of the earth in mind. God's election of Abraham and God's covenant with him is the first clear expression of God's redemptive

---

Eden] and keep it" (Gen 2:15), indicating *God's concern about the earth*, and human beings' stewardship responsibility to care for creation.

68. While this study will not deal with the ecological dimension of redemption and mission in a consistent manner, this study affirms that, from a biblical perspective, the comprehensive scope of mission must include the redemption of the whole creation.

69. Wright, *Mission of God*, 194–95.

70. Flemming, *Recovering the Full Mission of God*, 23–24.

71. Some scholars observe a similar pattern between Genesis 1–11 and 12 and views the call of Abraham as a continuity of the sin-judgment-grace pattern. See Muilenburg, "Abraham and the Nations"; Kaiser, *Mission in the Old Testament*, 1–8.

concern for all nations,[72] which was already hinted at the Noahic Covenant in Genesis 9:8–17.

On the other hand, the Abrahamic Covenant encapsulates how God's blessing for all nations will be carried out: "through you" (Gen 12:3). As Andreas J. Köstenberger and Peter T. O'Brien say, "Abram will become the means of blessing for all humankind."[73] Wright states: "The tension between the universality of the goal (all nations) and the particularity of the means (through you) is right there from the very beginning of Israel's journey through the pages of the Old Testament."[74] Based on Genesis 12:1–3, Blauw summarizes the whole history of the people of Israel, saying that "the whole history of Israel is nothing but the continuation of God's dealings with the nations, and that therefore the history of Israel is only to be understood from the unsolved problem of the relationship of God to the nations."[75] It implies not only the missional purpose of God's choosing the people of Israel, but also the significance of their missionary role in the midst of the nations because God redemptively engages with the nations through the people of Israel. On the one hand, the ultimate goal of God's mission in Scripture is *universal* in scope. On the other hand, God in the biblical narrative constantly engages with the world through his *particular* people. In this regard, the biblical narrative is not merely about God's dealing with his people, but, more accurately from a missional perspective, about God's redemptive engaging with all nations and even the whole creation by calling, shaping, renewing, and transforming his people into his missionary people.

Thus, in light of God's twofold commitment in his mission, it can be safely argued that both the church and the world are the objects of *missio Dei*. In *missio Dei*, God shapes his people toward becoming his missionary people so that God can redemptively engage with the world through them. God commits himself to the missional formation of his particular people in order to accomplish his universal mission through them. In this view, it can be even concluded that the missional conversion of the church is not merely part of *missio Dei* but, rather, a *central* part of *missio Dei*. With the concept of *missio Dei* taken as a biblical-theological concept that guides this study of the church's missional conversion, this study will focus on how God in the biblical narrative calls, shapes, renews, and transforms his

---

72. Glasser et al., *Announcing the Kingdom*, 57. For a thorough study on the missiological meaning of the Abrahamic Covenant, see Kim, "Biblical Foundations."

73. Köstenberger and O'Brien, *Salvation to the Ends of the Earth*, 30.

74. Wright, *Mission of God*, 222.

75. Blauw, *Missionary Nature of the Church*, 19.

people toward being a missionary people who faithfully participate in his mission in and for the world.

H. Research Questions

As explained in the Theological Framework section, this study approaches the missional conversion of the church by taking the concept of *missio Dei* as a guiding biblical-theological concept. Thus, this study approaches the church's missional conversion as the work of God. Given this theocentric theological framework, the major research question that guides this research is: How does the triune God in the biblical narrative shape the people of God toward their missionary vocation so that they may continuously and faithfully participate in God's mission? This research question is twofold: (1) What is the missionary vocation of God's people given by God in the biblical narrative? (2) How does God shape the people of God toward their missionary vocation in the biblical narrative? This twofold research question is approached with four sub-questions as listed below.

1. [Yahweh and Israel's Missional Conversion] How does Yahweh shape Israel toward her missionary vocation in the Old Testament narrative?
2. [Jesus and His Disciples' Missional Conversion] How does Jesus shape his disciples toward their missionary vocation throughout his early ministry?
3. [The Holy Spirit and the Earliest Church's Missional Conversion] How does the Holy Spirit shape the earliest church toward its missionary vocation in the book of Acts?
4. [Missiological Implications for the Church Today] What are the theoretical and practical implications of these biblical-theological research findings for the church today?

I. Delimitations

As addressed in the Hermeneutical Method section, this study views the whole Bible as the story of God's mission, of which the missional conversion of God's people is a central part. Nonetheless, covering all of Scripture in this study is impossible. In order to limit its research scope, this study focuses on selected biblical cases relevant to the topic of this study, ones in which God engages with his chosen people in order to shape them for his redemptive mission for the whole creation. Particularly, this study chooses biblical cases primarily from narratives in Exodus, Judges, Numbers, Kings, Chronicles, the Gospels, and Acts; these books provide biblical accounts of God's dealings with his people within the context of his redemptive mission. While this study looks into biblical narratives that reveal how God shapes his chosen people for his mission, this focus on biblical narratives does not mean that non-narrative biblical texts—such as poetry, wisdom, prophecy, epistles, and apocalypse—are completely excluded from this study. Non-narrative texts, which are related to the biblical narratives in this study, are incorporated into this study as well and are examined in a supplementary way within the context of and in light of the biblical narratives that this study delves into.

2

Israel's Encounter with Yahweh and Her Missional Conversion

MICHAEL GOHEEN OBSERVES, "UNFORTUNATELY, too many treatments of the missional church do not pay enough attention to its Old Testament foundations."[1] It is true that the New Testament is "a missionary document,"[2] but, on the other hand, as Blauw stated more than five decades ago, "When we speak about the Church as 'the people of God in the world' and enquire into the real nature of this Church, we cannot avoid speaking about the roots of the Church which are to be found in the Old Testament idea of Israel as the people of the covenant."[3] In this sense, the full understanding of mission requires the assumption that, as Wright boldly articulated, "mission is what the [whole] Bible is all about."[4] Thus, as Goheen asserts rightly, to understand the relationship between the church and mission, "one must begin in the Old Testament . . . because the missional nature of the church is rooted in the calling of Israel."[5]

In this regard, any attempt to find the biblical foundation for the missional nature of the church should begin with the Old Testament. It would be worthwhile to explore the ways that God dealt with Israel to shape her missionary nature in the Old Testament. That being said, this chapter looks at how Yahweh shaped and wrestled with Israel in order to fulfill her missional purpose as revealed especially in the Abrahamic Covenant.

---

1. Goheen, *Light to the Nations*, 23.
2. Bosch, *Transforming Mission*, 15.
3. Blauw, "Mission of the People of God," 91.
4. Wright, *Mission of God*, 29.
5. Goheen, *Light to the Nations*, 23.

A. Yahweh Has a Missional Intention in His Liberation of Israel

As already discussed, the particular-universal relation in the Abrahamic Covenant in Genesis 12:1–3 implies that the Israelites, the descendants of Abraham, will be *a missionary people*, namely a particular means of God's universal mission, from their beginning and onward.[6] In the biblical narrative, the first key event in God's attempt to transform the people of Israel toward that missionary vocation was the Exodus, the focus of this section.[7] This section identifies the ways that Yahweh shaped the missionary nature of the people of Israel through the Exodus, and demonstrates that Yahweh liberated them to shape them for the fulfillment of his mission revealed in the Abrahamic Covenant. In other words, if Yahweh's calling of Abraham was "election into mission,"[8] the Exodus was liberation *for the missional conversion of Israel*.

Yahweh's Faithfulness to the Abrahamic Covenant

One who reads the biblical narrative of the Exodus cannot fail to find the connection between the Abrahamic Covenant and the Exodus because, as John Goldingay states, "God's covenant commitment to Abram was the basis for the people's deliverance from Egypt."[9] Yahweh's commitment to the Abrahamic Covenant is clearly expressed in Exodus 2:24 (NIV): "God heard their groaning and *he remembered his covenant* with Abraham, with Isaac and with Jacob." As Wright comments, "On the one hand, he is pulled down by human cries to investigate and rectify injustice on earth. On the other hand, he is driven forward by his own declared intention to bless the nations and fulfill his covenant to Abraham."[10] In this sense, the Exodus was "the *next* phase of the story that unfolded in Genesis, the same story that had been launched by God's 'great commission' to Abraham and its accompanying words of promise,"[11] and foreshadowed earlier in the book of Genesis.

---

6. Wright, *Mission of God*, 65. For the biblical exploration on a missional dimension of God's particular people, see Newbigin, *Open Secret*, 66–90; Wright, *Mission of God*, 222–64.
7. Glasser et al., *Announcing the Kingdom*, 75.
8. Wright, *Mission of God*, 264.
9. Goldingay, *Israel's Gospel*, 370.
10. Wright, *Mission of God*, 274.
11. Wright, *Mission of God*, 273. Emphasis added.

That the Exodus is an expression of Yahweh's commitment to the Abrahamic Covenant is also indicated in the way that Yahweh introduced himself to Moses in Exodus 3:6 (NIV): "I am the God of your father, the God of Abraham, the God of Isaac and the God of Jacob." In identifying himself as not only the God of Moses's father but also the God of patriarchs, God intentionally revealed the connection between himself and the people of Israel.[12] Also, it suggests that, as Terence E. Fretheim comments, "the promising aspect of the divine story now begins to take the shape of fulfillment."[13] Similarly, Douglas K. Stuart remarks on Exodus 3:6, "God's faithful provision over all the many generations since Abraham, according to the promises made him . . . was beginning to come to fruition."[14] The Exodus indicates God's faithfulness in fulfilling his mission as revealed to Abraham.

The Missionary Distinctiveness of Israel Shaped by the Exodus

On the one hand, the Exodus is the event in which Yahweh revealed himself publicly to the nations.[15] On the other hand, as W. Ross Blackburn comments, "Israel came to know the Lord as supreme above all gods and earthly rulers, one of the primary purposes of 'I am the Lord' to this point in Exodus" through the Exodus.[16] Roger E. Hedlund rightly points out, "God's redemptive acts were the means for setting his people free and imparting to them the knowledge of the true God."[17] According to Wright, "The exodus stands in the Hebrew Scriptures as the great defining demonstration of YHWH's power, love, faithfulness, and liberation on behalf of his people. It was thus a major act of self-revelation by God, and also

---

12. Durham, *Exodus*, 31.

13. Fretheim, *Exodus*, 57.

14. Stuart, *Exodus*, 116.

15. Goldingay, *Israel's Gospel*, 293–94; Blackburn, *God Who Makes Himself Known*, 17. What God did in Egypt reached the surrounding nations to the extent that, as Goldingay observes, "The story of deliverance ends with Moses's Midianite father-in-law coming to hear what Yhwh did in defeating the Egyptians and delivering the people and to acknowledge that Yhwh is indeed greater than all gods (Ex 18:8–11)." Goldingay, *Israel's Gospel*, 294.

16. Blackburn, *God Who Makes Himself Known*, 55.

17. Hedlund, *Mission of the Church*, 51. Hedlund highlights the revelatory dimension of the Exodus. He states, "Israel's deliverance in the exodus from Egypt was political, social, economic, humanitarian, and religious. But it was also revelational. The exodus revealed God to Israel and the nations. It brought liberation, but that liberty began with the knowledge of God and his redemption." Hedlund, *Mission of the Church*, 54.

a massive learning experience for Israel."[18] The people of Israel came to know that Yahweh, who redeemed them, was "incomparable," "sovereign," and "unique."[19] Thus, what the people of Israel experienced about Yahweh shaped their view of Yahweh. As Ferdinand Deist remarks, the Exodus was "a revelation that was to have a major influence on the way Israel thought about God."[20] Because of Yahweh's self-revelation that the people of Israel eye-witnessed, they became *witnesses of Yahweh* with the knowledge of Yahweh in the midst of the nations.

Liberated to Serve a New King

The last point, which is significant for Israel's missional conversion, is that the Exodus is the event that led the people into the establishment of a unique relationship between Yahweh and Israel. In Exodus 19:4, Yahweh told them through Moses, "[I] brought you *to myself*."[21] Israel was delivered from slavery bondage in Egypt to the presence of Yahweh. As Walter Brueggemann rightly notes, "The Exodus narrative, which creates the context for the encounter at Sinai, is the tale of Yahweh wresting Israel from enslavement to the commands of pharaoh and bringing Israel under the command of Yahweh. Thus, it is the exchange of one command for another."[22] The Exodus is "an exchange of overlords."[23] This means, as Brueggemann points out, "Israel is a 'slave' (or 'servant,' *'ebed*) to Yahweh and shall not be a slave to anyone else. Israel's life is fully under the governance of Yahweh, whom Israel is bound to obey, because Yahweh is the new 'owner' of Israel."[24] Thus, the Exodus is the event in which Israel was converted from Pharaoh to Yahweh. As Wright

---

18. Wright, *Mission of God*, 75. Also see Rowley, "Living Issues in Biblical Scholarship"; Wright, *Old Testament against Its Environment*, 20–29; Matthew, "Yahweh and the Gods." While G. Ernest Wright and Ed Matthew ascribe the faith of Israel and the kingdom of Yahweh to the historical act of God, Harold H. Rowley highlights the role of Moses in establishing biblical monotheism.

19. Wright, *Mission of God's People*, 76.

20. Deist, "Exodus Motif," 60.

21. Scripture quotations, unless otherwise noted, are from the New Revised Standard Version (NRSV) of the Bible.

22. Brueggemann, *Theology of the Old Testament*, 182.

23. Brueggemann, *Theology of the Old Testament*, 182.

24. Brueggemann, *Theology of the Old Testament*, 182. Furthermore, Brueggemann observes the connection between the commandments of God and the Exodus, as he states, "The commandments are introduced in the very utterance of Yahweh, as situated in the memory of the Exodus. *The God who commands is the God who delivers*[Italics in original]." Brueggemann, *Theology of the Old Testament*, 184.

notes, "Israel's problem was not just that they were slaves and ought to be free. It was that they were *slaves to the wrong master and needed to be reclaimed and restored to their proper Lord.*"[25]

Yahweh's kingship over the Israelites means that they found themselves brought into a *new service* that would be given by him. Goldingay notes, "The exodus does not take Israel from serfdom to the freedom of independence but from service of one lord to service of another. . . . Freedom in Scripture is the freedom to serve Yhwh."[26] In this sense, the Exodus is the event that brought the people of Israel into a new mission, that is to serve Yahweh as their king.

Summary

The narrative of the Exodus reveals how Yahweh shaped Israel for the fulfillment of his mission as revealed in the Abrahamic Covenant. First, Yahweh's missional intent in liberating Israel is indicated by his remembrance of the covenant, and his self-introduction as the God of Israel's ancestors. Second, the Exodus, which was Yahweh's self-revelation to the nations, resulted not only in making him known to the nations, but also shaped Israel as a witness of Yahweh in the midst of the nations. Lastly, Israel was liberated not for her own independence but to serve Yahweh as her new king.

B. Yahweh Calls Israel to Participate in His Mission

This section focuses on the call and mission of Israel defined by the Sinai Covenant in Exodus 19:4–6a.[27] The Sinai Covenant consists of three elements: (1) Israel's true identity, (2) Israel's requirement to obey Yahweh, and

---

25. Wright, *Mission of God*, 284. Italics in original.

26. Goldingay, *Israel's Gospel*, 323. For Goldingay, this is what liberation theology misses, as he states, "This dynamic suggests another direction in which we might need to reframe the emphases of liberation theology," Goldingay, *Israel's Gospel*, 323. Wright also points to the problem of ignoring the relational dimension between Israel and God as the result of the Exodus, as he notes, "The problem is not with what it says but where it stops. An interpretation that limits the relation of the exodus to the political, social and economic realm, or prioritizes such issues at the expense or even to the exclusion of the spiritual question of whether or not people come to know the one living God and to worship and serve him in covenant commitment and obedience is simply not handling the text as a whole and is therefore seriously distorting it." Wright, *Mission of God*, 285.

27. Some scholars call this covenant the Mosaic covenant, but, in this study, the term *the Sinai Covenant* will be used for the covenant, to highlight that the covenant is not from Moses but from Yahweh.

(3) Yahweh's grace for Israel, which was demonstrated through the Exodus. In the following, the focus is given to what each of the three elements reveals about the nature of Israel's missionary vocation and how each of the three elements is related to the nature of her missional conversion.

God's Initiation to Transform Israel to Fulfill the Abrahamic Covenant

Israel encountered Yahweh through the Exodus, and now encountered him again at Mt. Sinai. In this divine encounter, he attempted to shape the call and mission of Israel by establishing the covenant at Mt. Sinai. The covenant reveals how he will fulfill his mission—all nations will be blessed through Abraham's descendants (Gen 12:3, 22:18). In the covenant, the missionary vocation of Israel is made explicit for the first time in the biblical narrative by revealing Israel's true identity and vocation (Exod 19:5–6).

With the Sinai Covenant, Yahweh began to reveal ways by which Israel would participate in his mission. At one level, it is true that the covenant defines the relationship between Yahweh and Israel. As scholars generally agree, the covenant is viewed as "pivotal for understanding Israel's life and identity under God."[28] At another level, the covenant has a missional intent because it is in continuation of the Abrahamic Covenant and shows how Israel will participate in the fulfillment of the covenant. As Wright notes, "The covenant with Abraham was reconfirmed and given broader substance in the national covenant with Israel, mediated through Moses at Mount Sinai."[29]

Israel's True Identity (1): "My Treasured Possession"

In Exodus 19:5–6a, three phrases are used to refer to the identity of Israel: "my treasured possession," "a kingdom of priests," and "a holy nation." Each of the three phrases reveals different aspects of Israel's call and mission, as will be explored below. The phrase, "my treasured possession," reveals that Israel is called into a special relationship with Yahweh. This aspect of the identity of Israel is well indicated by the fact that the Hebrew word for "treasured possession" is used in the case that a king claims "an estate or territory that belongs to him in person, not to the state."[30] John A. Davies states, "Its principal use

---

28. Wells, *God's Holy People*, 13.
29. Wright, *Mission of God*, 329.
30. Okoye, *Israel and the Nations*, 60. The identity of Israel as Yahweh's treasured

in the Hebrew Bible is as a metaphorical designation of the people of Israel in relation to God."[31] This special relationship between Yahweh and Israel echoes in the rest of the Old Testament, but is well articulated in the covenant formula, "I will be your God and you will be my people."[32]

Two Aspects of Israel's Call: to Serve Yahweh, and for the Nations

Israel's identity as God's treasured possession indicates two aspects of Israel's call. First, Israel is called to *serve Yahweh*. This point is indicated by three parallel examples—Akkadian, Ugaritic and the Old Testament. Davies finds two illuminating cases, in which two Semitic words—Akkadian *sikiltu* and Ugaritic *sglt*—(which are etymologically close to *segullah*, the Hebrew word for "treasured possession") are used in the context of one's devoted service to another.[33] Drawing on Davies's observation of the two cases, Peter J. Gentry and Stephen J. Wellum contend, "the use of word for 'personal treasure' is paired with the notion of servant. . . . 'Personal treasure' is used in the context of *devoted service* in a relationship defined by a treaty."[34] One example similar to these two cases is found in Malachi 3:17 (ESV), which reads, "They shall be mine, says the Lord of hosts, in the day when I make up *my treasured possession*, and I will spare them as a man spares *his son who serves him*." In this verse, Mitchell Dahood observes that the Hebrew word for "treasured possession" was also used in a context of one's devoted service to another.[35] On this verse, Gentry and Wellum observe, "What is parallel . . . to 'personal treasure' is 'son,' qualified by the concept of devoted services."[36] According to Davies, the nature of the relationship defined by "treasured possession" in the verse is "one where filial loyalty would be an appropriate response."[37] Agreeing with Davies, Gentry and Wellum point out that Israel is called to serve Yahweh with "the devoted service of a son and honoured king in a covenant relationship."[38] Supported by the Akkadian and Ugaritic cases, Malachi

---

possession is found in Deut 7:6, 10:14–15, 14:2, 26:18; Ps 135:4.

31. Davies, *Royal Priesthood*, 52.

32. Okoye, *Israel and the Nations*, 60. For a comprehensive study on the covenant formula, see Martens, *God's Design*; Rendtorff, *Covenant Formula*.

33. Davies, *Royal Priesthood*, 53.

34. Gentry and Wellum, *Kingdom through Covenant*, 317. Emphasis added.

35. Dahood, "Ugaritic-Hebrew Parallel Pairs," 24–25.

36. Gentry and Wellum, *Kingdom through Covenant*, 318.

37. Davies, *Royal Priesthood*, 54.

38. Gentry and Wellum, *Kingdom through Covenant*, 318.

3:17 implies that the privilege that Israel has in her special relationship with Yahweh is a privilege *to serve Yahweh*.[39]

The second relational aspect of the special relationship between Yahweh and Israel is that Yahweh's call of Israel is *ultimately for the nations*. The Sinai Covenant presents the relationship between Israel and Yahweh with a universal purpose. This universal dimension of the Sinai Covenant is indicated in the so-called chiastic structure,[40] with which the Sinai Covenant is framed. Drawing on R. Mosis's detailed grammatical study of Exodus 19:5–6,[41] Jo Bailey Wells suggests that the two verses are framed with chiastic structure, in which the metaphors for Israel's identity are outer parts and a universal context and Yahweh's universal ownership are located at the center.[42] According to Wells, one significant implication of the structural analysis is that "the text [Exodus 19:5–6] is not only concerned to establish the nature of Yhwh's relation to Israel, but also Israel's relation to others."[43] As Wells notes, "What the reader is given is not a description of Israel in isolation, but in relation to the world of God's earth."[44] Wright relates the particular-universal tension in verses 5–6 to the mission of Yahweh when he states, "*the particularity of Israel here is intended to serve the universality of God's interest in the world. Israel's election serves God's mission.*"[45] Thus, Yahweh invited Israel into a unique relationship with him, but this relationship had a missional purpose because Israel is called ultimately to serve God's universal mission.

---

39. Regarding the biblical concept of election, Harold H. Rowley stresses this point: "Election is for service. And if God chose Israel, it was not alone that He might reveal Himself to her, but that He might claim her for service." Rowley, *Biblical Doctrine of Election*, 43.

40. For a comprehensive study on the pattern known as chiasmus, or a chiastic structure of biblical scriptures, see Breck, *Shape of Biblical Language*. John Breck introduces chiasmus as "a rhetorical pattern, common to both Testaments, that in many cases reveals clearly and precisely the central theme the biblical author sought to develop and communicate to his reader," and, more simply as "a form of inverted parallelism that focuses about a central theme" located at the center of the structure. Breck, *Shape of Biblical Language*, 15–16. An example of a chiastic structure is A:B:C:B':A' or A:B:B':A.'

41. Mosis, "Ex.19,5b–6a."

42. Wells, *God's Holy People*, 44.

43. Wells, *God's Holy People*, 44.

44. Wells, *God's Holy People*, 49.

45. Wright, *Mission of God*, 257. Italics in original. Also see Okoye, *Israel and the Nations*, 64.

Relationship with the Other Two Phrases

Along with the meaning of "treasured possession" in verse 5, it is important to identify the relationship between the phrase "treasured possession" in verse 5 and the two other ones, "a kingdom of priests" and "a holy nation," in verse 6. Gentry and Wellum provide an insightful suggestion that verse 5 and verse 6 refer to the same thing but picture different aspects of it. They use an analogy of "Dolby Surround Sound or a 3D holographic image" to explain the relationship between verses 5 and 6 and between the two phrases in verse 6.[46] They state:

> Once the terms are explicated it will become clear that "royal priesthood" and "holy nation" taken together is another way of saying, "God's personal treasure." In other words, the term "royal priesthood" and "holy nation" constitute the right and left speakers of stereo sound, and then together they form the left speaker for which the term "personal treasure" is the right speaker.[47]

Wells makes a similar point, viewing "two titles [in verse 6] not only as explanation and intensification but also as qualification of ['treasured possession']."[48] Wright in a similar manner interprets the relationship between the two verses, but explains it in terms of *status* and *role*.[49] That being the case, the three phrases together define what Yahweh calls Israel to be.

Summed up, the entire discussion on the phrase "my treasured possession" in verse 5 and its relationship with two other phrases—"a kingdom of priests" and "a holy nation"—in verse 6 can be summarized this way: (1) Israel is called into a special relationship with Yahweh so that it may serve him, (2) Israel's service to Yahweh is ultimately for the sake of the nations, and (3) Israel's call to serve Yahweh for the sake of the nations is expected to be fulfilled by being "a kingdom of priests" and "a holy nation."

Israel's True Identity (2): "A Kingdom of Priests"

While there have been different interpretations proposed for the phrase "a kingdom of priests," biblical scholars generally agree that it refers to the

---

46. Gentry and Wellum, *Kingdom through Covenant*, 316.
47. Gentry and Wellum, *Kingdom through Covenant*, 316.
48. Wells, *God's Holy People*, 45.
49. Wright, *Mission of God*, 256. Also see Wright, *Mission of God*, 255.

corporate priesthood bestowed upon the whole people of Israel.[50] At least two particular biblical observations support this meaning. The first scriptural observation is the close relationship between "a kingdom of priests" and "a holy nation," indicated by the fact that the words "priest" and "holy" are frequently used together in the Bible.[51] Drawing on the close relationship between these two words, the corporate meaning of the term "a holy nation" also suggests that "a kingdom of priests" refers to Israel's corporate priesthood. Another scriptural observation that indicates Israel's corporate priesthood is a striking similarity between the covenant ratification ritual in Exodus 24:3–8 and the consecration ritual of priests in Exodus 29:20 and Leviticus 8:23–24. According to Richard E. Averbeck, this similarity implies that, as the priests were consecrated, the whole nation was consecrated. [52]Drawing on these observations, Averbeck remarks, "from the start . . . , the whole nation was a 'kingdom of priests'—they were 'a holy people.'"[53]

Israel's Relationship with the Nations in Her Priesthood

In light of the analogy between Israel's priesthood in the world and individual priests in Israel, scholars generally suggest that, as priests do to Yahweh and to a community, Israel's priesthood has two relational dimensions: Israel's relationship to Yahweh (a vertical dimension of Israel's priesthood) and to the nations (a horizontal dimension of Israel's priesthood). First, the phrase "a kingdom of priests (or priestly kingdom)" denotes the horizontal relationship between Israel and the nations in such a way that Israel is called to mediate between Yahweh and the nations as priests do for a people. Blauw connects this functional view of individual priests with Israel's priesthood when he articulates, "What priests are for a people, Israel as a people is for the world."[54] Fretheim develops this connection further, highlighting the mediating role of Israel's priesthood when he points out, "[Israel] is to be devoted as a nation to *a mediatorial role* between God and other kingdoms, to function among the nations as a priest functions in a religious community."[55]

---

50. For complexity in interpreting the phrase "a kingdom of priests," see Blackburn, *God Who Makes Himself Known*, 89–90.

51. Blackburn, *God Who Makes Himself Known*, 90.

52. Averbeck, "Priest, Priesthood," 633.

53. Averbeck, "Priest, Priesthood," 634.

54. Blauw, *Missionary Nature of the Church*, 24. Also see Wright, *Mission of God*, 330.

55. Fretheim, *Exodus*, 212. Italics in original.

Thus, as R. Alan Cole asserts, the phrase "a kingdom of priests" refers to "the universal priestly status of Israel."[56]

This analogy between Israel's priesthood and Levitical priests within Israel signifies what Israel's mission to the nations would look like: *Bringing the nations to Yahweh*. James Chukwuma interprets Israel's mission to the nations in light of priests' role in a community, as he states, "What priests do is that priests serve a community by bringing them closer to God and serve God by mediating God's revelation and decrees to the community. The surprising thing here is that God promises to make priests of the entire community of Israel."[57] Wright interprets the priestly mission of Israel as making Yahweh known to the world and drawing the world to Yahweh when he comments:

> The job of priests, then, was to bring God to the people and bring the people to God. So now, with rich significance, God says to Israel as a whole people: "*You will be for me to all the rest of the nations what your priests are for you. Through you I will become known to the world, and through you ultimately I will draw the world to myself.*" That is what it meant for Israel to be God's priesthood in the midst of the nations.[58]

Blackburn also understands Israel's mission as representing Yahweh to the nations, making him known to the nations, when he states, "as the priests represented the Lord to Israel, so Israel was to represent him to the nations. . . . Israel was to reflect the Lord's own presence. In representing the Lord to the nations, Israel makes him known to the world."[59]

Thus, the mission to which Yahweh calls Israel involves what Israel is supposed to be, "a kingdom of priests." Israel as a kingdom of priests is called to be a bridge between Yahweh and the nations for the sake of drawing the nations to Yahweh. Drawing from the analogy between individual

---

56. Cole, *Exodus*, 145.

57. Okoye, *Israel and the Nations*, 62. Israel's corporate priesthood foreshadows the priesthood of believers in the New Testament.

58. Wright, *Mission of God's People*, 121. Italics in original. Also see Wright, *Mission of God*, 330–33. Wright observes that Paul views evangelism as a priestly task. He states, "Certainly this was exactly how Paul saw his own life's work as a missionary to the Gentiles—the nations. He reminds the Romans of 'the grace God gave me to be a minister of Christ Jesus to the Gentiles. He gave me *the priestly duty* of proclaiming the gospel of God, so that the Gentiles might become an offering acceptable to God, sanctified by the Holy Spirit.' . . . In other words, Paul saw his role as bringing God to the nations and bringing the nations to God, and he pictures himself as a priest in doing so. . . . *Evangelism is a priestly task* [italics in original]." Wright, *Mission of God's People*, 122.

59. Blackburn, *God Who Makes Himself Known*, 92.

priests' mediatory role and Israel's mission, it can be concluded that, as a kingdom of priests, Israel is called to bring Yahweh to the nations, and the nations to Yahweh.

Israel's Relationship with Yahweh in Her Priesthood

Israel's priesthood not only implies that it has a priestly role to the nations (the horizontal dimension of Israel's priesthood) but also indicates that Israel has a priestly privilege to be near the presence of *Yahweh* (the vertical dimension of Israel's priesthood).[60] Davies brings out this point by proposing the *ontological* view of Israel's priesthood when he states, "We are not to be looking... for a functional definition of priesthood, but for an *ontological* one."[61] He defines priesthood in terms of "access to the divine presence."[62] Thus, he contends:

> The words of the declaration speak of relationship rather than function. They indicate primarily *the people's standing before God, rather than their obligation towards the other nations* as is often supposed (intercession, service, mission), though it is not denied that there may be implications for human relationships of what it means to be the chosen people of God.[63]

While being too critical of the functional view of Israel's priesthood, Davies's critique of the functional view of Israel's priesthood sheds light on the significance of Israel's priestly role in her direct relationship with Yahweh. Priests in the Old Testament are primarily defined and referred to as "the ones who draw near to Yhwh" or "those who approach Yhwh."[64] As Davies points out, "The essence of the priestly prerogative consisted in access to the presence of God, particularly the presence of God associated with the altar, and above all the sanctuary."[65] Deborah W. Rooke observes from so-called

---

60. For T. Desmond Alexander, the origin of Israel's privilege of being near the presence of Yahweh goes back to the intimate divine-human relationship before the Fall in the book of Genesis. He states, "In Eden [Adam and Eve] experienced as priests the privilege of having immediate access to God's presence (Gen 3:8); in this context priests are those who may approach God and serve him directly." Alexander, *Exodus*, 97.

61. Davies, *Royal Priesthood*, 97.

62. Davies, *Royal Priesthood*, 98.

63. Davies, "Royal Priesthood," 157. Emphasis added.

64. Davies, *Royal Priesthood*, 162. For biblical texts that define priests this way, see Exod 19:22; Lev 10:3; Ezek 42:13, 43:19.

65. Davies, *Royal Priesthood*, 162.

priestly materials—Exodus, Leviticus and Numbers—"Priestly service is understood in terms of 'coming near to the Lord.'"[66]

The Relationship between Two Relational Dimensions of Israel's Priesthood

In light of the role of priests in a community, three points are made clear regarding the relationship between these two aspects of Israel's priesthood. First, the vertical dimension of Israel's priesthood is the condition for the horizontal dimension of Israel's priesthood. This point is obviously true of priests. As Albert Vanhoye states, "The *central element* is the favorable acceptance obtained before Yahweh. The priest is primarily the man of the sanctuary. If he is not accepted by God, he is a useless person."[67] Priests must be able to approach the presence of Yahweh and serve him before his presence because, otherwise, they cannot mediate between Yahweh and the community, failing to represent Yahweh to the community. Likewise, the mediatory role of Israel's priesthood essentially demands her intimate relationship with Yahweh. The relationship between priests and Yahweh is even extended to the whole people of Israel through their priestly mediation. In doing so, the whole people of Israel are intended to be a people who, through their priests' mediation, live with Yahweh who dwells in their midst, and, by extension, a people who represent Yahweh to the nations. Israel's privilege to be near and serve Yahweh before his presence should not be viewed as obtained by their volition or worth, but bestowed on them by God's choice and grace.

Second, the vertical dimension of Israel's priesthood exists for the horizontal dimension of her priesthood.[68] In other words, Israel's intimate

---

66. Rooke, "Priests and Priesthood," 194.

67. Vanhoye, *Old Testament Priests and the New Priest*, 30. Italics in original.

68. It seems unlikely that the horizontal dimension of Israel's priesthood (Israel's mediatory role to the nations) exists for the vertical dimension of her priesthood (Israel's intimate relationship with Yahweh), while the former may have an influence on the latter. At least three reasons support this point. First, the horizontal dimension of Israel's priesthood cannot exist without the vertical dimension of her priesthood because, as noted earlier, the latter is the condition for the former. In other words, the horizontal dimension of Israel's priesthood is derived from the vertical dimension of her priesthood. Second, in most of, if not all, the biblical cases in the Old Testament, Israel's relationship with the nations did not have a positive effect on her relationship with Yahweh. As discussed later in this chapter, Israel was often attracted to the nations and, by extension, turned away from God. Third, while Israel's struggles with the nations often led to the restoration of her relationship with Yahweh, this case is primarily about the relationship between Yahweh and Israel, revealing Yahweh's commitment to Israel.

relationship with Yahweh has a missional purpose. This point is drawn from the priests' role for the sake of a community's benefits. As Vanhoye observes, the priests' close relationship with Yahweh is not only for their own personal benefit, but also for the benefit of the community.[69] After analyzing all the functions of a priest, Roland de Vaux concludes, "All these various functions [of a priest] have a common basis.... [H]e is always an intermediary.... [T]he priest was *ipso facto* a mediator, for the priesthood is an institution for mediation."[70] Likewise, Israel's special relationship with Yahweh is not for her own benefit only, but exists for the sake of the nations. Thus, as Martin Noth states, "Israel has the role of the priestly member in the number of earthly states; it has the priestly privilege of 'drawing near' to God to do 'service' for all the world."[71] The nations can be brought to communion with Yahweh through the mediation of Israel's priesthood. Vanhoye excellently makes this point clear when he states:

> It is easy to see that the sum total of all this activity [at the sanctuary for the benefit of the community] answers a profound aspiration: the desire to live in communion. The role of the priest is to open to the people the possibility of communion with God and community with all humanity, since the one necessarily involves the other. In other words, priesthood is to be defined as an undertaking of mediation.[72]

A third point is derived as a consequence of the two points made above: The ultimate goal of Israel's priestly mediatory role among the nations is to bring the nations into communion with God. Israel's priesthood can be viewed as an extension of the priests' priesthood because priests brought the whole people of Israel into communion with Yahweh, thus shaping Israel's priesthood. In this sense, priests in Israel exist for the purpose of shaping the priesthood of Israel in the midst of the nations. By extension, the priesthood of Israel exists for the sake of shaping the priesthood of the nations by bringing the nations into communion with Yahweh. Through the mediatory role of Israel's priesthood, her priesthood expands to the nations. In this

---

In this case, the restoration of Israel's relationship with Yahweh was not a consequence of her priestly role among the nations. This point is true particularly in light of the fact that Yahweh used the Gentile nations as his means to test Israel's loyalty to him or bring her back to him (e.g., Judg 3:1–6; Isa 9:8–21).

69. Vanhoye, *Old Testament Priests and the New Priest*, 31.
70. Vaux, *Ancient Israel*, 357.
71. Noth, *Exodus*, 157.
72. Vanhoye, *Old Testament Priests and the New Priest*, 31.

view, Israel as a kingdom of priests is called for the sake of a *priestly formation of the nations* (see Figure 2 below).

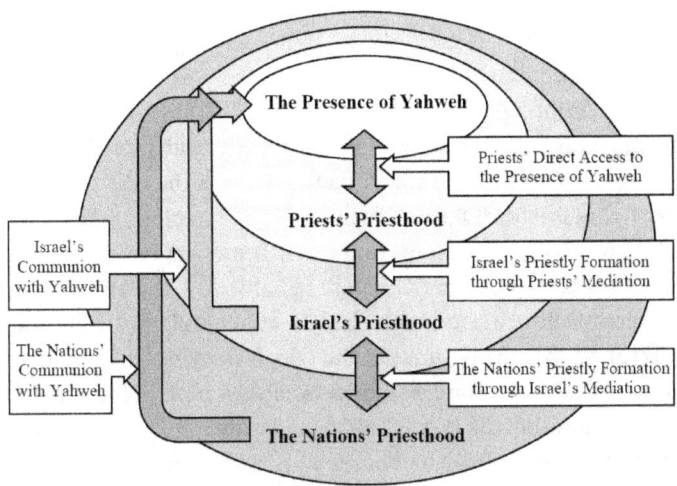

Figure 2. The priestly formation of the nations through Israel's priesthood.

Israel's True Identity (3): "A Holy Nation"

As in the Sinai Covenant, the Old Testament often uses the word "holy" as a term that refers to the characteristic of Israel as a whole. Wells states, "The notion of holiness characterizes Mosaic Yahwism and much of the Pentateuch, Israel's foundational Torah."[73] Wells even related the concept of holiness with the purpose for which Yahweh chose Israel when he comments, "The concept of holiness encompasses the present reality and the future plan for Israel as God's elect."[74] Johannes Hänel describes the whole faith of Israel as a "religion of holiness."[75] Without the concept of holiness, any efforts to decode Israel's call and mission would be incomplete, because, as in the Sinai Covenant, the Old Testament makes this clear.

---

73. Wells, *God's Holy People*, 13.
74. Wells, *God's Holy People*, 13.
75. Quoted in Eichrodt, *Theology of the Old Testament*, 1:270.

Yahweh as the Original Source of Holiness

The proper starting point in discussing the concept of holiness from a biblical perspective should be Yahweh himself because, as J. E. Hartley states, "In Scripture, holiness is exclusive to Yahweh. . . . [B]ecause only God is holy, there is nothing either within humans or on earth that is inherently holy, and no Scripture attempts to define 'holy.'"[76] Thus, as Allan Coppedge points out, "human holiness cannot be properly understood without reference to divine holiness."[77] Given that Yahweh is the one true source of holiness, holiness in the Old Testament, first and foremost, refers to Yahweh himself. In other words, holiness in the Old Testament is a concept that descriptively refers to the essential nature of Yahweh.[78] The fact that holiness is the inherent nature of God in the Old Testament is indicated by the biblical observation that many times in the Old Testament, Yahweh associated himself with the word "holy." Based on his observation of the close relation between the name of God (I AM) and the adjective "holy," Coppedge states, "the chief idea being revealed about God is his holiness."[79] Edmond Jacob also agrees with Coppedge when he states, "the relation between holiness and the name reveals the identity of holiness with deity."[80] Drawing on the relationship between the name and identity of a person in the Bible, Hartley points out, "Because key names were intricately tied to the bearer's identity in the ancient Semitic world, this means that holiness is the quintessential nature of God."[81] Furthermore, the word "holy" is commonly used when the Bible refers to the three persons of the triune God.[82] In light of these scriptural evidence, it can be said that the concept of holiness, first and foremost, refers to the essential nature of Yahweh.

---

76. Hartley, "Holy and Holiness, Clean and Unclean," 420.

77. Coppedge, *Biblical Theology of Holiness*, 16.

78. Schultz, *Old Testament Theology*, 2:173; Snaith, *Distinctive Ideas of the Old Testament*, 46; Brunner, *Christian Doctrine of God*, 157; Jacob, *Theology of the Old Testament*, 86; Purkiser, *Exploring Christian Holiness*, 27; Routledge, *Old Testament Theology*, 115.

79. Coppedge, *Biblical Theology of Holiness*, 42–43.

80. Jacob, *Theology of the Old Testament*, 88.

81. Hartley, "Holy and Holiness, Clean and Unclean," 420.

82. Coppedge, *Biblical Theology of Holiness*, 46.

Holiness and the Presence and Character of Yahweh

The view of holiness as the essential nature of Yahweh is evidenced by the fact that the holiness of Yahweh in the Old Testament is often associated with the *presence* and *character* of Yahweh.

Holiness and the *Presence* of Yahweh

Before the concept of holiness is understood as a moral concept, it is primitively a term associated with the presence of a divine being. Rudolph Otto develops this primitive view of divine holiness. In constructing the most primitive idea of the holy, he calls the most pure and primitive form of religious experience "mysterious tremendum," which is a phrase he coined from two concepts—(1) the presence of a *mystery*, which is inexpressible and above all creatures, and (2) *tremor*, which refers to a feeling of fear as the most primitive form of human response to the mystery.[83] In short, the idea of holiness is a human primitive response to the presence of a divine being.

When the Old Testament speaks of holiness as a term for the essential nature of Yahweh, it does not speak of an abstract concept of a divine being, but rather associates it with *the presence of Yahweh*. Wells observes that holiness is "a characteristic which is associated with the *presence* of Yhwh."[84] An example is the biblical account of the burning bush in Exodus 3.[85] The burning bush itself represented the presence of Yahweh in the moment when Moses witnessed it; the presence of Yahweh made *holy* the place of the burning bush. Likewise, Mt. Sinai and the tabernacle (and temple) in the Old Testament were holy because Yahweh was present there. These biblical cases show that it is the presence of Yahweh that makes objects and individuals holy in the Old Testament. That is why the distance from the presence of Yahweh is one major symbolic way to measure the degree of holiness in the Old Testament. In this sense, as Hartley states, one aspect of the Israelites' being holy meant that "God was present in their midst."[86]

---

83. Otto, *Idea of the Holy*.

84. Wells, *God's Holy People*, 31.

85. Oswalt states, "Note that this is the first time 'holy' appears in the Bible. Furthermore, there are only four previous occurrences of derivative forms of the root." Oswalt, *Called to be Holy*, 25.

86. Hartley, "Holy and Holiness, Clean and Unclean," 427.

Holiness and the *Character* of Yahweh

While the primitive idea of holiness is commonly found in other religions, the concept of holiness in the Old Testament moves beyond the primitive idea of holiness. The concept of holiness in the Old Testament is unique because it is a term for the uniqueness of Yahweh. James Muilenburg states, "Yahweh's uniqueness is the uniqueness of his holiness."[87] Brueggemann points out, "The term *holiness* . . . refers to the radical otherness of Yahweh,"[88] by which he means the "incompatibility" of Yahweh.[89] Gerhard von Rad states, "[the concept of the holy] is . . . the 'wholly other.'"[90] Thus, the underlying idea of the holiness of Yahweh is that Yahweh is *radically unique*.

One way that the Old Testament refers to the uniqueness of Yahweh is through the character of Yahweh, which began to be explicitly revealed by means of two biblical events—the Exodus and the Sinai Covenant. Hartley states, "God mightily revealed his holy character to Israel at the sea and at Sinai."[91] The character of Yahweh as revealed to Israel through the act of redemption and his initiation of the Sinai Covenant is *moral* and *relational*. Through the Exodus, Yahweh demonstrated his faithful love for the Israelites. Israel praised the incomparable power and character of Yahweh after they crossed the Red Sea, singing, "*Who is like you, O Lord, among the gods? Who is like you, majestic in holiness, awesome in splendor, doing wonders?*" (Exod 15:11). Then, in Exodus 15:13, they praised Yahweh not only for his incomparable power but also his incomparable character as revealed in his mighty act of redemption: "In *your steadfast love* you led the people whom you redeemed."[92] On the phrase, "your steadfast love," Philip Graham Ryken comments, "By 'unfailing love,' Moses meant God's covenant-keeping love, his absolute loyalty to his people, and his faithfulness to his promise. God had proved his love to Israel over and over. Everything that had happened to this point in the book of Exodus was motivated by God's love."[93] By proving his faithful love for Israel, Yahweh explicitly revealed his moral and relational character through the Exodus.

---

87. Muilenburg, "Holiness," 619.

88. Brueggemann, *Theology of the Old Testament*, 288. Italics in original.

89. Brueggemann, *Theology of the Old Testament*, 288.

90. von Rad, *Old Testament Theology*, 205.

91. Hartley, "Holy and Holiness, Clean and Unclean," 430.

92. The phrase "steadfast love" is translated differently in different English translations. It was translated as "unfailing love" in NIV, "lovingkindness" in NASB, "mercy" KJV, and "love" in JPS Tanakh.

93. Ryken, *Exodus*, 409.

Along with the Exodus, the moral and relational character of Yahweh is made further explicit in the context of the Sinai Covenant. Brueggemann observes God's relatedness from the biblical picture of "a God bound in covenant,"[94] and states, "covenant requires of Yahweh a practice of faithfulness and steadfast love, an enduring engagement with and involvement for Israel."[95] John Oswalt states, "by making a covenant with his people God seeks to reveal his holy character,"[96] and identifies three moral characteristics of Yahweh revealed in the context of the covenant: grace, ethical righteousness, and faithfulness.[97] The unique character of Yahweh, revealed in and by the covenant, is moral and relational.

The moral and relational aspect of holiness is a unique aspect of holiness in Israel, rooted in the moral and relational character of Yahweh.[98] The Exodus and the Sinai Covenant reveal that the character of Yahweh is characterized by virtues such as love, grace, faithfulness, mercy, justice, and ethical righteousness.

Israel's Distinctiveness Shaped by the Holiness of Yahweh

The relationship between Yahweh's holiness and Israel's holiness implies that Israel's call to be a holy nation presupposes Israel's constant and intimate relationship with Yahweh. Israel can be holy only in her connection or relation with Yahweh because Yahweh is the original and only source of holiness. Consequently, Israel is expected to be a people that *reflects God's holiness* in her life. This point is made explicit as in Leviticus 19:2b: "You shall be holy to me; for I the Lord your God am holy." The Israelites' being a holy nation means that they are called to reflect the holiness of Yahweh in their life. Because the holiness of Yahweh is associated with the presence and character of Yahweh, it can be said that Israel was called to reflect the holiness of Yahweh by living a life profoundly shaped by the presence and character of Yahweh. Blackburn echoes this point when he states, "The difference [between Israel and the nations] lay not in Israel's nationhood, but in the fact that Israel was the Lord's, and she alone reflected his character" and "Israel somehow reflects the Lord's presence."[99]

94. Brueggemann, *Theology of the Old Testament*, 297.
95. Brueggemann, *Theology of the Old Testament*, 297.
96. Oswalt, *Called to be Holy*, 38.
97. Oswalt, *Called to be Holy*, 21–38.
98. According to Hartley, "in most other religions, holiness and the ethical are not connected." Hartley, "Holy and Holiness, Clean and Unclean," 420.
99. Blackburn, *God Who Makes Himself Known*, 94. According to Blackburn, "The

Israel's Life Shaped by the *Presence* of Yahweh

In light of the inseparable relation between holiness and the presence of Yahweh, Israel's call to be a holy nation implies that Israel is called to reflect the *presence* of Yahweh. What enables Israel to reflect the presence of Yahweh to the world is Yahweh's determination to be bonded with Israel. Yahweh wills to dwell in her midst as in Exodus 39:45: "I will *dwell among the Israelites*, and I will be their God." As Brueggemann points out, the Old Testament presents Yahweh as "the Holy One in/of Israel."[100] Israel is called not merely to be a people but to be a people in the midst of whom Yahweh dwells.

The presence of Yahweh in the midst of Israel creates a context of dealing with the particular issue of how Israel should live with the holy Yahweh. This issue of holiness is related to Israel's whole cultic system, including the state of being clean or unclean. Brueggemann states, "holiness as pertains to Yahweh has cultic footage and concerns the proper use, ordering, and protection of cultic matters."[101] The ritually purifying system creates boundaries between cleanness and uncleanness, but its purpose is not separation. The purifying ritual system is indispensable if Israel is to live with the holy Yahweh who dwells in her midst. Hartley states:

> These rules on ritual purity were not designed either to separate the Israelites from dealing with foreigners or to set up classes within Israelite society, as was often the case in other cultures .... The purpose of these rules was to establish boundaries in the routine of daily life in order that the Israelites might live as a holy people serving Yahweh, who is holy. The primary boundary was to prevent any impure person or thing from entering sacred space; therefore, all had to be ritually clean before entering the sanctuary lest holiness consume them.[102]

Regarding Leviticus 11, which deals with clean and unclean food and animals, Brueggemann notes similarly, "The holiness of Yahweh is understood, in texts like Leviticus 11, as the careful management of the mystery of access [to the presence of Yahweh], which in turn opens the mystery of life."[103] In other words, Israel's whole ritual system with clean and unclean categories

---

expectation that Israel is to reflect the Lord's character, implicit in the use of [the Hebrew root of the word 'holy'] in Exodus, but becomes explicit in Leviticus: 'be holy, for I am holy' (Lev. 11:44–45; cf. 19:2; 20:26; 21:8)." Blackburn, *God Who Makes Himself Known*, 94n24.

100. Brueggemann, *Theology of the Old Testament*, 289.
101. Brueggemann, *Theology of the Old Testament*, 288.
102. Hartley, "Holy and Holiness, Clean and Unclean," 426.
103. Brueggemann, *Theology of the Old Testament*, 289.

was intended not to build separation but to "make Yahweh's holy, life-generating, life-guaranteeing presence available and certain in Israel."[104] In this regard, Israel is called to live a life carefully aligned with the rules associated with the presence of Yahweh in her midst. In this way, Israel's life is to reflect the presence of Yahweh who is in her midst.

Israel's life shaped by the *character* of Yahweh

If the holiness of Yahweh is a term that points to the character of Yahweh, Israel's being holy means that the people are called to *reflect the character of Yahweh*. In other words, the people of Israel are intended to be a people whose distinctive life corresponds to and, by extension, displays the character of Yahweh. In this way, Israel is called not only to be a people in the midst of whom Yahweh dwells, but also to be a people who are *like Yahweh*. Brueggemann puts it this way: "The premise of the command of Sinai is that Yahweh is holy . . . and Israel, who is contingently holy, is to *imitate Yahweh* and so become holy likewise."[105] Hartley states, "To heed this call [to be holy as Yahweh is holy] the Israelites were to respond to God *by becoming like God*; that is, they were to develop in themselves characteristics such as those God possesses."[106] Wells notes similarly, "[Israel] can, in some way, become like God."[107] In this way, Yahweh is to be made visible through Israel's distinctiveness which is profoundly shaped by the character of Yahweh.

Two Relational Dimensions of Israel's Holiness

Out of the discussion of the concept of holiness above, two relational dimensions of Israel's holiness are identified. First, regarding Israel's relationship with Yahweh, Israel's holiness is a derived holiness. Second, as for Israel's relationship with the nations, Israel's holiness has a missionary dimension.

---

104. Brueggemann, *Theology of the Old Testament*, 288. For the relationship between Israel's ritual (or cultic) system and the presence of Yahweh, see Brueggemann, *Theology of the Old Testament*, 192–93.

105. Brueggemann, *Theology of the Old Testament*, 290. Emphasis added.

106. Hartley, "Holy and Holiness, Clean and Unclean," 427. Emphasis added.

107. Wells, *God's Holy People*, 31.

Israel's Holiness as a Derived Holiness

The view of Yahweh as the sole source of holiness implies that the holiness of Yahweh is *the* model of, reason for, and foundation for the holiness of Israel. First, the holiness of Yahweh is the *model* of Israel's holiness. In light of the view of Yahweh as the source of holiness, Israel's holiness is always derived holiness. The quality of the holiness of Yahweh determines the quality of Israel's holiness. This means that the people of Israel are called to be distinctive in a way that their presence and life display the holiness of Yahweh. In this aspect of Israel's holiness, the emphasis is countercultural, whereas an incultural[108] aspect of her holiness is not absent.[109]

Second, the holiness of Yahweh is the *reason* for Israel's holiness. In other words, her pursuit of being a holy nation should be motivated by the holiness of Yahweh. In Leviticus 19:2b, Yahweh says, "You shall be holy to me; for I the Lord your God am holy." There is no reason given to Israel, other than Yahweh's holiness, for her to be holy. Yahweh makes his holiness the reason for Israel's pursuit of holiness.

Third, the holiness of Yahweh is the *foundation* for Israel's holiness. As Judy Yates Siker points out, "Holiness depends on relationship to God."[110] Coppedge states, "One of the consequences of this fact [that the holiness of all other things becomes a secondary holiness, not a primary holiness] is that while God is holy always and forever, persons and things may lose their holiness . . . . So we may safely say that derived holiness is not automatically a permanent possession."[111] In this sense, the Israelites' being holy requires *their constant faithful relationship with Yahweh*. The unfolding story of Israel, which will be looked at later, demonstrates this point: when Israel failed to be faithful to the covenant relationship with Yahweh, it failed to be Yahweh-like, becoming instead like other nations.

---

108. Antithetical to the term *countercultural*, the term *incultural* basically means "translated into a culture," or "culturally relevant," denoting a positive relationship with a particular culture. Another term, which is equivalent to the term *incultural* is the term *indigenous*. According to David Bosch, the term *inculturation* refers to one aspect of contextualization. For the discussion of the history, essence, meaning of the term *inculturation*, see Bosch, *Transforming Mission*, 447–57.

109. One way to see the incultural aspect of Israel's distinctiveness is the similarity between Israel's religion and ancient Near East religions.

110. Siker, "Holiness," 477.

111. Coppedge, *Biblical Theology of Holiness*, 49. For Coppedge, a biblical example that illustrates this relationship between the original divine holiness and derived holiness is the case of Jerusalem city, which ceased to be the holy city when the glory of God departed from it (Ezek 10).

The Missionary Nature of Israel's Holiness

Israel's relationship with Yahweh highlights Israel's distinctiveness, which is rooted in the holiness of Yahweh, but her distinctiveness has a missionary purpose. The missionary dimension of her holiness can be explained in terms of the relationship between being distinctive in the midst of the nations and reaching out to the nations. On the one hand, as discussed above, Israel is called to reflect the holiness of Yahweh by being a people whose life is profoundly shaped by the presence and character of Yahweh. In this way, Israel's holiness is primarily about being a contrast people amid the nations, instead of Israel's outward ministry to the nations.

On the other hand, Israel's holiness has a missionary purpose because, through her holiness, Israel is able to present the holiness of Yahweh to the nations. John Durham highlights the visibility of the distinctiveness of the people when he states:

> Israel as a "holy people" then represents a third dimension of what it means to be committed in faith to Yahweh [i.e., along with a treasured possession and a kingdom of priests]: they are to be a people set apart, different from all other people by what they are and are becoming—*a display-people*, a showcase to the world of how being in covenant with Yahweh changes a people.[112]

In a similar vein, Wells asserts, "being 'holy' does not infer a separation in terms of isolation" between Israel and the nations. Rather, it "demands a relationship with others, for Israel is invested with God's presence, then it may represent it and mediate it to others."[113] Blackburn put it this way: "What . . . did it mean that Israel was a holy nation? Simply put, Israel was set apart as a nation for the purpose of rendering priestly service in order to *reflect the character of God to the nations*. In other words, through Israel, God would *make himself known to the world*."[114] In this sense, what generates Israel's missionary role to the nations is the visibility of Israel's holiness. Hence, if Israel should lose her holiness, she would become like the nations. As a consequence, Israel would no longer be able to perform her missionary role among the nations.

---

112. Durham, *Exodus*, 263. Emphasis added.
113. Wells, *God's Holy People*, 56–57.
114. Blackburn, *God Who Makes Himself Known*, 95. Emphasis added.

The Relationship between the Priesthood and Holiness of Israel

As discussed above, the phrases, "a kingdom of priests" and "a holy nation," highlight different aspects of the missionary vocation of Israel. If Israel's priesthood defines the relationships between Yahweh and Israel and between Israel and the nations, Israel's holiness is the *condition* of the relationships, one that enables the relationships. Wright observes this relationship between Israel's priesthood and holiness, as he points out, "the priestly role . . . required holiness of Israel, just as it required holiness of their own priests in the midst of the ordinary people of Israel."[115] For Wright, holiness is "a condition of priesthood" and priesthood is "a dimension of mission."[116]

Regarding the vertical view of priesthood (a priest's intimate relationship with Yahweh), a priest's holiness is an essential condition for his qualification to serve before Yahweh. When a priest fails to be holy, the priest is disqualified from being near the presence of Yahweh and, thus, serving him before his presence. As a result, the defiled priest cannot fulfill his priestly role before the presence of Yahweh. Regarding the horizontal dimension of priesthood (a priest's mediatory role between Yahweh and Israel), a priest in Israel is called for the sake of Israel's communion with Yahweh. When a priest fails to be holy, the priest is unable to serve as a bridge between Yahweh and Israel. As a result, the priest cannot fulfill the mediatory role, leaving the community disconnected from the presence of Yahweh. R. K. Duke well summarizes this view of a priest's holiness as a condition for the priest's mediatory role when he states:

> To be a priest was to operate in the danger zone of encroaching upon the divine realm for the purposes of representing the divine will to the community and representing the community before God. To be in the presence of the holy God was to risk death. . . . Those set aside to be priests were placed in a special state of holiness that allowed them access to the 'dwelling' of God. . . . The priests' position of having a greater status of holiness than that of the layperson not only put them at greater risk of dying but also placed them in a position of being able to serve the community of faith effectively."[117]

Likewise, without being holy, Israel cannot have an intimate relationship with Yahweh. This means loss of the vertical aspect of her priesthood, namely failure to have an intimate relationship with Yahweh. It also results in loss of

---

115. Wright, *Mission of God*, 372.
116. Wright, *Mission of God*, 372.
117. Duke, "Priests, Priesthood," 652.

the horizontal aspect of her capability to reflect the holiness of Yahweh, being disconnected from Yahweh, who is the origin of her holiness. As a consequence, without being holy, Israel cannot present the holiness of Yahweh to the nations, thus failing to make Yahweh visible to the nations. Ultimately, Israel becomes unable to fulfill the horizontal aspect of her priesthood—bringing Yahweh to the nations and the nations to Yahweh.

Out of the analysis of the relationship between the priesthood and holiness of Israel, two implications about Israel's missionary vocation are derived: First, the fulfillment of Israel's missionary vocation involves the restoration of her holiness, which is required for her priestly role to the nations, and, therefore, second, the fulfillment of Israel's missionary vocation requires that she succeed in keeping an intimate relationship with Yahweh because he is the very source of her holiness.[118]

Requirement of Obedience

Israel's call and mission are built on Yahweh's covenant with the people and come with one conditional statement, "if you obey me fully and keep my covenant," in verse 5a.[119] The requirement of obedience in the Sinai Covenant brings up a particular issue to be considered in order to identify the nature of Israel's missionary vocation: *How is the requirement of human obedience related to the fulfillment of Israel's missionary vocation?* Regarding this question, two points can be identified as discussed below: (1) Israel's obedience as the essential condition for fulfilling her missionary vocation and (2) Yahweh's faithfulness as the context of the conditionality of the Sinai Covenant.

Obedience as the Key for the Fulfillment of Israel's Missionary Vocation

The discussion of the phrase "treasured possession" above shows that the relationship between Yahweh and Israel is characterized by Israel's devoted service to Yahweh. This aspect of the relationship becomes explicit with

---

118. These implications highlight one biblical theme—the presence of God, which will be discussed later.

119. According to Terence E. Fretheim, "In [Exod] 19:5, . . . keeping covenant is essentially equivalent to obeying God's voice, but with the specific reference back to Abraham." Fretheim, *Exodus*, 211. Following his interpretation on the verse, our discussion on the conditional statement in Exod 19:4 will assume that the two phrases—obeying God and keeping his covenant—in Exod 19:4 are not different items and that they simply refer to a human obedient response to God.

the conditional statement of obedience in such a way that such a relationship is actualized only when Israel is fully obedient to Yahweh. Likewise, Israel's missionary vocation as being a kingdom of priests and a holy nation also can be fulfilled only when the people are faithful to the requirement of obedience to Yahweh. Wright states, "this identity and role [of Israel] was dependent on the condition [of obedience]."[120] Thus, the obedience requirement in the Sinai Covenant has a missional dimension in that what Yahweh intends Israel to be for the sake of the nations demands her full obedience to him. In this sense, what makes Israel a missionary people depends on her full obedience to Yahweh.[121] Wright echoes this point when he states, "How are we to be such a holy people? This brings us back to our text, to verse 5a. 'Now if you obey me fully and keep my covenant....' (Ex. 19:5a). *Obedience* is the key to being priestly and holy."[122]

This aspect of the requirement of obedience in the Sinai Covenant implies one significant nature of Israel's transformation to be God's missionary people: Israel's becoming missional essentially involves her becoming *obedient* to Yahweh because the fulfillment of her missionary vocation is impossible apart from her fully obedient relationship with Yahweh. Thus, a fundamental condition for Israel's being missional is Israel's *faithfulness* in her relationship with Yahweh. This relationship is characterized by her full obedience to him, which is not merely legalism, but involves love (e.g., Deut 6:5) and trust (e.g., Josh 1:9; Ps 112:7; Isa 26:3).

Conditionality in the Context of Yahweh's Unceasing Faithfulness

Regarding the conditional statement—"if you obey" (Exod 19:5)—in the Sinai Covenant, one question needs to be considered for a proper understanding of the nature of Israel's missionary vocation: Does the conditional statement of the Sinai Covenant suggest that the fulfillment of the Sinai Covenant depend *merely on human obedience*?

One clue to the question is found in the relationship between the Sinai Covenant and the Abrahamic Covenant. At a surface level, it appears as though the fulfillment of the covenant hinges upon human obedience.

---

120. Wright, *Mission of God*, 333. Also see Wright, *Mission of God's People*, 126.

121. The significance of Israel's obedience for her missionary vocation is further supported by Duane A. Garrett's observation of a chiastic structure within the Sinai Covenant text. According to Garrett's construction of the chiastic structure, the central element is the conditional statement of obedience. It implies that the most central part of the Sinai Covenant is obedience. For the chiastic structure observed by Garrett, see Garrett, *Commentary on Exodus*, 459.

122. Wright, *Mission of God's People*, 126. Italics in original.

The covenant is often categorized as a conditional covenant, but Gentry and Wellum remark, "the categories of conditional and unconditional often used in characterizing covenants are not helpful or fruitful because they result in failing to hear the different emphases in the biblical text."[123] Taking this approach, Davies argues that the conditional statement should be understood "within the framework of an already established relationship."[124] Victor P. Hamilton notes, "The purpose of the Lord's offering Israel a covenant is not to 'make' Israel God's people. They already are God's people. Earlier in Exodus the Lord has already called Israel 'my people,' 'my firstborn son,' 'my son.' . . . Also, Moses in conversation with Lord has called Israel 'your people' (5:23)."[125] Fretheim also echoes the same view, based on his observation that Yahweh refers to himself as God of the ancestors of Israel.

> [T]he recurring references to the God of Abraham, Isaac, and Jacob, and the promises sworn to them, simply assume that this people is already God's people, the inheritor of the promises given to their ancestors (3:15–17; 6:4, 8). . . . This suggests that for Exodus *the covenant at Sinai is a specific covenant within the context of the Abrahamic covenant.*[126]

This observation about the already-established relationship between Yahweh and Israel before the establishment of the Sinai Covenant reveals that, as Fretheim asserts, "the covenant at Sinai is a specific covenant within an *already existing* covenant."[127] More specifically, Hamilton views the Sinai Covenant as a covenant which "elevates to a more intimate, dynamic level an *already-existing* relationship between two parties."[128]

In this regard, the Sinai Covenant is in continuation of the Abrahamic Covenant,[129] by which Israel has already been brought into a relationship with Yahweh. Davies points out, "The Abrahamic covenant . . . is very much

---

123. For the conventional way of the categorization of covenants based on whether they are conditional or unconditional, see Davies, *Royal Priesthood*, 178–81.

124. Davies, *Royal Priesthood*, 46.

125. Hamilton, *Exodus*, 301.

126. Fretheim, *Exodus*, 209. Italics in original.

127. Fretheim, *Exodus*, 209.

128. Hamilton, *Exodus*, 301.

129. While seldom recognized among scholars, the Noahic Covenant (Gen 9:8–17), which is God's everlasting covenant, serves as a larger context and a preliminary condition of the Abrahamic Covenant and other following biblical covenants. Already noted in the Theological Framework section of chapter 1, God's post-Fall initiation of redeeming the whole creation already began with the Noahic Covenant. For the discussion of (1) the significance of the Noahic Covenant in God's mission and (2) its implications for mission today, see Snyder and Scandrett, *Salvation Means Creation Healed*, 117–34.

in view as providing the framework for the exodus and Sinai covenant."[130] William J. Dumbrell even brings these two covenants into a close relationship, based on similarities between the Abrahamic Covenant and the Sinai Covenant in such a way that "the Sinai Covenant was in fact a particularization of Gen. 12:1–3 in the experience of Israel."[131] If the Sinai Covenant is in continuation of the Abrahamic Covenant, by which Yahweh's relationship with the people of Israel is *already* established, the requirement of obedience in the Sinai Covenant is *not* a condition based on which Israel can obtain the status of Yahweh's treasured possession.[132] As already noted above, it is a condition that fulfills what Yahweh expected Israel as his *already* chosen people to *look like*. It is a requirement that would enable the people of Israel to play their missionary role among the nations. Fretheim states, "The condition would be that a disobedient Israel would not be able to be the kind of people God has called them to be, and hence God would not be able to use them for this purpose as God would like."[133]

Another biblical clue to the nature of the Sinai Covenant's conditionality comes from how Yahweh dealt with Israel's covenantal infidelity. As illustrated in the story of the golden calf (Exod 32–34), which is the first biblical case of Israel's covenantal unfaithfulness, Yahweh continued to keep his covenant with the people of Israel even in the cases where they failed to obey him. The story of the golden calf finds its culmination not in Yahweh's breaking the covenant, but in his renewing and re-establishing it (Exod 34:10–28).[134] In light of this biblical case, Dumbrell even suggests the prospect for the *unconditionality* of the Sinai Covenant, which "could not lie with a national Israel,[135] but with God's continuous faithfulness to fulfill the covenant. God's unceasing faithfulness to fulfilling the Sinai Covenant does not mean that the Sinai Covenant operates regardless of Israel's obedience requirement. Rather, it suggests that God continuously brings Israel back to

---

130. Davies, *Royal Priesthood*, 180.

131. Dumbrell, "Prospect of Unconditionality," 153.

132. In his considerable discussion on the nature of the Sinai Covenant's conditionality, Davies concludes that the condition statement in the covenant can be viewed as a *privilege* given to Israel as part of the relationship already established between Yahweh and Israel. Thus, for the Israelite, the obedience requirement is not viewed as a burden or duty, but it was something they were *joyful* about because they were *privileged* in an already established relationship between them and Yahweh. See Davies, *Royal Priesthood*, 46–47.

133. Fretheim, *Exodus*, 213.

134. Dumbrell, "Prospect of Unconditionality," 150–52.

135. Dumbrell, "Prospect of Unconditionality," 152. For the discussion on the unconditional aspect of the Sinai Covenant, see Waltke, "Phenomenon of Conditionality"; Davies, *Royal Priesthood*, 181–82.

a covenant relationship with him. God's unceasing faithfulness to the covenant does not negate Israel's requirement of obedience, but leads Israel to becoming a people who faithfully obey God.

In conclusion, the discussion of the nature of the Sinai Covenant does not suggest that the Sinai Covenant is purely a conditional covenant whose fulfillment depends merely on human obedience, but suggests that the conditional nature of the Sinai Covenant is within the context of Yahweh's unceasing faithfulness to fulfill the covenant. Thus, Yahweh's faithfulness to the covenant is a *central* factor for the fulfillment of Israel's missionary purpose. Davies states, "It would thus appear just as valid to speak of unconditionality with respect to the Sinai Covenant as it is with the Abrahamic or Davidic, if by this is meant the certainty that God will abide by *his commitments*."[136] From this point, one aspect of how Israel would fulfill her missionary vocation is identified: The fulfillment of Israel's missionary vocation that hinges upon her covenant relationship with Yahweh, is led by *Yahweh's faithfulness* in fulfilling her missionary purpose revealed in the Abrahamic Covenant.

The Grace of Yahweh

The Sinai Covenant begins by addressing Yahweh's act of grace already demonstrated for the people of Israel, as found in Exodus 19:4 in which he reminds Israel of what he had done for her through the Exodus: "You have seen what I did to the Egyptians, and how I bore you on eagles' wings and brought you to myself." Two aspects of how Yahweh shapes Israel as his missionary people are indicated by two observations about the mention of the Exodus in the Sinai Covenant. First, as already discussed above, it is true that Israel's obedience to Yahweh is a central part of the Sinai Covenant and *the* necessary condition for Israel to fulfill her call and mission. However, Israel's obedience is not merely a duty nor obligation; rather, Israel's obedience is her *joyful and grateful response* to Yahweh's grace. This point is derived from the relationship between the Exodus, through which Yahweh demonstrated his grace for Israel, and the Sinai Covenant, in which Israel is called to obey Yahweh. The relationship between the Exodus and the Sinai Covenant is indicated in the fact that Yahweh invited Israel into the Sinai Covenant by reminding her of what Yahweh had done for her in verse 4. Davies contends, "The past dealings of Yhwh with this people provide the basis for the undertaking of vv. 5–6."[137] Hedlund echoes the same point when he states, "the terms of the agreement were expressed in covenant law, yet the

---

136. Davies, *Royal Priesthood*, 182. Emphasis added.
137. Davies, *Royal Priesthood*, 104.

basis of the relationship was entirely of grace."[138] John Bright views the Sinai Covenant even as "a covenant of Grace."[139]

The role of Yahweh's reminder of the Exodus in the establishment of the Sinai Covenant between him and Israel can be seen more concretely in light of the immediate context, in which Yahweh invited Israel to the covenant and Israel responded to his invitation. Hamilton observes how the immediate context of the Sinai Covenant would impact the establishment of the Sinai Covenant. He asks, "Of interest here is that the Lord does not speak to his people anytime before chap. 19 about a covenant. So why wait until now? Why wait until after the Exodus, until the sea has been crossed, until they are well into the journey to Canaan?"[140] Hamilton finds a convincing answer to the question from Moshe Greenberg's quote, which is from a halakic midrash on the book of Exodus:

> Why didn't the Torah begin with the Decalogue? A parable will explain it: A man entered a country and said, "Make me your king." The people replied, "What have you even done for us that we should make you our king?" So, he built them walls, made them water-works, fought wars on their behalf. Then he said to them, "Make me your king," and they said, "Yes indeed!" Thus God liberated Israel from Egypt, divided the sea for them, gave them manna from heaven, provided them with a water supply, provisioned them with quail, fought Amalek on their behalf, then said to them, "Make me your king," whereupon they replied, "Yes indeed!"[141]

Oswalt notes similarly:

> God addresses the Israelites, after he has graciously delivered them, and invites them to enter into a relationship with him wherein he would be their God, and they would be his people (Ex. 19:3-6).... After all, they have seen what God had done to the Egyptian gods and the sea and to the Amalekites. To have a God like that as one's own would certainly be of great benefit! It is at this point that God offers the covenant.[142]

---

138. Hedlund, *Mission of the Church*, 60.
139. Bright, *Kingdom of God*, 28.
140. Hamilton, *Exodus*, 301.
141. Quoted in Hamilton, *Exodus*, 301. Later, the midrash was translated into English, and the English version of the midrash is available now. For the quote in the English version of the midrash, see Lauterbach, *Mekhilta De-Rabbi Ishmael*, 2:313-14.
142. Oswalt, *Called to be Holy*, 27.

In this regard, as Goldingay points out, Yahweh was "showing who is *king*" to Israel through the Exodus.[143] Thus, through the Exodus, Yahweh proved to the people of Israel that he deserves their full obedience as their new king. In this sense, Yahweh's grace was *the evidence* to the people of Israel that Yahweh deserved their single-minded allegiance to him, *the reason* for them to accept the covenant, and *the motivation* for them to keep the covenant.[144] Therefore, the covenant relationship is characterized by Israel's obedience to Yahweh as her grateful and joyful response to Yahweh's grace. The Israelites accepted Yahweh's invitation to the Sinai Covenant gratefully because what Yahweh had done for them was so gracious. They accepted the Sinai Covenant joyfully because their experience of Yahweh's grace had created a positive expectation about a new life that they would live with Yahweh who was so gracious to them.

A second aspect of Israel's formation into God's missionary people is that the fulfillment of Israel's missionary vocation is interrelated with her relationship with Yahweh. This point was already suggested in the above discussion of Israel's identity and the requirement of obedience and is also indicated in the way that Yahweh described the Exodus in Exodus 19:4b, in which Yahweh says, "[I] brought you to myself." On this verse, Davies comments, "The 'bringing to myself' expresses the underlying motivation of the preceding divine actions and focuses on relationship rather than location."[145] On the verse, Chukwuma states, "The action of deliverance was a demonstration of Yahweh's good will toward these former slaves in Egypt and of Yahweh's desire to have them for Yahweh alone."[146] Blackburn notes, "The Lord did not deliver Israel for her own sake, henceforth to live independently, but rather for relationship with him. In effect, this relationship with the Lord was the goal of the Egyptian deliverance."[147] In light of this point, two relational dimensions of Yahweh's work for Israel's missional formation are identified. On the one hand, as already argued, Yahweh's act of grace for Israel aimed at the fulfillment of her missionary vocation for *all nations*. On the other hand, Yahweh initiated the Exodus, motivated by his desire for the relationship with *Israel*. Hence, Yahweh's work for the fulfillment of Israel's missional purpose—all nations will be blessed—is intertwined with his desire to have the relationship with Israel. Yahweh is driven both by his faithfulness to fulfill Israel's missionary vocation and his desire to have the

---

143. Goldingay, *Israel's Gospel*, 320. Emphasis added.
144. Gentry and Wellum, *Kingdom through Covenant*, 312.
145. Davies, *Royal Priesthood*, 40–41.
146. Okoye, *Israel and the Nations*, 58–59.
147. Blackburn, *God Who Makes Himself Known*, 88.

relationship with her. One implication that logically comes out here is that the missional purpose Yahweh has for Israel is intrinsically related to the relationship that he desired to have with Israel. This implication indicates that Yahweh's work of fulfilling Israel's missionary vocation necessarily involves the restoration of her relationship to him.

Summary

In the Sinai Covenant, Yahweh made explicit the way that Yahweh intended to fulfill the missional purpose he had for Israel among the nations. The discussion of the Sinai Covenant in this section decoded the covenant in relation to the Exodus and with the focus on three elements of the covenant—three identity-defining phrases, the requirement of obedience, and Yahweh's grace. Several aspects of how Israel would fulfill her missionary vocation are derived from the analysis of the Sinai Covenant as recapitulated below.

First, Israel's missionary purpose would be fulfilled by Yahweh's faithfulness to the Abrahamic Covenant. As in the case of the Exodus, the Sinai Covenant is in continuation of his faithfulness to fulfill Israel's missionary purpose revealed in the Abrahamic Covenant. The covenant was initiated not by Israel but by Yahweh. Yahweh's commitment to shape Israel as his missionary people is clearly indicated by the point that Israel's obedience requirement in the Sinai Covenant should be understood as God's commitment to continuously bring Israel back to the obedient relationship. This point implies that Israel's missional conversion would take place in the context of *Yahweh's unceasing faithfulness* in fulfilling his plan about Israel's missionary purpose.

Second, the missionary nature of Israel's call has two relational dimensions. The three phrases in the Sinai Covenant, which refer to the missionary vocation of Israel, show the interrelatedness of two relational dimensions of Israel's missionary vocation: between Yahweh and Israel, and between Israel and the nations. These two relational dimensions of Israel's missionary vocation are further supported by two divine motivations of the Exodus: Yahweh's faithfulness to fulfill his mission of bringing his blessing to *all nations* and his desire to have the relationship with *Israel*. Furthermore, the analysis of the three identity-defining phrases in the Sinai Covenant affirms that these two relational dimensions of Israel's call are related to each other in such a way that Israel's relationship with Yahweh is a condition for her missionary role to the nations. In other words, Israel's mission among and for the nations flows from the uniqueness of her relationship with Yahweh. Therefore, the way that Yahweh shapes Israel as his missionary people indispensably involves the restoration of her relationship with Yahweh.

Third, Israel's mission is primarily about being distinctive among the nations, rather than intentionally reaching out to the nations, though it necessarily involves both. Yahweh invited Israel into the Sinai Covenant for the sake of the missional purpose he had for Israel, but her mission was not primarily a crosscultural missionary task. Israel's mission as revealed in the Sinai Covenant was to *be* a contrast people, who present the holiness of Yahweh to the nations through the visibility of Israel's distinctive life which reflects the holiness of Yahweh who was in her midst. Hence, Israel's mission in the Old Testament period was primarily not centrifugal (reaching out to the nations), but rather centripetal because the nations were to be drawn to Yahweh through Israel's distinctiveness which reflects the holiness of Yahweh. However, the centripetal movement of Israel's mission should not be viewed as absence of the centrifugal movement in her mission. Israel was not in isolation from the nations, but was sent among the nations by Yahweh. The sent-ness of Israel's presence among the nations was the centrifugal force of Yahweh's mission to the nations. In this sense, Israel's distinctive presence, which is publicly visible and identifiable among the nations, was to be Yahweh's act of proclamation about who he is to the nations.

Fourth, Israel is called to become a *particular* kingdom of Yahweh. A kingdom has a king who reigns over it. The Sinai Covenant was Yahweh's invitation to Israel into a new life under his kingship. This point is made clearer in the meaning of the phrase, "my treasured possession," and the requirement of obedience. Martin Buber calls the Sinai Covenant "a kingly covenant" in which Israel came under the rule of Yahweh and the people were constituted as his domain.[148] Bright also states, "For Israel had begun its history as a nation summoned by God's grace to be his people, to serve him alone and to obey his covenant law. *The notion of a people of God, called to live under the rule of God, begins just here, and with it the notion of the Kingdom of God.*"[149] That being said, the Sinai Covenant revealed not only *a kingship of Yahweh*, but also *a particular people* over whom he would reign. Through the establishment of the Sinai Covenant, he created his kingdom with a particular people who were called to serve him as their king. Israel was called to be a particular kingdom of Yahweh.[150] In this sense, Yahweh's

---

148. Buber, *Kingship*, 121–35.

149. Bright, *Kingdom of God*, 28. Italics in original.

150. To say that Israel is the particular kingdom of Yahweh does not mean that Yahweh's reign is limited to Israel. Bruce K. Waltke identifies two kinds of the kingdom of God in the Old Testament: God's universal kingdom and God's particular kingdom. God's universal kingdom refers to "the activity of God . . . in exercising his sovereignty

missional formation of Israel, through the establishment of the Sinai Covenant with Israel, can be viewed as *particularization* of the kingdom of Yahweh. However, in light of the role of Yahweh's grace in establishing the Sinai Covenant between Yahweh and Israel, the requirement of obedience to Yahweh was not primarily a matter of obligation in a legalistic sense, but was to be Israel's *grateful and joyful response* to Yahweh's grace. Israel as a particular kingdom of Yahweh began with Yahweh's grace for her and her grateful and joyful response to Yahweh's grace for her. From the very moment that Yahweh called the people, he provided them with a reason to serve him with thankfulness (for what Yahweh had done for them) and joy (at the new life that they would live with him as their king).

C. Yahweh Gives the Missional and Holistic Law to Israel

The discussion on the Sinai Covenant argued that Israel was called to present and represent the holiness of Yahweh to the nations. For the sake of that missionary vocation, Israel was to reflect the holiness of Yahweh by living a life which was profoundly shaped by the holiness of Yahweh. This section will explore the relationship between the law and Israel's holiness, focusing on the *missionary* and *holistic* nature of the law.

The Missionary Nature of the Law

The law in the Old Testament is missionary by nature because, by keeping the law, Israel's life can make Yahweh visible to the nations. The missionary nature of the law is derived from the fact that *the law reflects the lawgiver*, who is Yahweh. Drawing from the relationship between speeches and speakers, James W. Watts identifies a mirroring relationship between the law in the Old Testament and the lawgiver, Yahweh. Watts states, "Speeches always indirectly characterize their speaker by providing readers the basis for inferring what kind of person talks this way. So *the law codes voiced directly by God in Exodus, Leviticus, and Numbers provide a powerful impression of the divine character.*"[151] Similarly, Cole sees the role of moral law as a mirroring relationship between Yahweh's holiness and Israel's holiness when he points out:

---

over all things," and God's particular kingdom means "God's activity in exercising his authority over his subjects who, out of their faith in him and love for him, serve only him." Waltke, "Kingdom of God in the Old Testament," 49–50.

151. Watts, "Legal Characterization," 1. Emphasis added.

> [T]he basic idea of the Hebrew root [of the word 'holy'] seems to have been 'set part' and therefore 'different' from common things. . . . It is in [God's] moral nature that the God of Israel is different: therefore 'holiness' in Israel has a moral content. That is why He will reveal Himself in the 'ten worlds,' which are a moral rather than an intellectual revelation, although they have an intellectual content.[152]

Drawing on Watts's idea on the relationship between the law and the character of Yahweh, Blackburn notes that the law is related to the missionary nature of Israel's holiness when he states, "

> By its very nature, law functions to reveal the character of the lawgiver, since a law code reflects the concerns of the one giving it. . . . The context of the law . . . would serve to make the Lord's character known to all who encountered it, whether Israel who heard it from Moses, or the nations who were to see it manifest in the life of Israel. In other words, specific laws would make a public statement concerning the Lord's character.[153]

Commenting on Deuteronomy 4:6–8, which links the visibility of Yahweh with the law, Wright notes the missionary nature of the law when he points out, "The motivation for God's people to live by God's law is ultimately to bless the nations. After all, what would the nations actually see? *The nearness of God is by definition invisible. What, then, would be visible? Only the practical evidence of the kind of society that was built on God's righteous laws.*"[154]

Furthermore, the law given to Israel also reflects the *presence* of Yahweh since, as noted earlier, cultic regulations in the law dealt with the issue of how Israel can live with Yahweh dwelling in her midst. In this sense, the law can be viewed as by nature missionary. Because the law reflects the presence and character of Yahweh, Israel could make invisible Yahweh visible to the nations by keeping the law.

In light of the discussion of the missionary nature of the law, it can be said that the law was central to the fulfillment of Israel's missionary vocation. As defined in the Sinai Covenant, Israel was called to present the holiness of Yahweh—his presence and character—to the nations in order to bring the nations to Yahweh. For the sake of this missionary purpose, Israel's life was to reflect the holiness of Yahweh, which points to his presence and character. It was by keeping the law that Israel could be holy and,

---

152. Cole, *Exodus*, 22–23.
153. Blackburn, *God Who Makes Himself Known*, 100.
154. Wright, *Mission of God*, 380. Emphasis added.

thus, reflect the holiness of Yahweh, because the law reflects the presence and character of Yahweh. In this way, Israel could make invisible Yahweh visible to the nations through the visibility of her distinctive life which was profoundly shaped by the holiness of Yahweh. Therefore, keeping the law was essential for Israel to fulfill her missionary vocation.

The Holistic Nature of the Law

In addition to the missionary nature of the law, the law in the Old Testament is holistic by nature because the law is comprehensive in scope. The law given to Israel covers all aspects of the Israelites' life. This holistic nature of the law is rooted in the *relational* nature of Israel's holiness based on the relationship between Yahweh's holiness and Israel's holiness. Israel's holiness involves the relationship between her and Yahweh and the relationship between individuals. It is spiritual because Israel's holiness deals with her constant relationship with the presence of Yahweh who is present in her midst; it is social because her holiness reflects the moral character of Yahweh. The two aspects of the relational nature of Israel's holiness are parallel to two categories of practical holiness: ceremonial (or ritual or symbolic) and moral (or social or ethical) holiness.[155]

Ceremonial Holiness

As already explained in the discussion of how the life of Israel is to be shaped by the presence of Yahweh in her midst, ceremonial holiness has to do with the presence of Yahweh who dwells in the midst of Israel. When Israelites came to the presence of Yahweh, they had to be ceremonially holy because, otherwise, Yahweh's holiness would consume them.[156] In order to deal with this holiness issue, Yahweh gave Israel the ceremonial law, which covered the system of clean and unclean categories and regulations associated with the categories. If Israelites wanted to access the presence of Yahweh, they had to keep the ceremonial law. Thus, as already mentioned,

---

155. Israel's holiness in the Old Testament is categorized as follows: holiness as status, and holiness as practice. On the one hand, the Old Testament says that Israel is *already* holy. In this case, holiness means Israel's status as "being set apart," implying that Yahweh chose them for a certain purpose. On the other hand, Israel is called to be holy as in Leviticus 19:2. In this case, holiness means a particular way of life that Israel ought to live as Yahweh's holy people. Practical holiness falls into this category of holiness. Regarding *practical* holiness, Wright states, "Israel was to live out in daily life the practical implications of their status as God's holy people." Wright, *Mission of God*, 372.

156. Hartley, "Holy and Holiness, Clean and Unclean," 426.

the purpose of ceremonial holiness was not to create and keep boundaries among Israelites, but to provide a way by which they can access the mysterious and life-giving presence of Yahweh. Thus, ceremonial holiness was all about the constant relationship between Yahweh and Israel. The life of Israel is to be profoundly shaped by the presence of Yahweh who dwells in her midst. By keeping ceremonial holiness, Israel would be constantly reminded that Yahweh is present in her midst. Israel's life is intended to reflect the presence of Yahweh who dwells in her midst.

Moral Holiness

Another aspect of practical holiness is moral. Wright states, "being holy meant living lives of integrity, justice and compassion in every area—including personal, family, social, economic, and national life."[157] The moral aspect of Israel's holiness also involves the land.[158] As already discussed, moral holiness is theologically rooted in the moral and relational character of Yahweh. Since keeping the law was a practical way for Israel to be holy, the moral aspect of Israel's holiness, which is rooted in the moral and relational character of Yahweh, requires them to keep the moral law. Cole observes this connection between God's holiness and Israel's holiness, on the one hand, and the moral law, on the other hand. Cole points out, "Since God's holiness is defined as being moral, to be a 'holy people' . . . meant that stern moral demands are made of her. . . . Since YHWH is holy, there is no need for more explanation: the new relationship, brought about by grace, makes inexorable moral demands."[159] In this sense, the moral law was given to Israel for her moral holiness. In other words, Israel's holiness could be moral by keeping the moral law, which reflect the moral and relational character of Yahweh. In doing so, Israel could reflect the moral and relational character of Yahweh and present it among the nations.

The moral law was to characterize the social distinctiveness of Israel's life, dealing with the relationship between individuals and Israel's relationship with the land.[160] However, given the relationship between the moral

157. Wright, *Mission of God*, 373.

158. For Israel's land in relation to her holiness and mission, see Wright, *God's People in God's Land*; Wright, *Old Testament Ethics*, 76–99; Snyder and Scandrett, *Salvation Means Creation Healed*, 117–34.

159. Cole, *Exodus*, 23.

160. While implicit, the moral law deals with how Israel should treat the land, in view of the fact that agriculture was Israel's primary economic system. Thus, land in ancient Israel was the primary source of Israel's socio-economic life. The way that individuals in Israel treat one another is closely related to the way that they treat the land.

law and the character of Yahweh, the basis of the moral law is not inherent human dignity, but rather the moral and relational character of Yahweh. The Israelites' moral law has its origin and basis not in themselves,[161] but in the moral and relational character of Yahweh. In this way, Israel's social life, which would reflect the character of Yahweh, was to serve as a showcase of the character of Yahweh among the nations.

Holiness and Law in Leviticus 19

One particular biblical text that clearly shows the relationship between Israel's holiness and the law is Leviticus 19. Its structure and content reveal the missionary and holistic nature of the law.

The Missionary Nature of the Law in the Structure of Leviticus 19

Leviticus 19 begins with the holiness command given to the whole people of Israel, "The Lord spoke to Moses, saying: Speak to *all the congregation of the people of Israel* and say to them: *You shall be holy, for I the LORD your God am holy*" (Lev 19:1–2). The following verses of the chapter list the laws that Israel ought to keep. The relationship between holiness and the law is made clear in light of this structure of Leviticus 19: *by keeping the law, Israel can be holy as Yahweh is holy*. On the relationship between Israel's holiness and the law in Leviticus 19, Wright comments, "The bulk of the Leviticus 19 shows us that the kind of holiness that reflects God's own holiness is thoroughly practical, social and very down-to-earth."[162] Jacob Milgrom makes the same point when he states, "all the commandments enumerated in Leviticus19 fall under the rubric of holiness."[163] Regarding the message of Leviticus 19, Milgrom contends that the laws in Leviticus 19 "emphasize Yahweh's holy nature and that Israel should emulate it."[164] In this regard, Leviticus 19 presents the law as a practical way through which Israel can be holy, reflecting the holiness of Yahweh, and, in doing so, presenting it to

---

For this aspect of Israel's relationship with the land, see Wright, *God's People in God's Land*; Wright, *Old Testament Ethics*, 76–99.

161. The moral and relational characteristic of the life that human beings are called to live is already foreshadowed in the creation narrative in which they are created in the context of a community (the social relationship between man and woman) to bear the image of God. See Cho, "Nature of the Church's Mission," 121.

162. Wright, *Mission of God*, 374.

163. Milgrom, "Holy, Holiness, Old Testament," 852.

164. Milgrom, "Holy, Holiness, Old Testament," 852.

the nations. Therefore, the law's missionary nature is identifiable because, by keeping the law, Israel was intended to be a showcase of the holiness of Yahweh in the midst of the nations.

The Holistic Nature of the Law in the Content of Leviticus 19

While Leviticus 19 highlights the moral law,[165] Leviticus 19 also includes the ceremonial law.[166] Thus, the scope of the law in Leviticus 19 is both ceremonial and moral, indicating the holistic nature of the law. In the Old Testament, the law given to the whole people of Israel is holistic, in the sense that the law covers *every* dimension—religious, spiritual, personal, social, and environmental—of Israel's life. On the holistic nature of the law in the Pentateuch, Duke is right when he points out, "The modern tendency to separate cultic law from ethical law was unknown [in the Pentateuch]."[167] Israel's holiness is characterized by the *holistic* nature of the law. Hartley states, "Observance of both the ceremonial regulations and the moral law was required for the fulfillment of this call to be holy."[168] Similarly, Milgrom points out, "the commandments, the observance of which generates holiness, are performative as well as prohibitive, ethical as well as ritual."[169] The law given to the people of Israel deals with their relationship with Yahweh who dwells in their midst, and with other individuals.

The Holistic Nature of the Ten Commandments

This holistic nature of the law in Leviticus 19 is clearly evident because Leviticus 19 reflects the Ten Commandments (or the Decalogue).[170] Baruch A. Levine comments, "Chapter 19 may be characterized as a brief torah (instruction). . . . More specifically, it echoes the Ten Commandments."[171] The holistic nature of the law in the Old Testament is also found in the holistic nature of the Ten Commandments. The Ten Commandments embody two kinds of relational obligations: relationships with Yahweh and with one another. As David L. Baker notes, "The decalogue sets out ground rules for the

---

165. Wright, *Mission of God*, 374.
166. Milgrom, *Leviticus*, 212.
167. Duke, "Priests, Priesthood," 649.
168. Hartley, "Holy and Holiness, Clean and Unclean," 425.
169. Milgrom, "Holy, Holiness, Old Testament," 855.
170. The term *Decalogue* is derived from the Greek word for "ten words."
171. Levine, *Leviticus*, 124.

people of God, covering both their relationships with God and others."[172] Mark E. Biddle observes the significance of the structure of the Ten Commandments, which embraces the two relational dimensions:

> [I]t is important to note that the Decalogue is structured in two groupings focusing on two planes of reference. The first four commandments deal with Israel's relationship to YHWH; the remaining six with the relationship of individual Israelites to one another. The significance of this structure cannot be overemphasized. In this manner, the Decalogue established unmistakably the fundamental connection between *religion* and *ethics*. As Jesus put it, the Torah can be summarized in the two great commandments of love for God and for one's neighbor.[173]

C. W. Christian calls this twofold structure of the Ten Commandments, "the inclusiveness of the law."[174] He states, "If the law addresses and unites the two fundamental relations in life—the relation to God and to the world about us—then it is clear that it is *inclusive*. By this we mean it encompasses life in all of its aspects."[175] The two relational categories in the Ten Commandments clearly reveal the holistic nature of the law.

While the Ten Commandments do not explicitly mention land, the two relational aspects of the Ten Commandments do not exclude but implicitly embed Israel's relationship with the land. Snyder keenly observes "the *ecological* setting of the Ten Commandments."[176] This point is derived from the Old Testament claim that the land and even the whole earth belongs to Yahweh (e.g., Lev 25:23; Deut 10:14; Ps 24:1). Yahweh is the creator of the whole earth and the land giver. In light of Yahweh's relationship with the land, the primary role of Israel in relation to the land is not that of owner but that of *steward*. The people of Israel could enjoy what the land produces, but at the same time they were to care for the land which belongs to Yahweh. Furthermore, the land in Israel is not only a theological concept but also a socio-economic resource which enables Israel's socio-economic life by enjoying, consuming, sharing, and exchanging what the land produces. However, Israel's way of producing and exchanging resources derived

---

172. Baker, *Decalogue*, 35. The second part of the commandments, which are ethical principles, has the potential to be easily acceptable even to people outside Israel because, according to Baker, four of them "were widely accepted in the ancient world." Baker, *Decalogue*, 36.

173. Biddle, *Deuteronomy*, 106. Italics in original.

174. Christian, *Covenant and Commandment*, 72.

175. Christian, *Covenant and Commandment*, 72. Emphasis added.

176. Snyder and Scandrett, *Salvation Means Creation Healed*, 83–85.

from the land is not set by their own desires but by Yahweh, the owner of the land.[177] Thus, Israel's relationship with the land is deeply embedded in the two relational dimensions of the Ten Commandments. Shaped by their commitment to Yahweh and grounded in God's ownership of the land, Israel's life that involves the land was to reflect Yahweh in their midst and consequently present him to the surrounding nations.

In conclusion, Yahweh, who called Israel to be holy, gave the people the law as the practical way by which they could be holy as he is. The law given by Yahweh is both missionary and holistic, rooted in the relational nature of Israel's holiness, reflecting his holiness. First, the law is missionary in nature and purpose because the law reflects the presence and character of the lawgiver, Yahweh. By keeping the law, Israel could make Yahweh visible among the nations. Second, the law is holistic, dealing with two relationships: with Yahweh and with individuals and their environment. One implication of the holistic nature of the law is that Israel's holiness is holistic. Hartley holistically understands Israel's holiness when he states, "Israel's being holy meant: (1) they were in a covenant relationship with God; (2) God was present in their midst; (3) they were to promote justice throughout the community by keeping divine instructions; and (4) they were to observe the rules of ritual purity."[178] Because of the missionary and holistic nature of the law, by keeping the law, Israel was to present and embody both the *presence* and *character* of Yahweh to the nations.

D. Yahweh Dwells in the Midst of Israel

One of the points made in the previous sections is that Yahweh was and would be continuously faithful in fulfilling Israel's missionary vocation. This point is consolidated by a biblical theme of *the presence of Yahweh*.[179] This section argues that *the presence of Yahweh* in the midst of Israel is *the fulfilling factor* of her missionary vocation.

The Presence of Yahweh and the Mission of Israel

From the moment that Yahweh called Abraham for his mission, Yahweh shaped the missionary nature of the people of Israel through his divine

---

177. Wright, *Old Testament Ethics*, 148; Barram, *Missional Economics*, 90.

178. Hartley, "Holy and Holiness, Clean and Unclean," 427.

179. For biblical approaches to the theme of the presence of God in relation to Christian mission, see Beale, *Temple*, 25; Lister, "The Lord Your God," 11; Booth, *Tabernacling Presence of God*.

presence in action among them. The theme of the presence of Yahweh is dominant particularly in two Old Testament books—Genesis and Exodus—which are significant for Israel's missional formation. Genesis 12–50 presents Yahweh's presence working in the lives of the patriarchs from Abraham to Joseph.[180] When they were faithful to him, his divine presence in their lives was noticeable even in the eyes of people around them. The theme of the presence of Yahweh is more dominant in the book of Exodus than in any other books in the Bible. Durham not only observes that the presence of Yahweh is predominant in the book of Exodus,[181] but also regards the two key biblical events—the Exodus and the establishment of the Sinai Covenant—in the book of Exodus as united under and derived from the theme of the presence of Yahweh. Durham states:

> Two additional themes are natural extensions of the Presence theme in the Book of Exodus. The first of these themes is Deliverance, or Salvation, or Rescue. The second of them is Covenant, the provision of a means of Response to Deliverance.... And binding together and undergirding both Rescue and Response is Presence, the Presence of Yahweh from whom both Rescue and Response ultimately derive.[182]

Israel's missional formation through the Exodus and the establishment of the Sinai Covenant was the result of the presence of Yahweh who worked in and for Israel.

The Presence of Yahweh in the Exodus

The Exodus was an event in which Yahweh's presence in action was revealed. Blackburn states, "Exodus, is simply the Lord's effort to make himself known among the nations for who he is, the God who rules over the universe and redeems those who call upon him."[183] As Wright notes, the Exodus "was... a major act of self-revelation by God, and also a massive learning experience for Israel."[184] The words Yahweh spoke to Pharaoh through Moses, the plagues Yahweh sent against the Egyptians, and the miracle he did at the Red Sea were the undeniable evidence of his presence in action.

---

180. Frame, *Doctrine of God*, 96.
181. Durham, *Exodus*, xxi.
182. Durham, *Exodus*, xxiii.
183. Blackburn, *God Who Makes Himself Known*, 17.
184. Wright, *Mission of God*, 75.

Throughout the Exodus, the presence of Yahweh was undeniably evident in the eyes of Israel. On the side of Israel, the Exodus was the event in which Israel depended fully on the presence of Yahweh who was taking the lead. The Exodus demanded Israel's absolute trust in the presence of Yahweh. Blackburn articulates, "the people [of Israel] have been consciously dependent on the Lord from the beginning. In fact, it was precisely the promise of the Lord's presence that encouraged Israel to leave Egypt in the first place. . . . Israel's confidence, and ultimately her ability to walk out of bondage into freedom, comes in knowing that *the Lord is with her.*"[185] The presence of Yahweh in the midst of the people of Israel was *both the aim and means* in delivering Israel. On the one hand, Exodus 19:4, in which Yahweh proclaims to Israel through Moses, "[I] brought you to myself," reveals that one purpose of the Exodus was the presence of Yahweh in the midst of Israel because, as a result of the Exodus, Israel was brought to, in Childs's words, "his dwelling."[186] On the other hand, the same verse implies that the presence of God was the means by which the goal was accomplished. It was "I," which refers to Yahweh, who brought them into his presence. Thus, as Terrain notes, "Presence [of God] is that which creates a people."[187]

The Presence of Yahweh in the Establishment of the Sinai Covenant

In the book of Exodus, the Sinai Covenant is being established within the context of and under the influence of the *public* presence of Yahweh. How the presence of Yahweh is related to the establishment of the Sinai Covenant is indicated in Exodus 19:9, in which Yahweh says to Moses, "I am going to come to you in a dense cloud, in order that the people may hear when I speak with you and so trust you ever after" (Exod 19:9). Norah Whipple Caudill observes that the *public* presence of Yahweh authenticated the Sinai Covenant. Caudill states, "it is likely that the cloud served as . . . a visible phenomenon 'in' which God's presence would be found," and, "The cloud will provide a visible location from which the people would hear God's voice."[188] Regarding the purpose of the public presence of Yahweh, she observes, "the purpose for God speaking with Moses in a public fashion is to authenticate him in the eyes of the people."[189] Fretheim also echoes Caudill's points when he notes, "God will speak in such a public way to Moses for this purpose:

185. Blackburn, *God Who Makes Himself Known*, 201. Emphasis added.
186. Childs, *Book of Exodus*, 367.
187. Terrien, *Elusive Presence*, 124.
188. Caudill, "Presence of God," 84.
189. Caudill, "Presence of God," 85.

to convince the people—now and forever—that Moses is a mediator of the word of God and not his own opinion."[190]

These findings from the verse imply that the public presence of Yahweh was crucial and necessary for the establishment of the Sinai Covenant. Yahweh invited Israel into the Sinai Covenant in the context of his public presence because Israel would come to know that the Sinai Covenant came not from Moses but from Yahweh.

The Presence of Yahweh as the Fulfilling Factor of the Covenant

Israel's holiness demands her constant dependence on the presence of Yahweh who is the original source of her holiness. This point is made clear in Moses's intercessory prayer for Israel's sin of making and worshiping the golden calf in Exodus 33. Wright notes: "Moses knows that without God's presence, the covenant is as good as dead."[191] Thus, as John M. Frame points out, "God is not merely present in the world; he is *covenantally* present."[192] Frame states, "God commits himself to us, to be our God and to make us his people. He delivers us by his grace and rules us by his law, and he rules not only from above, but also *with us and within us*."[193] The fulfillment of the covenant absolutely needs the presence of Yahweh. Arthur F. Glasser states:

> In the Old Testament, God intervened in human affairs though electing Israel and choosing this people to constitute a theocracy. This meant that they would live under his direct rule and thus foreshadow the coming of the Kingdom of God. At Sinai, God made Israel his people. With the conquest, Israel became a nation among the nations of the ancient world. God did not endow the Israelites with superhuman faculties. But *because of his theocratic presence in their midst*, it was possible for them to function as an incipient Kingdom of God in the midst of the kingdoms of other peoples.[194]

---

190. Fretheim, *Exodus*, 215.
191. Wright, *Mission of God*, 335.
192. Frame, *Doctrine of God*, 94. Italics in original.
193. Frame, *Doctrine of God*, 96. Emphasis added. The degree of the intimacy between God and his people gradually increases from the Old Testament, in which God dwells in the tabernacle (later temple) *among* them, to the New Testament, where God dwells *in* them (through the Holy Spirit).
194. Glasser et al., *Announcing the Kingdom*, 91. Emphasis added.

Concluding a study of the Old Testament concept of Israel's mission to the world, Robert Martin-Achard views mission as being derived from the work of God who *dwells in the church*, when he articulates, "mission . . . is entirely dependent on the hidden activity of God within His Church, and is the fruit of a life really rooted in God. The evangelization of the world is not primarily a matter of words or deeds: it is a matter of presence—*the presence of the People of God in the midst of [hu]mankind and the presence of God in the midst of His People*."[195]

Thus, the presence of Yahweh in the midst of Israel is neither optional nor merely one of the ways of fulfilling the covenant, but is central and essential for the fulfillment of the covenant. If the covenant is about the *what* of the Israelites' missionary vocation, the presence of Yahweh is about the *how* of their missionary vocation—their missionary vocation is fulfilled by the presence of Yahweh in their midst.

The Accessibility of Yahweh through the Tabernacle

The view that the presence of Yahweh is the fulfilling factor of the covenant leads to the next point to be made: For the sake of the fulfillment of Israel's missionary vocation, he made his presence accessible to Israel *on a daily basis through the tabernacle (and later temple)*. As Childs states, "The tabernacle serves as a portable sanctuary of the presence of God," and Yahweh, who was present at Mt. Sinai, "is continually present in the portable tabernacle."[196] It was, in Snyder's words, "a mobile symbol" of "God's presence with his people."[197] The tabernacle, rebuilt as the temple later in the monarchy period, was built primarily as the means by which Yahweh dwells among the Israelites so that he may meet them on an ongoing basis.[198] The purpose of the tabernacle as Yahweh's dwelling place is stated in Exodus 25:8 (NASB), "Let them construct a sanctuary for me, that I may dwell among them." R. B. Dillard and T. Longan III state, "the location, architectural design, building materials, and accessibility of the tabernacle all highlight the fact that a holy God dwelt in the midst of the Israelite people."[199] The purpose of Yahweh's dwelling in the midst of Israel was to meet the people, as mentioned in Exodus 29:42–43 (NIV), in which Yahweh says, "There I

---

195. Martin-Achard, *Light to the Nations*, 79. Italics in original.
196. Childs, *Book of Exodus*, 540.
197. Snyder, *Radical Renewal*, 58.
198. See Snyder, *Radical Renewal*, 55–64.
199. Longman and Dillard, *Introduction*, 77.

will meet you and speak to you; there also I will meet with the Israelites, and the place will be consecrated by my glory."[200]

Thus, through the tabernacle, Yahweh provided Israel a way to encounter him on a regular basis. It was a means by which the people encountered him continuously. Goldingay points out, "The Israelites left Egypt not merely to meet with God at the mountain, but to meet with God on an ongoing basis. The sanctuary is where this meeting takes place."[201] As Childs notes, "What happened at Sinai is continued in the tabernacle."[202] Through the tabernacle, Yahweh made his presence accessible to Israel.[203]

Yahweh's work for the missional formation of Israel in the book of Exodus did not end with the Sinai Covenant and the laws, but with the instructions on the tabernacle. This implies that, as Childs states, "The tabernacle represents the fulfillment of the covenant promise,"[204] in an initial sense, but not in the full sense. The tabernacle, which represents Yahweh's dwelling in the midst of Israel, was Yahweh's *finalizing* but *central* piece of Israel's missional formation at Mt. Sinai. Leviticus 26:11–12 links Yahweh's presence in the midst of Israel with her covenant relationship with Yahweh: "I will place my dwelling in your midst, and I shall not abhor you. And I will walk among you, and will be your God, and you shall be my people." Yahweh commits himself to fulfill the covenant by placing his divine presence in the midst of Israel. The covenantal-missionary journey, imposed on the shoulders of Israel among the nations, counts not on the people, nor on them-with-Yahweh, but on *Yahweh-among-them*.

Therefore, in order to fulfill their missionary vocation, the people of Israel needed to trust in and depend on Yahweh who was in their midst, as they did throughout the Exodus. They began a journey toward the promised land by completely depending on the lead of Yahweh's presence in their midst, as described in Exodus 40:36–37 (NIV): "In all the travels of the Israelites,

---

200. In these verses, the term "the tent of meeting" is used to refer to the tabernacle. According to Waldemar Janzen, "Of the 133 occurrences of [the tent of meeting], thirty-two are found in the tabernacle texts, but most of the rest also refer to the tabernacle." Janzen, "Tabernacle," 447. Averbeck observes that the terms "tabernacle" and "the tent of meeting" are used with emphases of different dimensions of the tabernacle and that the latter highlights its function as a place of meeting. Averbeck, "Tabernacle," 810–12.

201. Goldingay, *Israel's Gospel*, 399.

202. Childs, *Book of Exodus*, 540.

203. As noted earlier, the tabernacle (and the temple later) symbolized the dwelling of Yahweh among the people of Israel, but was not the only way for the people of Israel to come to the presence of Yahweh. As discussed later in this chapter, one particular example of this exception is the way that the prophets encountered Yahweh in the Old Testament.

204. Childs, *Book of Exodus*, 541.

whenever the cloud lifted from above the tabernacle, they would set out; but if the cloud did not lift, they did not set out—until the day it lifted." During that period, the presence of Yahweh over and in the tabernacle manifested as the cloud over it and the glory of Yahweh in it.[205] The people of Israel, who were just delivered by Yahweh, had no one other than him whom they could trust at the outset of their journey. They had to *completely* trust in and depend on the guidance of the presence of Yahweh as they set out on their missionary journey in the midst of the nations.

The Presence of Yahweh and His Kingship over Israel

Another aspect of the tabernacle as representing the presence of Yahweh is that the tabernacle was to be a means by which Yahweh would rule over Israel in her actual life. This point is made clear when the tabernacle is viewed as an extension of Mt. Sinai, where Yahweh demanded her obedience to him and gave the people the law to keep. Blackburn finds this role of the presence of Yahweh in the midst of the Israelites, based on "the structural and lexical similarities between Mt. Sinai and the tabernacle."[206] Blackburn argues that the tabernacle communicates Yahweh's kingship over Israel:

> Mount Sinai is where the Lord gave Israel his law and where Israel pledged to obey. . . . The connection between Sinai and the tabernacle suggests that, despite the lack of direct kingship language in the tabernacle section, the tabernacle is the place where the Lord continued to exercise his reign over Israel. That the tabernacle is associated with the Lord's ruling over Israel is further supported by two considerations: the meetings between Moses and the Lord in the Holy of Holies were for the purpose of the Lord's commanding Israel . . . , and more implicitly, the tablets containing the commandments were to be placed in the ark in the Holy of Holies.[207]

The tabernacle was designed not merely for Yahweh's ongoing meeting with Israel, but also for his reigning over her, while his presence and activity were not confined to the tabernacle. Israel was called to be a people among whom Yahweh dwelled as their king.

---

205. The covering cloud is also found when Solomon completed the temple and performed the dedication of it as written in 1 Kgs 8:10–11.

206. Blackburn, *God Who Makes Himself Known*, 132. Also see Clements, *God and Temple*, 22; Rodriguez, "Sanctuary Theology," 131–37; Sarna, *Exploring Exodus*, 203–4; Blackburn, *God Who Makes Himself Known*, 131–32.

207. Blackburn, *God Who Makes Himself Known*, 132–33.

The Story of the Golden Calf

One biblical case that illustrates the significance of the presence of Yahweh for the fulfillment of Israel's missionary vocation is the case of the golden calf recorded in Exodus 32–34. This narrative can be structured roughly with three subsections: Israel's Rebellion in Yahweh's absence (Exod 32), Moses's intercessory request to Yahweh (Exod 33), and the renewal of the covenant (Exod 34). This structure indicates the connection between the presence of Yahweh and the fulfillment of Israel's missionary vocation.

Exodus 32: Israel's Rebellion in Yahweh's Absence

While Moses was absent from the sight of the Israelites for a long period of time, they sought to have their own god by making the image of a calf out of gold. This was absolutely a sin against Yahweh. Two observations of the context in which they committed the sin are crucial. First, the Israelites disobeyed after only about fifty days since swearing to Yahweh that they would obey all the words of Yahweh given through Moses.[208] What the Israelites proved about them in forty days after their articulation of commitment to Yahweh was their unfaithfulness to and lack of trust in Yahweh, as he admitted that they were "a stiff-necked people" (Exod 33:5). Second, their rebellion against Yahweh can be viewed as a consequence of their failing to recognize his presence.[209] Given that Moses served as a mediator between Yahweh and the Israelites, Moses's absence from their sight means that, as Durham notes, "with Moses gone, access to Yahweh is cut off."[210] Then, they felt that "another deity is needed,"[211] creating their own god, which was what Yahweh banned as in the first of the Ten Commandments, in order to satisfy their need. This biblical observation that Israel failed to obey Yahweh during the period when they felt his absence proves the absolute necessity of the presence of Yahweh to keep them faithful to what they ought to be among the nations. As Blackburn points out, "*Israel's faithful obedience depends upon knowing the Lord's presence in her midst.*

---

208. The whole people of Israel swore to Yahweh, saying, "All that the Lord has spoken we will do, and we will be obedient" (Exod 24:7). Then Moses went to Mt. Sinai, waiting there for seven days, and being with Yahweh inside the cloud for forty days (Exod 23:9–18). Israel's rebellion against Yahweh happened while Moses was with Yahweh on Mt. Sinai.

209. Some biblical texts that indicate the link between the absence of God's presence and sin include Ps 10:11, 94:6–7; Isa 47:10; Ezek 9:9.

210. Durham, *Exodus*, 419.

211. Durham, *Exodus*, 419.

Indeed, as Israel's idolatry stemmed from believing the Lord to be absent, so does unfaithfulness through the Scriptures."[212]

Exodus 33: Moses's Intercessory Request to Yahweh

Brueggemann states, "There can be little doubt that Exodus 33 is the most sustained and delicate attempt to deal with the problem of Yahweh's presence/absence in Israel."[213] Especially significant is Moses's response to Yahweh who said to him that he would give the promised land to the Israelites but would not go with them after they made and worshiped a golden calf. Moses replies to Yahweh by asking a crucial question: "If your presence does not go with us, do not send us up from here. . . . What else will distinguish me and your people from all the other people on the face of the earth?" (Exod 33:15–16). Moses was well aware that, as Goheen states, "it is precisely God's presence with his people that distinguishes them from other peoples."[214] Terrien comments on the verses, "The distinctiveness of Israel, the mark which sets the people apart from other nations is strictly theological. *Israel has no ethnic meaning unless the presence of Yahweh remains with the people.* The peoplehood of Israel, in contrast to all other peoples, lies in this unique relationship, failing which it vanishes."[215]

Thus, as Durham states, "*without Yahweh's Presence*, Israel and Moses are not just certain to fail the destiny set before them."[216] The gold-calf section, particularly Exodus 33, reveals that the very foundation that shapes and fulfills the missionary vocation of Israel is not in her, but in the presence of Yahweh in her midst.[217]

Exodus 34: The Renewal of the Covenant

One more thing to be noted is that this narrative of the golden calf does not end with Yahweh's decision to withdraw his presence from Israel, but with the renewal of the covenant on Yahweh's side and the renewed commitment to him on Israel's side. What is significant for our purpose here is that the Israelites' rebellion against him was dealt with within the context of

---

212. Blackburn, *God Who Makes Himself Known*, 201. Emphasis added.
213. Brueggemann, "Crisis and Promise of Presence in Israel," 48.
214. Goheen, *Light to the Nations*, 45.
215. Terrien, *Elusive Presence*, 142. Emphasis added.
216. Durham, *Exodus*, 447. Emphasis added.
217. Brueggemann, "Crisis and Promise of Presence in Israel," 49.

the presence of Yahweh among them. While Moses's intercessory role was crucial, it was Yahweh among them who brought them back to covenant relationship with him. Yahweh recognized their rebellion against him, and led them to be deeply regretful of their sin (Exod 33:4). This narrative ends with the restored relationship between Yahweh and Israel.

As a result of Yahweh's intervening presence, their hearts to worship him were restored (Exod 33:7–9), and he re-established the covenant with the Ten Commandments on a new stone (Exod 34:1–27). This biblical case shows how the presence of Yahweh in the midst of Israel restored her missionary vocation, bringing her heart back to Yahweh. Thus, as Blackburn concludes, "the issues raised in [Exodus] 32–34 make it abundantly clear that the Lord's dwelling presence with Israel is foundational for Israel's relationship to the Lord as his people and the ongoing purpose to which she is called."[218]

The biblical story of the golden calf illustrates that the presence of Yahweh amid the people of Israel is vital to the fulfillment of their missionary vocation. The people of Israel, even though chosen by Yahweh, were incapable of fulfilling their missionary vocation without him. Consequently, the presence of Yahweh in the midst of Israel is central to the fulfillment of her missionary vocation. It is Yahweh amid them who enables Israel to fulfill their missionary vocation. That being said, the presence of Yahweh in the midst of the Israelites can be viewed as the *fulfilling factor* of their missionary vocation. As Martin-Achard states, "Israel's task is . . . to be *the nation in which Yahweh is at work* and whose existence is meaningless apart from the intervention of God."[219] Yahweh not only called the Israelites for the missional purpose he had for them, but also commits himself to fulfill her missionary vocation by dwelling among them and meeting them on an ongoing basis. Therefore, As Martin-Achard points out:

> God plays the decisive role in making the calling of Israel effectual for the heathen. It is His actions alone that make His People the light of the nations and lead the peoples to worship Him. The conversion of the world is the result of what He has wrought for Israel's sake; mission is a theocentric concept in the sense that it is brought into being and put into effect by God Himself and at the same time furthers His glory.[220]

However, the view that the presence of Yahweh among the people of Israel is vital to the fulfillment of their missionary vocation does not suggest that their role in fulfilling their missionary vocation was merely passive,

218. Blackburn, *God Who Makes Himself Known*, 201.
219. Martin-Achard, *Light to the Nations*, 76. Emphasis added.
220. Martin-Achard, *Light to the Nations*, 76.

since Yahweh intended to enable them to what they were called to be for his mission. The point is that the presence of Yahweh among them *enables* them to be his missionary people.

E. Yahweh Wrestles with Israel

Yahweh provided Israel with all she needed to be a contrast people who present the holiness of Yahweh among the nations. The covenant was established, the law was given, Yahweh himself was present among the Israelites with the completion of the tabernacle. Now Israel departs on their way from Mt. Sinai to the promised land (Num 10:11–36), accompanied by the tabernacle. The study on the period of wilderness, conquest, and judges in this section focuses on how Yahweh continues to deal with Israel to fulfill her missionary vocation. This section argues that these particular periods in the history of Israel demonstrate two factors related to how Yahweh *reshaped* Israel toward her missionary vocation—(1) Israel's continuous failure to fulfill her missionary vocation, and (2) Yahweh's faithfulness in fulfilling her missionary vocation—and highlight her relationship to Yahweh as *the* foundation of her missionary vocation among the nations.

During the Period of Wilderness

From the very beginning of the Israelites' journey in the wilderness and onward, the biblical narrative testifies to their lack of trust in and their unfaithfulness to Yahweh. The first case of it is found in Numbers 11. In Numbers 10, the Israelites depart from Mt. Sinai, but in the following chapter, Numbers 11, they quickly show their lack of trust in Yahweh, complaining to him about their hardship on the journey in the wilderness in Numbers 11:1: "Now when the people complained in the hearing of the LORD about their misfortunes, the LORD heard it and his anger was kindled." Yahweh responded to their complaint in two ways: (1) giving the punishment to them (Num 11:2), and (2) meeting their need with some instructions they ought to follow (Num 11:18–23, 31–32). Then, they failed to obey his command again, resulting in another punishment from Yahweh (Num 11:33–35).

This case not only illustrates that the Israelites failed to trust in Yahweh, but also shows that they were very prone to being attracted by the nations. Instead of being grateful for what Yahweh had done for them and being content with what he had provided them, they felt nostalgia for their previous life in Egypt in Numbers 11:4–6, in which they say, "If only we had meat to eat! We remember the fish we used to eat in Egypt for nothing, the cucumbers, the melons, the leeks, the onions, and the garlic; but now our strength is dried up, and there is nothing at all but this manna to look at." From the content of their complaint, two observations seem important: (1) "the refusal to be satisfied with the gifts God has given"[221] and (2) the positive memory of their previous life in Egypt. These two factors together resulted in their rebellion against Yahweh. On these verses, Cole comments, "In the midst of their austerity in the desert setting, they had become nostalgic over their former food supply while forgetting the bondage and oppression from which the Lord had so dramatically delivered them. The failure to remember God's grace and faithfulness was the second aspect of their rebellion."[222] When they faced a challenge, they quickly chose to forget what Yahweh provided for them and to be attached to what they had enjoyed in Egypt from where they were delivered. Hence, it becomes clear that the failure of Israel's missionary vocation involved her forgetfulness of the grace of Yahweh and the temptation to become like the nations.

This analysis of Yahweh's wrestling with Israel in Numbers 11 shows a typical pattern of Israel's missional conversion. This pattern follows the sequence of, first, Israel's sin that resulted from her lack of trust in Yahweh and his punishment for her sin, and, then, his response to Israel's cry to restore the covenant relationship. This pattern repeats throughout Israel's journey in the wilderness.[223] R. Dennis Cole observes the repetition of this pattern in the following biblical narrative of Israel. Cole states, "This initial rebellious incident cited in the text sets the stage and pattern for the successive acts of sedition."[224] Throughout her journey in the wilderness, Israel continued to prove her unfaithfulness to Yahweh,[225] but Yahweh did not give up on Israel. Rather he took initiatives, in David L. Stubbs's words, "to purge Israel of sinfulness."[226] Yahweh's intention in punishment was to get Israel's relationship with him right.

---

221. Olson, *Numbers*, 65.

222. Cole, *Numbers*, 184.

223. David L. Stubbs observes eight rebellions of Israel against Yahweh in the book of Numbers: seven rebellions in Num 11:1—21:35, and a final rebellion in Num 25. See Stubbs, *Numbers*.

224. Cole, *Numbers*, 180.

225. David L. Stubbs provides an excellent summary of lack of trust and unfaithfulness of Israel to God. See Stubbs, *Numbers*, 112–14.

226. Stubbs, *Numbers*, 112.

Achan's Sin during the Period of Conquest

The pattern of Israel's failure to keep the covenant and Yahweh's initiatives to restore the covenant is also found during the period of conquest in the land of Canaan. In Joshua 7, because of the sin of Achan who secretly took some of the devoted things which were sacred to Yahweh and must go into his treasury (Josh 6:17–19), Israel was defeated in a fight against the city of Ai. While it was a sin committed by one individual, Yahweh regarded it as a sin of breaking the covenant by the whole people of Israel (Josh 7:10–11).[227] The whole people were brought to encounter Yahweh in punishment, and, then, they were brought back to being faithful to Yahweh with the success of their attack against the city of Ai. It is only after their encounter with Yahweh in removing their sin that the covenant was renewed in Joshua 8:30–35. This biblical example also shows that their encounter with Yahweh in punishment was not the end of the covenant, but was instead aimed at restoring the covenant.

During the Period of Judges

Israel's failure to obey Yahweh continued after the death of Joshua, beginning with her disobedience to Yahweh's command to drive out all the Canaanites (Judg 1:1—2:5). Strikingly, a new generation of Israel after the death of Joshua "did not know the LORD or the work that he had done for Israel" (Judg 2:10).[228] Not only that, Israel chose to abandon Yahweh and to worship the gods of the land of Canaan (Judg 2:11–12). In doing so, Israel lost the very foundation of her missionary vocation by following the ways of the nations. The consequence of this can be understood as loss of Israel's holiness, which was a condition for her priestly mediatory role in the midst of the nations, because Israel's holiness demands her constant relationship with Yahweh, the original source of holiness. As a result, Israel became just like other nations. With no difference between Israel and the nations, Israel became unable to be a contrast people who were supposed to embody the holiness of Yahweh in their life and present it to the nations. However, Yahweh did not give up on Israel. Rather, he took initiatives in order to bring the people back to him.

---

227. According to David M. Howard Jr., the extension of Achan's sin to the whole people of Israel is an example of what has been called "corporate solidarity," a concept originally introduced by H. W. Robinson. See Howard, *Joshua*, 193–94.

228. Goldingay understands the word "know" as "commitment" in the context of Deuteronomy. If so, this verse implies that the people of Israel did not commit themselves to God. See Goldingay, *Israel's Gospel*, 534.

Yahweh's instrument, for bringing Israel back to him and testing her obedience to him, was her neighbor nations (Judg 3:1–4). When Israel turned away from him, he used the nations against Israel; in response to his punishment, Israel cried out to Yahweh and repented of her sin against him. As Goldingay notes, Israel's crying out to God was an "expression of returning to Yhwh" and "a recognition that Yhwh is sovereign to bring oppression and deliverance."[229] Responding to Israel's cry, Yahweh delivered her through a judge he chose in ways that revealed to Israel the mighty and sovereign presence of Yahweh over the nations.[230] Therefore, the purpose of Yahweh's dealing with Israel's sin against him was not the ending of the covenant, but restoration of it.

Throughout the period of judges, the pattern of (1) Israel's apostasy, (2) Yahweh's punishment, (3) Israel's crying out, and (4) Yahweh's deliverance (with a judge) repeated, revealing Israel's unfaithfulness to the covenant, on the one hand, and Yahweh's faithfulness in fulfilling the missional purpose he had for the people, on the other hand. The conclusion of the book of Judges is an indication that Israel would be *unable* to fulfill her missionary vocation *on her own*: "all the people did what was right in their own eyes" (Judg 21:25b). This also implies the necessity of Yahweh's unceasing faithfulness in fulfilling Israel's missionary vocation.

In sum, Israel's journey during the period of the wilderness, conquest, and judges is characterized by the cyclical pattern comprised of (1) the rebellion of Israel against Yahweh, (2) the intervening act of Yahweh, and (3) the restoration of Israel's relationship with Yahweh. This pattern shows Israel's continuous failure to fulfill her missionary vocation, on the one hand, and Yahweh's faithfulness in fulfilling it, on the other hand. Israel continued to fail her missionary vocation, but Yahweh, who was faithful in fulfilling her missionary vocation, continuously encountered the people, and, as a consequence, Israel's relationship with Yahweh, which is the foundation of her missionary vocation, came to be restored.

One finding in the survey over the period of wilderness, conquest, and judges is the constant emphasis on Yahweh's concern with the Israelites' relationship with him. Israel's sin that Yahweh dealt with during the period was primarily about Israel's relationship with him. Israel turned against, did not remember, and even abandoned Yahweh. In this way, Israel became like other nations, following the way of the nations.

---

229. Goldingay, *Israel's Gospel*, 536.

230. One particular example is the case of Gideon, in which Yahweh brought victory with only 300 men at the war against Midian. In this way, Yahweh revealed his mighty and sovereign presence to the people of Israel because the victory was attributed not to Gideon nor to the men at the war but to Yahweh himself.

However, Yahweh continuously intervened to convert Israel back to him, re-establishing the relationship between him and the people. This biblical narrative shows that Israel's relationship with Yahweh is *the* foundation of her missionary vocation among the nations because, when Israel lost the foundation, she lost her mission altogether.

F. Yahweh Encounters Israel through Prophets

This section looks at the ministry of the prophets through whom Yahweh encountered the people of Israel to bring them back to their missionary vocation during the period of monarchy.[231] This section demonstrates that the ongoing dynamic—between Israel's failure to fulfill her missionary vocation, on the one hand, and Yahweh's commitment to fulfill it, on the other hand, during the period of judges—continued in the period of monarchy.

Israel's Apostasy

Israel experienced a dramatic socio-political change with the transition from the period of judges to the period of monarchy, but the beginning of this new period in Israel's history resulted from her rejection of Yahweh's kingship over her. The motivation that led to this transition disappointed Yahweh because Israel's request for a human king meant that she rejected his kingship over her (1 Sam 8:7). Thus, Samuel says, "the wickedness that you have done in the sight of the Lord is great in demanding a king for yourselves" (1 Sam 12:17). Although Yahweh approved the Israelites' request, Samuel reminded them that Yahweh still remained their king when he said to them, "Only fear the LORD, and serve him faithfully with all your heart" (1 Sam 12:24).

The period of monarchy was not different from the previous period in the sense that Israel still repeatedly went astray from Yahweh in the period of monarchy. The cyclical pattern of Yahweh's dealing with the sin of Israel continued in the period of monarchy. William Sanford LaSor states, "the apostasy of kings and people in the monarchic period caused the cycle of apostasy, judgment, repentance, and salvation to be suspended by the exile."[232] On the

---

231. Moses is often viewed as the first prophet and the model or prototype of a prophet. See Cook, *Hear O Heavens and Listen O Earth*, 41–44; Routledge, *Old Testament Theology*, 211; Cook, "Prophets and Prophecy," 204–5. For the view that identifies Abraham as a prophet, see Schmitt, "Prophecy (Preexilic Hebrew)," 482; Peterson, "Prophet, Prophecy," 624.

232. LaSor, "Prophets," 68.

one hand, some of the kings (of the southern kingdom of Judah) were good in the eyes of Yahweh, purifying their kingdom from sins. On the other hand, the overall characteristic of this period was one of apostasy, culminating in the destruction of both kingdoms of Israel as a divine punishment for their unfaithfulness to God. J. Daniel Hays gives a concise picture of the Israelites' apostasy generated by their kings in that period:

> Beginning in 1–2 Samuel and developing throughout 1–2 Kings, the Israelite monarchy grows both in power and in corruption. Especially in 1–2 Kings, the king often controls the priesthood and thus brings the worship system and its organization into his administration and under his control, often with an idolatrous orientation. Frequently, these Israelite kings worship idols and thus lead the entire nation into idol worship through their control of the priesthood.[233]

Because of the apostasy of Israel, Yahweh wrestled with her throughout the period of the monarchy, striving to bringing her back to him. Goldingay states, "Israel designates a body with which 'God *struggles*,' and God does so especially during Israel's time as a state. In this wrestling match, kings often take the lead in *frustrating* Yhwh's purpose."[234]

Prophets as Yahweh's Primary Instrument to Deal with Israel's Apostasy

In spite of the apostasy of Israel, Yahweh did not abandon her, but continued to be committed to bringing her back to a covenant relationship with him by giving warnings and chances to repent *through prophets*. LaSor states, "YHWH is patient, and he gave his people the opportunity to repent. He also attempted various means of persuasion: war, drought, famine, and pestilence (See Amos 4:6–11)."[235] However, as Goldingay states, the prophets were "a chief means of Yhwh's wrestling."[236] Hays points out, "The role of the prophets takes on a special significance in times when the

---

233. Hays, *Message*, 24. As indicated in this quote, one major factor that led to Israel's apostasy was the priests' failure to shape Israel's priesthood. For the relationship between priests and Israel's priesthood, see the section on the Sinai Covenant, particular the discussion on the meaning of "a kingdom of priests" above. For a helpful study on Levitical priests' role in shaping Israel, see Haydock, *Theology of the Levitical Priesthood*.

234. Goldingay, *Israel's Gospel*, 613. Emphasis added.

235. LaSor, "Prophets," 64.

236. Goldingay, *Israel's Gospel*, 668.

Israelite monarchy and the Israelite priesthood turn away from God."[237] The prophets were Yahweh's primary divine means through whom he encountered Israel. Former prophets such as Elijah and Elisha confronted those in the ruling position such as kings. The pattern in Yahweh's confrontation through the prophets includes "confrontation with the king and other ruling powers, a call to repent and return to faithful obedience to Yahweh, and warnings to judgment on those who fail to heed the voice of Yahweh."[238] This pattern is also found in the so-called literary prophets or classic prophets in many ways.[239]

The Divine Origin of the Office, Message, and Ministry of Prophets

The prophets' ministry to Israel originated directly from Yahweh. As Carroll Stuhlmueller states, prophets "were called directly by God," so their prophecy "derived its authority directly from God" and was "not commissioned by priest or king."[240] The prophets played the role of Yahweh's intervening agents, motivated not by their own agendas but by Yahweh's direct commission, such as in the case of Moses. They were sent with a mission to Israel by Yahweh. Brueggemann observes the divine origin of the office of prophets from how Yahweh commissioned prophets:

> The prophet purports to narrate the direct encounter with Yahweh whereby the prophet was pressed into service as a messenger for Yahweh. . . . The call narrative characteristically intends to assert that Yahweh holds the initiative for any particular prophetic activity or utterance, and that prophets on occasion are compelled to speak, even against their will.[241]

The divine origin of the office of prophets indicates that the message of the prophets came from Yahweh. The primary role of prophets was to be Yahweh's spokesmen, so the message of the prophets was not their own, but came directly from Yahweh himself. He spoke directly to Israel through the prophets. The divine origin of the message of prophets is evidenced by the so-called messenger formula such as "thus says the Lord, or said the Lord."[242]

---

237. Hays, *Message*, 24.
238. Hays, *Message*, 24.
239. Hays, *Message*, 24.
240. Senior and Stuhlmueller, *Biblical Foundations for Mission*, 79.
241. Brueggemann, *Theology of the Old Testament*, 630.
242. On the messenger formula, see March, "Prophecy," 149–53; Brueggemann,

Thus, as Goldingay states, when the prophets speak, "what people are immediately aware of are words that come from God."[243]

Furthermore, the former prophets such as Elijah and Elisha were not merely Yahweh's messengers with the words of Yahweh. They manifested the presence of Yahweh by exercising the power of Yahweh. Goldingay states, "The use of their powers can mean Elijah and Elisha drive people to recognize Yhwh alone . . . and specifically they demonstrate that Yhwh indeed has power and puts earthly kings in their place. . . . They can also demonstrate that the human agents of these marvels are indeed the agents of Yhwh."[244] Goldingay views Elijah and Elisha as "not only Yhwh's representatives but almost Yhwh's embodiments" to the extent that "[t]hey exercise Yhwh's power, execute Yhwh's decisions, manifest Yhwh's insights and reveal Yhwh's plans," so "people's attitude to them *is* their attitude to God."[245]

In sum, the office, message, and ministry of prophets originated directly from Yahweh. Prophets served as God's divine means through which the people of Israel clearly recognized the presence of Yahweh, and he clearly revealed his divine will to them. Yahweh provided them with the way to maintain a constant, intimate relationship with him, but, when the people of Israel failed it, he used the prophets as a primary means of her *divine* encounter with him.

Yahweh's Message through the Prophets on Calling Israel to Repent

In dealing with Israel's apostasy, Yahweh encountered Israel through the prophets with the message of *repentance*. In that period marked by Israel's apostasy, the major role of the prophets sent by Yahweh was to warn Israel of her sins so that she might repent and be converted fully to Yahweh again. Goldingay points out:

> A prophet . . . resembles the sentinel on a city's walls warning of danger approaching. . . . A prophet's task is to admonish the people or testify against them. . . . In a sense Yhwh is the admonisher speaking by means of prophets and seers . . . , but in another sense the prophets are the admonishers. . . . Their task

---

Theology of the Old Testament, 630.
    243. Goldingay, *Israel's Gospel*, 680.
    244. Goldingay, *Israel's Gospel*, 675.
    245. Goldingay, *Israel's Gospel*, 677. Italics in original.

is to point out the wrong the people have done and to urge them to turn from their wrong ways and to Yhwh.[246]

The Hebrew verb *subh* is most commonly used for the word "repent" in the Old Testament in general and by the Old Testament prophets in particular. The meaning of the verb shows what Yahweh intended to speak to Israel through the prophets' message of repentance.[247] David A. Lambert states, "The Hebrew term *shuv* apprehends a situation from the perspective of the one in motion, indicating a reversal in his or her trajectory. . . . To state *shuv* depicts the actual process of motion, the turning, while 'return' focuses on its result, the arrival back."[248] When this primary meaning of the verb is used in the context of the covenant, it reflects a change of Israel's attitude or relationship toward Yahweh. In his study of the verb *subh*, William L. Holladay establishes a biblical case for this point. He identifies biblical examples of what he calls the "covenantal usage of the verb" in which the verb is used to express "a change of loyalty on the part of Israel or God, each for the other."[249] Lampart observes the verb *subh* is used for a restoration of the covenant relationship with Yahweh, but also for cessation of sin.[250] Thus, the meaning of repentance reflected by the Old Testament use of the verb *subh* is both a matter of faith (in Yahweh) and of obedience (to the commands of Yahweh), including the change of both the hearts and deeds of the people of Israel.

This brief survey of the verb *subh* indicates the *relational* and *holistic* nature of repentance. On the one hand, the fundamental issue at stake in the prophets' message of repentance is Israel's relationship with Yahweh. By

246. Goldingay, *Israel's Gospel*, 683.

247. Lambert, *How Repentance Became Biblical*, 71. The primary meaning of the verb is "to (re)turn." David A. Lambert argues that the meaning of the verb indicates "a dramatic change in direction," instead of a resultant status of turning. Lambert, *How Repentance Became Biblical*, 71.

248. Lambert, *How Repentance Became Biblical*, 73. The term *shuv* is another variation of the English transliteration of the Hebrew verb *shub*.

249. Holladay, *The Root šûbh in the Old Testament*, 2. Holladay discovers that the verb is used in both of the opposite ways of change: (1) become apostate and (2) repent. It means that, as Lambert explains, "whereas *shuv* lends the sense of a particular kind of turn, it is the prepositions with which *shuv* is paired that determine whether the emphasis in the verse is placed on what the agent turns toward or what he or she turns away from." When this verb is used in a positive sense with prepositions such as "to," or "toward," Yahweh calls Israel to return to (or turn to God). When this verb is used in a negative sense with prepositions such as "away from," Yahweh gives Israel a warning against her because she failed to return to Yahweh or turned away from Yahweh. For this way of use of the verb *subh*, see Holladay, *Root šûbh in the Old Testament*, 147–49; Lambert, *How Repentance Became Biblical*, 74–75.

250. Lambert, *How Repentance Became Biblical*, 75–88.

calling Israel to repent, Yahweh aimed at the renewal or reestablishment of Israel's relationship with him. On the other hand, the meaning of repentance aims at Israel's holistic change of life toward living a life according to the law given by Yahweh. By calling Israel to repent, Yahweh intends to restore Israel back to being a contrast people whose life holistically reflects the holiness of God by keeping the law, which is holistic. This relational and holistic aspect of repentance indicates that Israel's missional re-formation as her response to Yahweh's calling her to repent was to involve (1) the restoration of her relationship with Yahweh, and (2) the holistic change of her life.

The Sinai Covenant as the Basis of the Prophets' Message[251]

As R. E. Clements points out, "the prophets did not regard themselves as introducing a new doctrine of God in Israel, or as teaching a new morality."[252] The theological basis of the prophets' message was the Sinai Covenant, which defined Israel's missionary vocation. Yahweh's primary purpose in his encounter with Israel through the prophets was to restore the covenant relationship with her so that she may fulfill her missionary vocation as being a kingdom of priests and a holy nation in the midst of the nations. Gentry and Wellum excellently sum up the relationship between the message of the prophets and the Sinai Covenant when they state:

> The messages of the prophets are sometimes quite shocking. Prophets functioned as spokesmen for God, raised up to call attention to the failure of the people of God to be covenant keepers. They confronted the people of God and exposed the clever and devious ways by which they had gradually slipped away from the standards defined by *the covenant at Sinai* for a proper relationship with God and proper treatment of each other. The prophets were giants in the art and skill of communication, . . . yet all their sentences, their promises and threats, are *based on the covenant God made with Israel*, especially as found in its fullest form in the book of Deuteronomy.[253]

Robin Routledge observes the covenant as the point of reference in the prophets' speech, as he asserts, "Though prophets before Jeremiah make

---

251. The close relationship between the prophets' message and the Sinai Covenant is strong particularly in the classic prophets, including prophets such as Amos, Isaiah, Jeremiah, and Hosea.

252. Clements, *Prophecy and Covenant*, 16.

253. Gentry and Wellum, *Kingdom through Covenant*, 577. Emphasis added.

relatively few specific references to the Sinaitic covenant, the relationship between God and the people of Israel is a central concern of their preaching. Even where they do not use [the Hebrew term for covenant,] their theology is *deeply rooted in Israel's covenant traditions.*"[254] Stuhlmueller sees prophets as "God's instruments for purifying and reinvigorating Israel's religious attitudes."[255] He highlights their challenge against the people of Israel who turn away from what God *originally* intended them to be.[256] Stuhlmueller states, "Prophecy sought to reform Israel's religious and civil institutions by reverting to the free, uncomplicated, and heroic times of Moses and Joshua and to the moment when Israel was acting more immediately under God's leadership. Those were the days when the impact of God's will was felt directly within Israel's secular, daily life."[257] Thus, the Sinai Covenant was the basis of the prophets' message. The prophets envisaged Israel turning back to the covenant relationship established in the period of Moses.

The Comprehensive Nature of Israel's Sin

Sinai-covenant-centeredness in the message of the prophets is made explicit in light of the nature of Israel's sins that Yahweh dealt with through the prophets. These sins that Yahweh rebuked through the prophets are consistent with the holistic nature of the law, which is both the relationship between Yahweh and Israel and the relationship between individuals. In his survey of the nature of sin and dominant strategies for dealing with sin particularly in the Hebrew canonical division called Prophets, Mark J. Boda observes two relational aspects of sin. On the one hand, Boda observes that, in the Old Testament books commonly called the Former Prophets,[258] Yahweh pointed out their "violation of the Deuteronomic exclusive worship values" and "a lack of trust in Yahweh."[259] On the other hand, Boda points out, "While violations of Deuteronomy's exclusive worship values dominated the presentation of history in the Former Prophets, violations

---

254. Routledge, *Old Testament Theology*, 246. Emphasis added. Also see Clements, *Prophecy and Covenant*, 16–19; Bright, *Covenant and Promise*, 41–43, 83–94.

255. Senior and Stuhlmueller, *Biblical Foundations for Mission*, 55. Interestingly, Stuhlmueller mentions social and political aspects of Israel's apostasy, but does not mention a religious dimension of its apostasy even in his dealing with the biblical texts in which Israel worshiped pagan gods.

256. Senior and Stuhlmueller, *Biblical Foundations for Mission*, 55–82.

257. Senior and Stuhlmueller, *Biblical Foundations for Mission*, 58.

258. For Boda, the Former Prophets span from the book of Joshua to the First and Second Kings in the Old Testament.

259. Boda, "Prophets," 31.

of moral law are not lacking."²⁶⁰ Likewise, "The presentation of sin in the Latter Prophets continues the focus on the double axes (vertical and horizontal) already encountered in the Former Prophets."²⁶¹ Boda goes on to state, "The prophets showcased in the books of Isaiah, Jeremiah, Ezekiel and the Twelve, express deep concern over dysfunctional relational patterns exemplified by the people [of Israel] towards Yahweh and towards one another."²⁶² The comprehensive scope of Israel's sin not only included these two relational dimensions of Israel's life but also laid waste to the land given her,²⁶³ as indicated in Hosea 4:1–3. According to these verses, as the result of the Israelites' sin against Yahweh and one another, "the land mourns, and all who live in it languish; together with the wild animals and the birds of the air, even the fish of the sea are perishing" (Hos 4:1–3).

This comprehensive scope of Israel's sin that Yahweh dealt with through the prophets is parallel to the holistic nature of the law which is central for Israel to be faithful to the Sinai Covenant. The sin of Israel was nothing less than her unfaithfulness to the Sinai Covenant. In this sense, what Yahweh demanded of Israel through the prophets was her turning back to the foundation of her missionary vocation, namely the covenant relationship with Yahweh, as defined in the Sinai Covenant.

Yahweh's Grace Again

Yahweh's faithfulness in fulfilling Israel's missionary vocation is found in the Latter Prophets' concluding message because their message to Israel does not end with Yahweh's abandonment of Israel, but with the grace of Yahweh by which he will restore Israel to what he originally intended her to be in the future. This hope of restoration was given not because Israel deserved it, but because Yahweh is *gracious*. Boda strikingly observes it in relation to how the Latter Prophets dealt with Israel's sins. He states:

> Throughout the Latter Prophets sin is dealt with in a variety of ways. Isaiah 1 identifies two key strategies. Isaiah 1.2–20 highlights the role of the prophet confronting the people with their sin (Isa. 1.2–15) and then exhorting them to repent (Isa. 1.16–17). Isaiah 1.21–31 highlights the role of divine discipline to purify the people from their sin (Isa. 1.25). But all the prophetic

---

260. Boda, "Prophets," 31.
261. Boda, "Prophets," 34.
262. Boda, "Prophets," 34.
263. For a helpful study on the ecological dimension of sin, see Wright, *Mission of God*, 429–33; Snyder and Scandrett, *Salvation Means Creation Healed*, 76–78.

> books contain significant material related to the second strategy, highlighting the ultimate failure of the first strategy.... In the wake of this failure of the first strategy and employment of the second strategy, the prophets reveal a third strategy of dealing with sin: *the unilateral gracious initiative of Yahweh*.[264]

The final message from Yahweh regarding the unfaithfulness of Israel is not abandonment, but a new divine initiative to bring the people back to covenant relationship. Oswalt is right when he comments on the overall message of the book of Isaiah:

> Israel is declared as the means through whom God's light and blessing will come to the world. In the words of chs. 40–48, Israel is to be his witness. But this poses a nearly unanswerable question: How can this Israel become that Israel? The rest of the book functions as an answer to that question. In short, the answer is *God, God who has the power (chs. 7–39) and the grace (chs. 40–66) to make the impossible possible.*[265]

Summary

As in the earlier period, during the period of monarchy, Israel proved her inability to fulfill her missionary vocation on her own, failing to be faithful to the covenant relationship with Yahweh, and breaking the whole dimension of the law. However, through prophets, Yahweh sought to bring Israel back to what he intended her to be. Called and sent directly by Yahweh, the prophets presented the will of Yahweh to Israel. The message of the prophets was profoundly rooted in the Sinai Covenant, which defines the missionary vocation of Israel, and their message aimed at the restoration of the covenant. However, Israel's monarchy period culminated with destruction by the Gentile nations as the punishment from Yahweh for her continuing unfaithfulness to God and failure to repent. On the one hand, this ending of the period of monarchy was the most obvious proof that Israel cannot fulfill her missionary vocation on her own. On the other hand, it demonstrated that only Yahweh himself can fulfill Israel's missionary

---

264. Boda, "Prophets," 42. Emphasis added. For Boda, the New Covenant, Yahweh's forgiveness of Israel's sin, and a servant figure are part of Yahweh's divine initiative to restore Israel back to him. For Boda, this divine initiative of grace is the key for understanding sin in the Prophets, both Former and Latter. See Boda, "Prophets," 42–43.

265. Oswalt, *Isaiah 1–39*, 54. Emphasis added.

vocation. The prophets' conclusive message of restoration shows that Yahweh will fulfill Israel's missionary vocation.

G. Summary and Conclusion of the Chapter

This chapter explored Yahweh's mission to Israel in the Old Testament with focus on the way Yahweh shaped the people of Israel toward their missionary vocation in the Old Testament narrative. With this research focus, this chapter delved into the Exodus, the Sinai Covenant, the law, and the presence of Yahweh, and looked into how Yahweh continuously reshaped Israel toward what she was called to be for his mission from the period of wilderness to that of monarchy. This chapter identifies several aspects of the way Yahweh shaped the people of Israel for his mission as summarized below.

Two Relational Dimensions of Israel's Missionary Vocation

Through the Exodus, Yahweh liberated the Hebrew people, the descendants of Abraham, from slavery bondage in Egypt, resulting in the birth of Israel as a nation. The Exodus revealed Yahweh's faithfulness in fulfilling Israel's missionary purpose as revealed in the Abrahamic Covenant. Israel was brought into being as a consequence of Yahweh's act to fulfill her missionary purpose. Thus, on the one hand, Israel was liberated not for her own independence but ultimately for the nations, which would be blessed through her. On the other hand, this missionary purpose of Israel's existence is juxtaposed with another relational dimension of her reason for being. The people of Israel were not merely brought out of Egypt but brought into the presence of Yahweh as their new king. Through the Exodus, Yahweh led them to the conversion of Israel to Yahweh so that they might serve him as their new king. Given these two dimensions of the reason that Yahweh brought the people out of Egypt, it can be said that the mission commissioned to Israel in the midst of and for the nations is closely related to the king-servant relationship between Yahweh and Israel. This relationship between the two relational dimensions of Israel's missionary nature is made explicit in the meaning of three identity-defining phrases—my treasured possession, a kingdom of priests, and a holy nation—in the Sinai Covenant. The two relational dimensions are interrelated to each other in such a way that Israel's missionary role to the nations is a consequence of the relationship between Yahweh and Israel.

Israel as the Missional and Holistic Kingdom of Yahweh

The study of the Sinai Covenant shows that Yahweh's mission to Israel was a *particularization* of the kingdom of Yahweh because, by establishing the Sinai Covenant, Yahweh created his kingdom *with a particular people* over whom he reigns. In the Sinai Covenant, the relationship between Yahweh and Israel is characterized by Yahweh's kingship over Israel and her full obedience to Yahweh. The requirement of obedience in the covenant undergirds the king-servant relationship between Yahweh and Israel. The parallels between Mt. Sinai and the tabernacle highlights the role of Yahweh as a lawgiver. Therefore, Israel was to be the kingdom of Yahweh with a particular people.

However, Israel's obedience to Yahweh had a *missionary* purpose because the requirement of obedience was ultimately for her relationship with the nations. As discussed in this chapter, the key to the fulfillment of her missionary vocation was obedience because the missionary nature of Israel's distinctiveness was to be shaped by her obedient relationship with Yahweh. Israel was called to obey Yahweh not exclusively for her own benefit but ultimately for the sake of the nations.

If the requirement of obedience defines the relational dimension of the kingdom of Yahweh, the holistic nature of the holiness of Israel defines the holistic scope of the kingdom of Yahweh. The law given Israel as a practical way to be holy includes all relational dimensions—with Yahweh, with one another, and with the land, covering the whole life of Israel. Thus, Israel as a particular kingdom of Yahweh was to be holistic. Israel was called to present the *holistic* holiness of Yahweh to the nations in a *holistic* way of life.

The Mission of Israel Is Primarily about Being a Contrast People

Israel delivered by Yahweh was brought into a covenant relationship as she encountered Yahweh at Mt. Sinai where Yahweh gave Israel a missionary vocation to fulfill his mission as revealed in the Abrahamic Covenant. The missionary vocation of Israel as defined by three identity-defining phrases—*my treasured possession, a kingdom of priests*, and *a holy nation*—in the Sinai Covenant reveal that her mission was primarily about being distinctive among the nations rather than intentionally reaching out to the nations. Israel was called to present the holiness of Yahweh, which points to both the presence and character of Yahweh, to the nations by *being a contrast people* whose life is to be profoundly shaped by the holiness of Yahweh who is in their midst, among the nations. In other words, Israel was called to be as much different from the nations as Yahweh was different from the world in order to make Yahweh visible to the nations and, ultimately, in order for the nations to be drawn to Yahweh. Israel's missionary role to the nations would come from Israel being distinctive.

The Missional Faithfulness of Yahweh

The analysis of the way Yahweh shaped Israel toward her missionary vocation in the Old Testament narrative demonstrates that Yahweh was faithfully committed to shaping and fulfilling the missionary purpose he had for Israel. That is evidenced by Yahweh's motivation for and his goal of the Exodus, the grace-based nature of the Sinai Covenant, and Yahweh's desire for the covenant relationship with Israel and for dwelling in her midst. When it comes to the conditionality of the Sinai Covenant, on the one hand, the fulfillment of the missionary vocation of Israel requires her obedience to Yahweh. On the other hand, the conditionality of the Sinai Covenant should be understood within the context of Yahweh's unceasing faithfulness in fulfilling the Abrahamic Covenant. In this regard, the fulfillment of Israel's missionary vocation should not be viewed as being left in the hands of the people. Rather, it implies that Israel's missionary purpose would be fulfilled by Yahweh's faithfulness in accomplishing the Abrahamic Covenant.

Yahweh's faithfulness in fulfilling the missionary vocation of Israel is made explicit in the repetition of the pattern of (1) Israel's rebellion, (2) Yahweh's intervening initiative, and (3) the restoration of the covenant relationship during the periods of wilderness, conquest, and judges. Yahweh's constant efforts to bring Israel back to him through prophets also depicts his commitment to the fulfillment of Israel's missionary vocation. While the fulfillment of the missionary vocation of Israel depends on the condition of Israel's full obedience to Yahweh, he did not leave Israel alone laden with her responsibility to be obedient, but he determined to be the one who held Israel accountable to fulfilling her missionary vocation. Furthermore, this point is further indicated in the prophets' message about Yahweh's promise of the restoration of Israel back to what she was called to be.

The Missional Unfaithfulness of Israel

The biblical cases that this chapter touched on reveal that Israel repeatedly failed her missionary vocation, lacking trust in Yahweh, quickly forgetting what Yahweh has done for it, and being attracted by the nations. This point is clearly evidenced by the observation that Yahweh's engagement with Israel from the periods of wilderness, conquest, and judges are characterized by the cyclical pattern, comprised of (1) the rebellion of Israel against Yahweh, (2) the intervening initiative of Yahweh, and (3) the restoration of the covenant relationship. This pattern demonstrates Israel's unfaithfulness in fulfilling her missionary vocation, on the one hand, and Yahweh's faithfulness in fulfilling her missionary vocation, on the other hand. Furthermore, the fact that the period of monarchy ended with Israel's destruction by Gentile nations as Yahweh's punishment for Israel's continuous apostasy indicates that Israel would not be able to fulfill her missionary vocation on her own.

3

The Disciples' Encounter with Jesus and Their Missional Conversion

IN THE LATE TWENTIETH century, the significance of Jesus's earthly ministry for understanding the essential nature of the church's mission has been gradually brought to attention along with the emergence of the term and concept of missional church,[1] taking Jesus's earthly ministry as *the* model of mission that the church should imitate.[2] *Missional Church*, published in 1998, clearly anchored this way of understanding of the relationship between the church's mission and Jesus's earthly ministry, reexamining the origin of the church in light of the gospel Jesus proclaimed and embodied, as noted earlier.[3] The church's mission was viewed as the continuation of Jesus's mission of representing the reign of God.[4]

---

1. The missional implications of Jesus's earthly ministry for individual missionaries has been noted repeatedly in the history of Christianity (e.g., St. Francis), but was not articulated for the church's mission until the later twentieth century. Probably, the Assembly of the World Council of Churches (WCC) held in Uppsala, 1968, can be viewed as a *termus a quo* of this articulation. The assembly took "humanization" of Jesus Christ seriously as its theological keyword. At the assembly, based on the understanding of Jesus as the model of new humanity, Christian missions were held to realize the new humanity. The articulation of the missional dimension of the earthly ministry of Jesus under the rubric of the missional church should not be viewed as a new, unprecedented development in the twentieth century. However, strong emphasis on the earthly ministry of Jesus in conceptualizing the church's mission in the twentieth century seems to be a new factor in the history of mission theology.

2. See Shenk, "Recasting Theology of Mission," 126–30. In this article, Wilbert R. Shenk observes the emerging perception of the missional meaning and significance of the humanity of Jesus among mission scholars from the Majority World such as Rene C. Padilla and Samuel J. Escobar. Shenk also contends that the rediscovery of the humanity of Jesus shapes what missional ecclesiology means. Thus, missional ecclesiology is rooted in missional Christology.

3. Guder, *Missional Church*, 88.

4. Guder, *Missional Church*, 102–9. The view of the church's mission as a

The main theological focus in this view of Jesus's earthly ministry was *what* the church's mission is, not *how* the church becomes missional. This chapter intends to look into how Jesus's earthly ministry is related to the missional conversion of the church. The main thesis of this chapter is that Jesus's early ministry, which intentionally focused on the people of Israel, also can be viewed as the continuation of Yahweh's work for the missional conversion of Israel. This chapter pays attention to discovering ways that Jesus shaped the people of Israel, particularly his disciples, through his earthly ministry in order to fulfill Israel's missionary vocation originally given by Yahweh.

A. Jesus Continues the Father's Work of the Missional Conversion of Israel[5]

Israel's period of monarchy ended with God's judgment on her, culminating in destruction by the Gentile nations, because Israel failed her covenant relationship with him and, by extension, their missionary vocation.[6] However, that did not mean that God gave up on Israel's missionary vocation. As mentioned in the previous chapter, through prophets, God revealed his plan ultimately to restore the foundation of Israel's missionary vocation, namely, her covenantal relationship with him, by establishing the "new covenant" with Israel.[7]

God's Renewal of Israel toward Her Missionary Vocation

The missional intention in God's plan for the restoration of Israel is clearly revealed in the twofold ministry of the Servant of God in the book of Isaiah.[8] On the one hand, the Servant is sent by God for "the particularistic

---

continuation of Jesus's mission is also emphasized in the so-called emerging church movement. Eddie Gibbs and Ryan Bolger in their empirical research on emerging churches in North America and the United Kingdom, observed that, from the church leaders they interviewed, emerging churches "identify with the life of Jesus." See Gibbs and Bolger, *Emerging Churches*, 44–45, 47–54.

5. In the two chapters—chapters 3 and 4—about the New Testament narrative, "God" or "the Father" will be used instead of "Yahweh" because "Yahweh" is not used in the New Testament.

6. Goheen, *Light to the Nations*, 75–76.

7. See Gentry and Wellum, *Kingdom through Covenant*, 433–34. For God's restoration program with the New Covenant, which is found in the Latter Prophets, see Boda, "Prophets," 42–43.

8. In the book of Isaiah, four Suffering Servant songs are found (Isa 42:1–4; 49:1–6; 50:4–9; 52:13—53:12). Each song pictures different aspects of the servant's twofold

mission of the Servant to Israel"[9] in order to "bring Jacob back to him and gather Israel to himself" (Isa 49:5). On the other hand, the mission given to the Servant is global in scope as written in Isaiah 49:6 in which Yahweh says to the Servant, "I will also make you a light for the Gentiles, that my salvation may reach to the ends of the earth" (NIV). On the Servant's twofold ministry, Tennent comments, "Without diminishing God's mission to Israel, there is an even greater mission that encompasses all the nations."[10] Andreas J. Köstenberger and Peter T. O'Brien view the similarity between the twofold ministry of the Servant and the particular-universal relationship in the Abrahamic promise and suggest that Yahweh's work of fulfilling the Abrahamic Covenant continues with the Servant's twofold ministry. They state:

> Although the Servant's work is in the first instance bound up with the redemption of Jerusalem and Israel's return to the holy city, that work will affect the whole world. This sequence of his ministry, namely, first to Israel which then results in blessing to the nations, suggests not only a pattern similar to the Abrahamic promises but also a partial fulfillment of them (cf. Is. 49:6).[11]

Thus, the Servant's mission to the Israelites has a missional intention in that their restoration is closely associated with the ingathering of the nations. The intention of God's plan to restore Israel through his Servant shows God's continuous faithfulness in fulfilling Israel's missionary vocation.

Jesus Sent as the Suffering Servant of God to Fulfill the Old Testament Prophecy

Scholars generally agree that the New Testament writers identified Jesus as the Servant of God in the book of Isaiah. Tennent states, "The quotation of the Suffering Servant Songs in the New Testament and other early Christian writings demonstrates decisively that the early church understood that Jesus was the Suffering Servant."[12] In Matthew 12:15-21, which quotes Isaiah 42:1-4, the mission of the Servant is viewed as fulfilled through Jesus. In the Gospel of Luke, Jesus understood himself as the one who fulfills the ministry

---

ministry, but the second song (Isa 49:1-6) clearly describes the particular-universal dynamics of the ministry of the servant.

9. Tennent, *Invitation to World Missions*, 47.
10. Tennent, *Invitation to World Missions*, 118.
11. Köstenberger and O'Brien, *Salvation to the Ends of the Earth*, 46.
12. Tennent, *Invitation to World Missions*, 199-200.

of the Servant. In Luke 4:16–21, Jesus read Isaiah 61:1–2 and declared, "Today this scripture has been fulfilled in your hearing."[13] In Luke 22:37, he understood himself as the one who was fulfilling the prophecy: "For I tell you, this scripture must be fulfilled in me, 'And he was counted among the lawless;' and indeed what is written about me is being fulfilled." The fulfillment of the prophecy about the Servant's suffering in Isaiah 53 is found in the suffering and death of Jesus in the Gospels.[14]

The view of Jesus as the Servant of God in the book of Isaiah is also indicated by his self-identification, not as the one who sends, but as the one *sent* to complete the mission commissioned by the Father. While the endings of the Gospels present Jesus as the sender of his followers (Matt 28:16–20; Luke 24:44–48; John 20:21), Jesus in the Gospels spoke of himself primarily as the one *sent* to fulfill the will of the Father (e.g., John 4:34, 5:30, 5:38, 6:38–39). Regarding the relationship between the Father as the sender and Jesus as the sent one in the Gospel of John, Köstenberger and O'Brien state, "The Fourth Gospel's primary focus is the mission of Jesus: he is the one who comes into the world, accomplishes his work and returns to the Father; he is the one who descended from heaven and ascends again; he is the Sent One, who, in complete dependence [upon] and perfect obedience to his sender, fulfills the purpose for which the Father sent him."[15] Jesus's primary self-identification as the one who was sent by the Father supports the view that Jesus was sent as the Servant of God to fulfill the Old Testament prophecy about the restoration of Israel back to the covenant relationship with God, which was the foundation of Israel's mission. Jesus's identification with the Servant indicates that, through the earthly ministry of Jesus, God continued what he already initiated with Israel.

---

13. Scholars generally agree with the view that the speaker in Isa 61:1–2, "me" is the Servant of God in the book of Isaiah and also the Messianic feature. See Oswalt, *Book of Isaiah, Chapters 40–66*, 562–63; Smith, *Isaiah 40–66*, 630–31. Goldingay comments, "The 'I' is that of a prophetic king, or rather of a kingly prophet. The combination of features connects with the overlap between prophetic and royal features in the description of the servant of Yahweh in Isaiah 40–55, because a number of aspects of the self-description in 61.1–3 take up descriptions of Yhwh's servant." Goldingay, *Critical and Exegetical Commentary on Isaiah 56–66*, 291.

14. See Chisholm, "Christological Fulfillment."

15. Köstenberger and O'Brien, *Salvation to the Ends of the Earth*, 203. Also see Köstenberger, *Missions of Jesus and the Disciples*, 93–140. The relationship between the Father as the sender and Jesus as the sent one triggered a question on whether mission in the Gospel of John is theocentric or Christocentric. For the debate on this issue, see Köstenberger, "Challenge of a Systematized Biblical Theology of Mission."

The Earthly Ministry of Jesus and the Kingdom of God

The view of Jesus's earthly ministry, as a continuation of God's work of shaping Israel into her missionary vocation as defined in the Sinai Covenant, is further supported by the centrality of the motif of the kingdom of God in the earthly ministry of Jesus. The idea of the kingdom of God (or reign of God) was familiar to the Jews in the days of Jesus. As already discussed in chapter 2, the origin of God's kingship or lordship over the people of Israel goes back to the moment when God delivered them from Egypt and established a covenant with them at Mt. Sinai. The Exodus was a transition from one lord to another, and God's kingship was the basis of the Sinai covenant in which God calls them to obey him fully (Exod 19:5). Thus, Martin Buber calls the Sinai covenant "a kingly covenant" in which the people of Israel came under the rule of YHWH.[16] John Bright also makes the same point: "For Israel had begun its history as a nation summoned by God's grace to be his people, to serve him alone and to obey his covenant law. *The notion of a people of God, called to live under the rule of God, begins just here, and with it the notion of the Kingdom of God.*"[17] The people of Israel were originally to be a *particular* example of what the kingdom of God on earth would look like, but they failed to be.

God did not abandon his plan of shaping them to be his particular kingdom on earth, but rather took another divine initiative to restore Israel as a people he reigns over as their king, as Jesus took the concept of the kingdom of God (or of the kingdom of heaven in the Gospel of Matthew) as the central theme of his earthly ministry. Jesus's ministry began with the proclamation of the kingdom of God, as in Mark 1:15 where he proclaims, "The time is fulfilled, and *the kingdom of God* has come near; repent, and believe in the good news."[18] George R. Beasley-Murray contends that this verse is "a summary of the gospel preached by Jesus."[19] As Bright states, the theme of the kingdom of God was "the central thing with which [Jesus] was concerned."[20] The problem is that Jesus did not define the kingdom of God, and because of that problem, as Donald Senior points out, "[w]hat Jesus meant by this metaphor must be deduced from the overall message of his preaching, his lifestyle, his commitments."[21] Jesus did not provide us with a definition

---

16. Buber, *Kingship*, 121–35.
17. Bright, *Kingdom of God*, 28. Italics in original.
18. Beasley-Murray, *Jesus*, 71.
19. Beasley-Murray, *Jesus*, 71.
20. Bright, *Kingdom of God*, 17.
21. Senior and Stuhlmueller, *Biblical Foundations for Mission*, 146.

statement for the kingdom of God, but "a cumulative definition of what the kingdom of God meant" can be derived from his overall ministry.[22] In this sense, the kingdom of God was at the center of the whole earthly ministry of Jesus as the kingdom of God was announced, inaugurated, and characterized through the earthly ministry of Jesus.

In light of this connection between the kingship of God in the Old Testament and the centrality of the motif of the kingdom of God in the earthly ministry of Jesus, Jesus's ministry can be viewed as the fulfillment of God's plan to restore Israel, promised through his prophets in the Old Testament. Through the earthly ministry of Jesus, God sought to bring Israel back to what he originally intended her to be for his mission. This restoration of Israel was to entail the restoration of the reign of God over Israel, as defined in the Sinai Covenant. Through Jesus, God sought to reshape Israel into a particular kingdom of God which presents the holiness of God—the character and presence of God—to all nations, so that they may be drawn to him.

Jesus's Primary Mission as Renewing Israel's Missionary Vocation

As mentioned above, Jesus's identification with Isaiah's Suffering Servant shows that Jesus's earthly ministry to Israel was a continuation of God's work of shaping Israel toward her missionary vocation. Observing this continuity, Gerhard Lohfink states, "That God has chosen and sanctified his people in order to make it a contrast-society in the midst of the other nations was for Jesus the self-evident background of all his actions."[23] From this point of view, Jesus can be viewed as sent "to restore and renew his people, in order to carry out definitively and irrevocably [God's] plan of having a holy people in the midst of the nations,"[24] as Lohfink points out. Thus, Jesus's earthly ministry can be viewed as a renewal movement among the Israelites. Wright makes this point when he states, "Jesus did not intend to found a church because there already was one, namely the people of Israel itself. Jesus's intention was therefore to reform Israel, not to found a different community altogether."[25] In this regard, as Goheen points out, it can be said that one of the aims of Jesus's earthly ministry was to restore and gather the

---

22. Senior and Stuhlmueller, *Biblical Foundations for Mission*, 146.
23. Lohfink, *Jesus and Community*, 123.
24. Lohfink, *Jesus and Community*, 123.
25. Wright, *Jesus and the Victory*, 275.

people of Israel "as [an] eschatological community that takes up that missional role and identity again."[26]

This understanding of Jesus's earthly ministry as a continuation of God's work of shaping Israel toward her missionary vocation resolves the issue of the striking contradiction between the universal and particular dimensions of Jesus's ministry.[27] Johannes Nissen states, "The universality of the final commission contrasts strikingly with the particularity of the mission instruction in Matthew 10:5–6: 'Go nowhere among the Gentiles . . .', and with Jesus's words in 15:24: 'I was sent only to the lost sheep of the house of Israel.'"[28] One way that explains this particular-universal contrast in Jesus's earthly ministry is that Israel's missionary vocation must be restored first so that, through those who are renewed and gathered by Jesus, all nations may be brought to God. Nissen observes this twofold mission of Jesus as a two-stage mission:

> The best solution is probably to suppose that Matthew is operating with a two-stage scheme of salvation history implying two stages in the mission of Jesus. The mission of the earthly Jesus is a centripetal mission directed to Israel in the hope that the conversion of his people will inaugurate the 'eschatological pilgrimage of nations to the mountain of God' . . . and so lead to salvation of the world.[29]

God had a missional intention in renewing the Israelites so that, through them, all nations might be brought to him. Thus, as Bosch notes, "the first disciples are prototypes for the church,"[30] with which, the Gentile mission was launched right after the death and resurrection of Jesus. In this sense, the contrast between the particular and universal aspects of Jesus's earthly ministry indicates that, like God's work of shaping Israel in the Old Testament, the renewal movement of Jesus among the Israelites had a missional intention.

---

26. Goheen, *Light to the Nations*, 76.

27. For different interpretations of the particular-universal contradiction in Jesus's earthly ministry, see Hahn, *Mission in the New Testament*, 26–28; Bosch, *Transforming Mission*, 60.

28. Nissen, *New Testament and Mission*, 27.

29. Nissen, *New Testament and Mission*, 27–28. Also see Jeremias, *Jesus' Promise to the Nations*, 55–73; Soares-Prabhu, "Church as Mission."

30. Bosch, *Transforming Mission*, 74. Regarding the relationship between Jesus's disciples and Israel, Goheen views the twelve elected by Jesus as "a symbolic prophetic action of the beginning of a renewed and restored Israel." Goheen, *Light to the Nations*, 84.

B. Jesus Focuses on Israel in His Earthly Ministry

The view of Jesus's earthly ministry as a continuity of God's work of shaping Israel as his missionary people is identifiable in the fact that the people of Israel were the primary focus of Jesus's earthly ministry, while he did not reject the Gentiles who approached him.

Jesus's Mission Only to Israel

On the one hand, the ministry of Jesus has *universal* significance and relevance in a sense that what the church's mission to the whole world should look like is found and rooted in the person, teaching, and life of Jesus. The way that the church participates in God's mission should be modeled on the life and ministry of Jesus. Samuel Escobar states, "Jesus was sent by God the Father and was *God's best missionary, the true model* for Christian mission."[31] On the other hand, Jesus's earthly ministry was *particularistic*, intentionally limited to the Israelites. This point is made clear especially in the Gospel of Matthew.[32] Jesus said, "I was sent only to the lost sheep of Israel" (Matt 15:24). Even when Jesus sent out his twelve disciples, he said to them, "Go nowhere among the Gentiles, and enter no town of the Samaritans, but go rather to the lost sheep of the house of Israel" (Matt 10:5–6 ESV). Bosch observes, "Matthew never tells of Jesus actually taking the initiative and going out to Gentiles. They approach him, not he them."[33]

When Jesus spoke about mission to the Gentiles, he mentioned the Gentile mission mainly in terms of a promise for the future.[34] As Bosch notes, the Gentile mission is "referred to only in the future tense" until the death and resurrection of Jesus.[35] In his analysis of Jesus's teaching about the Gentile mission, Joachim Jeremias observes that the inclusion of Gentiles into the kingdom of God is mentioned only as a promise to fulfill in the future."[36] Thus, as Goheen states, "while affirming this ingather-

---

31. Escobar, *New Global Mission*, 99. Emphasis added.

32. For Jesus's intentionality in limiting his earthly ministry to the people of Israel, see Blauw, *Missionary Nature of the Church*, 67–68; Senior and Stuhlmueller, *Biblical Foundations for Mission*, 238–41; Bird, *Jesus and the Origins of the Gentile Mission*, 51–57.

33. Bosch, *Transforming Mission*, 61. Also see Köstenberger and O'Brien, *Salvation to the Ends of the Earth*, 83.

34. For a thorough study of Jesus's view of the Gentile mission as a future event, see Jeremias, *Jesus' Promise to the Nations*.

35. Bosch, *Transforming Mission*, 64.

36. Jeremias, *Jesus' Promise to the Nations*, 55.

ing of the nations, he limits his own [immediate] mission and that of his disciples to the Jews."[37]

While Jesus intended to limit his ministry almost exclusively to the Jews, his earthly ministry does not reveal any negative view of the Gentiles. Rather, while largely passive, he had an open attitude toward the Gentiles who approached him. Köstenberger and O'Brien observe, "Even during his earthly ministry, Jesus exceptionally ministered to Gentiles in response to their requests, though he never takes the initiative. What is more, sometimes he seems to take positive steps to avoid ministry to Gentiles."[38] His openness toward the Gentiles is well illustrated when he viewed the faith of the centurion in Capernaum as better than that of any among Israelites, saying in Matthew 8:10, "Truly I tell you, in no one in Israel have I found such faith." In his comprehensive analysis of Jesus's earthly ministry, Lohfink excellently draws together Jesus's relationships with the Jews and with the Gentiles: "*Jesus in no way excluded the Gentiles from salvation. But he himself directed his attention exclusively to Israel*."[39]

Thus, scholars generally observe that while Israel was the primary focus of Jesus's earthly ministry, it does not indicate his negative view of Gentiles. This biblical observation indicates that God's mission to Israel in the Old Testament narrative continues in Jesus's earthly ministry among the Jews. As God in the Old Testament did, Jesus intentionally concentrated on shaping Israel.

The Universal Vision of Jesus's Ministry to the People of Israel

As discussed above, Israel was the primary focus of Jesus's earthy ministry, but Jesus had a missional reason to focus on Israel. As Johannes Munck points out, "Jesus's apparent particularism is an expression of his universalism—it is because his mission concerns the whole world that he comes to Israel."[40] Jesus envisioned the universal impact of the restored people of Israel when he said in Matthew 8:11-12, "I tell you, many will come from east and west and will eat with Abraham and Isaac and Jacob in the kingdom of heaven, while the heirs of the kingdom will be thrown into the outer darkness, where there will be weeping and gnashing of teeth." In these verses, Jesus not only echoes the Old Testament utterances of the

---

37. Goheen, *Light to the Nations*, 80.
38. Köstenberger and O'Brien, *Salvation to the Ends of the Earth*, 94.
39. Lohfink, *Jesus and Community*, 17. Italics in original.
40. Munck, *Paul and the Salvation of Mankind*, 271.

eschatological pilgrimage of the Gentiles, but also links it with the people of Israel who are represented by Abraham and Isaac and Jacob. In his analysis of the verses, Jeremias states, "Jesus expected the incorporation of the Gentiles into the people of God," and asserts that this would happen through two consecutive events: "first the call to Israel, and subsequently the redemptive incorporation of the Gentiles in the Kingdom of God."[41] The priority of the Jews over the Gentiles in salvation history is found in early Christian writings. As Jeremias observes, "the promise of salvation given to 'the fathers' . . . and to 'the sons of the prophets and of the covenant' . . . must first be fulfilled, the children must first be fed, before the incorporation of the Gentiles into the people of God could be effected. This is the universal conviction of the earliest Christianity."[42]

However, the contrast between the inclusion of Gentiles and exclusion of the people of Israel in the kingdom of heaven in the verses above shows that God is not guilty of favoritism toward Israel. The point of the contrast is, as R. T. France comments, "that membership in the kingdom of heaven will not be on the basis of race, that believing Gentiles will take the place of unbelieving Jews."[43] The priority of Israel over the Gentiles is not in terms of significance but *in time*, in the sense that Jesus's concentration on Israel in his ministry does not mean that the ingathering of the Gentiles is a secondary event.[44] Jesus envisioned that, as renewed through his earthly ministry, the people of Israel would participate in God's mission of gathering all nations.

C. Jesus Bridges Israel's Mission and the Disciples' Gentile Mission

The earlier discussion about the earthly ministry of Jesus in this chapter shows that God continued to shape Israel toward her missionary vocation through Jesus who was sent to fulfill the mission of the Servant of God. This section focuses on one specific question about the aim of Jesus's earthly ministry to Israel: *What do the Gospels say about Jesus's missional vision for the restored and renewed Israel?*[45]

---

41. Jeremias, *Jesus' Promise to the Nations*, 71.
42. Jeremias, *Jesus' Promise to the Nations*, 72.
43. France, *Gospel According to Matthew*, 156.
44. deSilva, *Introduction to the New Testament*, 257, 262.
45. For helpful scholarly literature on the question on the aims of Jesus, see Wright, *Mission of God*, 506n8.

The Relationship between the Disciples and the Whole People of Israel

Lohfink suggests a way to approach this question. He contends that the question of "how Jesus envisioned, more exactly, the Israel which he sought to gather, the true people of God" is answered "decisively by Jesus's instruction of his disciples."[46] One particular strategy that Jesus used in his earthly ministry to Israel was to choose twelve people as his disciples among Jews, create a community with them, and work among them. Jesus began his ministry by announcing the kingdom of God, and what immediately follows is that he called the first four disciples (Matt 4:17–22; Mark 1:14–20).[47] In his survey of the Gospel of Mark, I. Howard Marshall observes, "the story concentrates on [the disciples'] association with Jesus."[48] However, as Lohfink points out, "the circle of disciples did not form a new community outside the old people of God, one assembled by Jesus as a *surrogate* or *replacement* for Israel. A concept of this sort would be thoroughly unbiblical."[49] Jesus's renewal movement within the people of Israel should not be viewed as being limited to the community of the disciples. Rather, the relationship between the disciples and the whole people of Israel is *symbolic* and *strategic*. The former was intended not to replace the latter, and yet be *representative* of the latter.

First, the relationship is symbolic because the disciples symbolically "represent the twelve tribes."[50] This symbolic view of the disciples in relation to the whole people of Israel is associated to the symbolic meaning of the number twelve, the number of the disciples symbolizing the twelve tribes of Israel (Matt 19:28; Luke 22:30; Rev 21:12–14).[51] Second, one way to understand the symbolic meaning of the relationship between the disciples and the whole people of Israel is to view the relationship in light of the strategic aspect of the relationship. The relationship is strategic in the sense that Jesus called the disciples as "the beginning and center of growth for the renewed, eschatological Israel."[52] The whole people of Israel were called to join the eschatological people of God he already created by calling the disciples. Thus, they were chosen for the sake of Israel as a whole. Lohfink makes this point

---

46. Lohfink, *Jesus and Community*, 31.
47. Bosch, *Transforming Mission*, 36.
48. Marshall, *New Testament Theology*, 67.
49. Lohfink, *Jesus and Community*, 34. Italics in original.
50. Lohfink, *Does God Need the Church*, 131.
51. Collins, "Twelve," 670; Jones, "Twelve," 690.
52. Lohfink, *Does God Need the Church*, 131. For this strategic aspect of Jesus's focus on the disciples, see Coleman, *Master Plan of Evangelism*, 21–32.

when he states, "all discipleship [in the Gospels] is . . . aimed at Israel and at the gathering of the whole people of God. With the disciples begins the eschatological re-creation of Israel, and in the re-creation of Israel the reign of God is revealed."[53] In this sense, the disciples are called to be an *example* of what the whole people of Israel would look like as a people gathered and renewed by Jesus.[54] Jesus's election of the community of the disciples can be viewed as a way that Jesus began to reshape the whole people of Israel toward their original missionary vocation. R. David Rightmire excellently sums up these symbolic and strategic aspects of the relationship between the disciples and Israel when he states:

> Jesus's choice of twelve disciples to form an inner circle of followers served to symbolize the truth that he had come to build a new house of Israel. The Twelve formed the nucleus of this new people of God, corresponding to the twelve tribes of Israel, and signifying God's saving activity at work in Jesus and his followers. Their number implies that they were destined primarily to work among the children of Israel. Although not confined to the Jews, the mission of the Twelve had special relation to the twelve tribes of Israel.[55]

The symbolic and strategic aspects of the relationship between the disciples and Israel indicates that the disciples were the primary focus in Jesus's earthly ministry to Israel. In this sense, this chapter focuses on how the whole earthly ministry of Jesus shaped the disciples into a nucleus of the eschatological people of God so that, with them, the renewal of the whole people of Israel for the mission of God may begin.

In-Between Context of Jesus's Earthly Ministry

Wright suggests that the way to approach the aim of Jesus's earthly ministry is to "observe what immediately preceded and what immediately followed Jesus's earthly ministry."[56] The Gospels clearly record that Jesus's ministry immediately followed that of John the Baptist. As Wright notes, "All the

53. Lohfink, *Does God Need the Church*, 131.
54. Lohfink, *Jesus and Community*, 35.
55. Rightmire, "Apostle," 34.
56. Wright, *Mission of God*, 506. Interestingly, Wright focuses only on what immediately followed Jesus's earthly ministry—the early church's mission to the nations. However, in his other book, *Knowing Jesus through the Old Testament*, he highlights what immediately preceded, focusing on the Old Testament values in Jesus's earthly ministry. See Wright, *Knowing Jesus*.

records agree that the ministry of Jesus began out of the ministry of John the Baptist" who launched "a prophetic ministry seeking the restoration of Israel."[57] When it comes to what immediately followed Jesus's earthly ministry, Luke's two-volume work—the Gospel of Luke and the book of Acts—shows that, as Wright points out, "very soon after Jesus's death and resurrection, we find his first followers crossing the boundaries of Jewish separateness from the Gentiles in order to share the good news about Jesus."[58] Thus, the origin of the early church's Gentile mission cannot be explained apart from Jesus's earthly ministry, but stemmed from what Jesus accomplished through his earthly ministry. As Senior articulates, "The catalyst that triggered the missionary consciousness of the early church and shaped its basic message was the person and ministry of Jesus. In him centrifugal forces . . . detected in the Old Testament reach their point of explosion; in him the worldwide perspective of early Christianity finds its source."[59] Wright observes Jesus's earthly ministry in this in-between context of the two before-and-after movements. He states:

> Jesus' earthly ministry was launched by a movement that aimed at the restoration of Israel. But he himself launched a movement that aimed at the ingathering of the nations to the new messianic people of God. The initial impetus for his ministry was to call Israel back to their God. The subsequent impact of his ministry was a new community that called the nations to faith in the God of Israel.[60]

Two aims of Jesus's earthly ministry to the people of Israel can thus be identified: (1) restoring them back to covenant relationship with God, and (2) preparing them for the Gentile mission. Thus, the aim of Jesus's earthly ministry is twofold, bridging the mission of Israel, as defined in the Sinai Covenant, and the Gentile mission by the disciples, as launched in the post-resurrection period.

Two Aims of Jesus's Earthly Ministry in the Old Testament

It should be noted that these two aims of Jesus's earthly ministry certainly did not originate in the New Testament because Jesus came to Israel to fulfill what

---

57. Wright, *Mission of God*, 506.
58. Wright, *Mission of God*, 506.
59. Senior and Stuhlmueller, *Biblical Foundations for Mission*, 141–42.
60. Wright, *Mission of God*, 506.

was already promised and prophesied in the Old Testament.[61] Rather, these two aims of Jesus's earthly ministry are firmly grounded in the Old Testament prophecies. As already discussed above, the New Testament writers view Jesus as the one who fulfilled the twofold mission of the Servant of God in the book of Isaiah. More specifically, how this twofold ministry of the Servant of God would impact Israel's mission is indicated in two biblical terms, "new covenant" (Jer 31:31–34) and "my witnesses" (Isa 43:10, 12).

At one level, the mission of Isaiah's Servant is to restore Israel back to God. This restorative prophecy finds more characterization in the New Covenant, which emphasizes the relationship between Israel and God, in a similar way that Israel's missionary vocation was defined in the Sinai Covenant. For example, the law, the central component of Israel's mission, is also found in the New Covenant (Jer 31:33).[62] This covenant is about bringing Israel back to God. At another level, the mission of the Servant to Israel is expected to shape her as a missionary people who witness about God to all nations: "You are my witnesses" (Isa 43:10, 12). The same identity of Israel is also found in Luke 24:48 and Acts 1:8.[63] Restored Israel's identity as "witnesses" of God in Isaiah 43 and the disciples' call to be "witnesses" of Jesus in Luke 24 and Acts 2 should not be viewed as different, but as fundamentally identical in light of the unity between the Father and Jesus. This point indicates that the disciples' missionary vocation as witnesses of Jesus "to the ends of the earth" (Acts 1:8) was already envisioned in the Old

61. Jesus himself understood his ministry as the fulfillment of Old Testament prophecies (e.g., Luke 4:1; 24:7). For a survey of the Old Testament prophecies fulfilled by Jesus, see Wright, *Knowing Jesus*.

62. Two observations from Jeremiah's New Covenant indicate that Israel's mission defined by the Sinai Covenant would be restored through the establishment of the New Covenant. First, the New Covenant defines Israel's covenant relationship with God in the same way that was defined in the early stage of Israel's history. This point is supported by the so-called covenant formula found in the New Covenant, "they will be my people, and I will be their God" (Jer 31:33). This covenant formula is the primary way that Israel's covenant relationship with God was defined before and when God called Israel as a nation for the first time in the Old Testament (e.g., Gen 17:7–8; Exod 6:7; Lev 26:11–12). Second, the law, which was the central component of Israel's mission as being a holy nation, is also mentioned in the New Covenant (Jer 31:33). "Minds" and "hearts" in the New Covenant does not seem to be new components because, when Jesus said to a teacher of the law that the most important commandment is loving God "with all your *heart* and with all your soul and with all your *mind* and with all your strength" and loving neighbors, the teacher of the law agreed with Jesus (Mark 12:28–34).

63. Scholars generally see the connection between the term "witness" in Isa 43 and the disciples' missionary identity as witnesses of Jesus in Luke 24 and Acts 1. See Johnson, "Jesus Against the Idols," 346–49; Evans, "Light to the Nations," 103; Wright, *Knowing Jesus*, 169.

Testament as a consequence of the ministry of the Servant of Isaiah. In his intertextual study of Isaiah's prophecies in the Gospel of Luke and the book of Acts, Craig A. Evans argues that the missionary identity of the disciples as witnesses of Jesus is grounded in Isaiah 43. He states:

> Most striking is the declaration of the risen Jesus: "You are witnesses of these things." Given the contribution that the prophecy of Isaiah has made to Luke's understanding of mission, it is very probable that the Evangelist would have us think of the Lord's solemn declarations in Isaiah: "You are my witnesses" (Isa 43:10, 12; 44:8). The disciples of Jesus now fulfill the task of being the Lord's witnesses. They are witnesses of what God has accomplished in his Son, Jesus the Messiah, whose death and resurrection have made salvation possible. This is what is meant by the words "witnesses of these things." The disciples have witnessed in Jesus the fulfillment of the Isaianic prophecies.[64]

In this sense, the disciples' Gentile mission through their witnessing was already expected in the Old Testament as the consequence of Jesus's earthly ministry.

Summary

To summarize, Jesus created a small community with his disciples in order to reshape Israel toward God's missionary people. Two aims of Jesus's mission to Israel are identified by the in-between context of Jesus's earthly ministry and the Old Testament prophecies about what Israel, restored by Isaiah's Servant of God, would look like. On the one hand, Jesus's mission to Israel was to restore Israel back to her mission defined in the Sinai Covenant, as indicated in the New Covenant. On the other hand, Jesus's mission to Israel was to shape Israel toward being a missionary people who witness to what God has done in and through Jesus to the ends of the earth. The rest of this chapter identifies ways that Jesus accomplished these two aims by shaping the disciples as a people who embody the kingdom of God, which is both *radical* and *inclusive*.

D. Jesus Shapes the Disciples as a *Radical* Contrast People

The view that God continued to shape Israel toward her missionary vocation through Jesus implies that there is continuity between what God intended

---

64. Evans, "Light to the Nations," 103.

her to be and what Jesus intended his disciples to be. This section focuses on ways that the essential nature of Israel's missionary vocation continues with Jesus's disciples by looking at three pieces of biblical evidence which connect Jesus's earthly ministry with God's mission to Israel in the Old Testament: (1) the relationship between Jesus and John the Baptist, (2) three biblical images in Matthew 5:13–16, and (3) Jesus as the new center of the disciples' holiness. Based on these biblical cases, this section demonstrates that the essential nature of Israel's missionary vocation not only *continued* with the disciples but also was *redefined* throughout the earthly ministry of Jesus.

John the Baptist and Jesus's Ministry

As discussed above, the continuity of Israel's missionary vocation with Jesus's disciples is indicated when the aim of Jesus's earthly ministry is seen as fulfillment of the prophetic promise of restoring Israel back to covenant relationship with God. This aim of Jesus's earthly ministry is made obvious when Jesus's earthly ministry is seen in connection with the ministry of John the Baptist, the background of whose ministry is Jewish expectation of Israel's restoration during the time of Jesus.

John the Baptist and Restoration of Israel

During the time of Jesus, Jews were saturated with the hope of the restoration of Israel, as promised by God through the Old Testament prophets.[65] As Wright points out, "It is indeed this framework of restoration hope that provides the context for understanding the ministry of John the Baptist."[66] In Luke 1:16, John the Baptist is identified as one who "will turn many of the people of Israel to the Lord their God." Wright states, "John's mission was to identify, through his call for repentance and baptism, the remnant of Israel who, by responding, was destined for cleansing and restoration as the true, eschatological people of God."[67] Ben F. Meyer views John's baptism as "designed to symbolize and seal the conversion of Israel."[68] Through John's ministry, "God called for the conversion and washing of the whole nation."[69] The view of John's ministry as the restoration of Israel back to God is further

---

65. Wright, *Knowing Jesus*, 143–44.
66. Wright, *Knowing Jesus*, 146.
67. Wright, *Knowing Jesus*, 147.
68. Meyer, *Aims of Jesus*, 116.
69. Meyer, *Aims of Jesus*, 116.

evidenced by the observation that the central message of John for her was *repentance*. As already explored, the Old Testament prophets as God's divine agents called the people of Israel to repent. The people of Israel hear the message of repentance from John the Baptist again.[70] Regarding John's ministry, Meyer points out, "In the face of judgment Israel was to be reconstituted *as in the beginning*."[71] The connection between the ministry of John and that of the Old Testament prophets shows that God's missional vision for Israel, which was revealed in the Sinai Covenant, continues in the New Testament.

Jesus and John the Baptist

The message of the Old Testament prophets about the restoration of Israel back to God continues not only with John the Baptist but with Jesus as Jesus accepted John's ministry and shared in the aim of his ministry. First, Jesus accepted John's ministry by being baptized by John (Matt 3:14–15). Jesus's act of being baptized by John implies that Jesus identified himself with those who desired Israel's restoration as John envisioned.[72] In so doing, Jesus joined "those who wanted to express their longing to be right with God, to be obedient to God's will and to see the coming of God's kingdom."[73]

In addition to accepting John's ministry, Jesus launched his own ministry with an aim which accords with John's own aim. Wright states, "Jesus identified himself with John's message and used it as the foundation of his own."[74] One significant evidence for this point is the message of repentance, which was the central message of John the Baptist. Jesus launched his own ministry with the message of repentance.[75] The repentance was "a demand both of John and Jesus." Meyer even states, "Radical repentance . . . remains among the most compelling facets of the Baptist's religious stance. Jesus refined and extended it."[76] In this regard, it seems that, as Meyer articulates, "like the Baptist, [Jesus] understood his own role in terms of the age-old scriptural promise of the restoration of Israel."[77]

The relationship between Jesus and John the Baptist supports the idea that one of the aims of Jesus's earthly ministry was to restore Israel to covenant

---

70. See Matt 3:3, 19; Luke 3:9.
71. Meyer, *Aims of Jesus*, 118. Emphasis added.
72. Wright, *Knowing Jesus*, 147.
73. Wright, *Knowing Jesus*, 147.
74. Wright, *Mission of God*, 506.
75. See Mark 1:15; Matt 11:20–24.
76. Meyer, *Aims of Jesus*, 123.
77. Meyer, *Aims of Jesus*, 128.

relationship with God, the foundation for Israel's missionary vocation to be a contrast people who present the holiness of God to the world.

Three Biblical Images in Matthew 5:13–16

In addition to the relationship between John the Baptist and Jesus, three biblical images Jesus used in Matthew 5:13–16 further reveal that Israel's missionary vocation continued with the disciples: "the salt of the earth," "the light of the world," and "a city set on a hill."

The Missionary Nature of the Images

The missional dimension of the disciples' identity is indicated in the images as they are called not to be merely salt, but to be the salt *of the earth*, not to be merely light, but to be the light *of the world*, not to be merely a city, but to be a city *set on a hill which is visible to the world*. David E. Garland states, "The disciples are to make an impression on *the earth* as salt . . . and on *the world* as light. They are also to make an impression upon *humanity* as doers of good works."[78] They are not isolated from the world as a sectarian group, but are sent into the world with a missionary role in the world. George M. Soares-Prabhu emphasizes this point when he calls Matthew 5:13–16 a "largely neglected mission command."[79] Thus, as Grant R. Osborne states, in the identify-defining images, "It is not just Judaism but the Gentiles who are also in view."[80]

Emphasis on Distinctiveness and Theocentricity

The view that the essential nature of Israel's mission continues with Jesus's disciples is clearly indicated in the observation that the identity-defining images emphasize two aspects of Israel' mission shown in the Old Testament: *distinctiveness* and *theocentricity*. First, like the missionary vocation of Israel defined in the Sinai Covenant, the images highlight the *distinctiveness* of Jesus's disciples. On the characteristic of the identity defined by the images, Osborne states, "There is a demand to be different and to act differently, that is, to be right with God and to act the way God demands, by following Jesus

---

78. Garland, *Reading Matthew*, 60–61. Emphasis added.
79. Soares-Prabhu, "Church as Mission," 259.
80. Osborne, *Matthew*, 177.

in *countercultural directions*."81 As John Driver interprets, these three biblical images define the disciples as "God's contrast-community."82 In a similar way, Lohfink interprets the meaning of "a city on the hill," by connecting the image with its Old Testament background, when he states, "If Matt. 5:13–16 is read in its context and against its Old Testament background, it is clear that the radiant city on the hill is a symbol for the church as a contrast-society, which precisely as *contrast-society* transforms the world."83 In this view, the three images highlight the distinctiveness of the disciples' mission. Soares-Prabhu points to the significance of distinctiveness in the church's mission in light of the images when he states, "Unless the Church lives as Church, . . . it cannot engage in authentic mission."84 In this sense, it can be said that, like Israel's mission in the Old Testament, the disciples were called to be a people whose lives are *different* from the world.

Second, like Israel's mission in the Old Testament, the ultimate goal of the disciples' mission is theocentric: to have the world "give glory to your Father in heaven" (Matt 5:16). Their mission is ultimately to *make God known to the world*. On the image of a city on a hill, Driver notes, "Like a mountaintop city which others will see, it will be a powerful *attraction*. . . . The restoration of a people who walk in the paths of the Lord and the fulfillment of the life envisioned in the law and the prophets will be a *magnet which attracts the peoples of the earth*."85 The disciples are called to be a contrast people to the extent that the world can recognize their distinctiveness and that, as a consequence of their countercultural mission, the world is drawn to the very source of their distinctiveness—God himself.

Summed up, the three biblical images Jesus used to refer to the identity of the disciples reveal that they share in the same essential nature of Israel's mission defined by the Sinai Covenant. As Daniel J. Harrington states, the identity of Jesus's followers defined by these images "is firmly rooted in Israel's identity as God's people."86 The images emphasize two aspects of Israel's mission—distinctiveness and theocentricity. The images define the disciples' mission as *being a contrast people* through whom God is known to the world as the world is drawn to God through their visible embodiment of the kingdom of God.

---

81. Osborne, *Matthew*, 177. Emphasis added.
82. Driver, *Images of the Church in Mission*, 171–73.
83. Lohfink, *Jesus and Community*, 66. Italics in original.
84. Soares-Prabhu, "Church as Mission," 259.
85. Driver, *Images of the Church in Mission*, 173. Emphasis added.
86. Harrington, *Gospel of Matthew*, 83.

Jesus as the New Center of the Disciples' Holiness

As already discussed in chapter 2, the law was given as a practical way for Israel to be holy in the Old Testament. Thus, the law was at the center of Israel's holiness. Likewise, Jesus advocated the significance of the law in the lives of the disciples, as indicated in Matthew 5:17–20.[87] In this sense, God through Jesus's ministry intended to *re*-shape them as a holy nation in the world. However, Jesus's relationship with the disciples indicates the holiness of the disciples is centered not on the law, but *on Jesus*. In his biblical analysis of holiness in the Gospel of Mark, Kent E. Brower observes Jesus as the new center of holiness of the people of God. Brower states, "Mark paints a picture of the restoration and re-creation of the holy people of God centered on Jesus. He makes this case through the narrative re-application of key biblical themes leading to a renewed understanding of holiness."[88] W. T. Purkiser makes the same point: "Holiness in the Gospels centers chiefly in the picture given of the character of Jesus. . . . Jesus is, in a way quite unintended by Protagoras who first used a similar phrase, 'the Man who is the measure of all things.'"[89]

Thus, what Israel was intended to be was *redefined* throughout the earthly ministry of Jesus.[90] What Jews were hoping for about God's restoration of Israel differed from the people of God as redefined by Jesus. In the days of Jesus, many Jews understood and hoped that God would restore Israel through a political revolution, an event like the Exodus in the Old Testament, which would lead up to the end of Israel's exile under pagan rule and God's judgment upon the pagan nations.[91] However, what Jesus envisioned about restored and renewed Israel was different from this political and national liberation.[92] Rather, Jesus was *redefining* Israel on the

---

87. For the discussion on Jesus's radical commitment to the law and its significance to the disciples' lives, see Snodgrass, "Matthew and the Law"; Dunn, "Law." Along with Jesus's attitude toward to the law, the Mosaic imagery in the Matthean presentation of Jesus who teaches the law indicates the continuity between God's work of shaping Israel as the people of God and Jesus's earthly ministry to Israel. For the thorough study of the Mosaic typology in the Gospel of Matthew, see Allison, *New Moses*.

88. Brower, "Holy One and His Disciples," 57.

89. Purkiser, *Exploring Christian Holiness*, 75.

90. In his thorough study of the ministry of Jesus, N. T. Wright convincingly demonstrated that Israel was redefined throughout the ministry of Jesus. See Wright, *Jesus and the Victory*.

91. For a Jewish political and nationalistic view of God's restoration of Israel, see Wright, *Jesus and the Victory*, 202–9.

92. In the four Gospels, Jesus did not raise or advocate a violent revolutionary movement for political and national liberation. Rather, for example, he told his followers,

basis of his teaching, life, and person. N. T. Wright states, "What we find in the gospels ... is a portrait of Jesus which both *reaffirms* the deep-rooted Jewish tradition ... and *redefines* it around his own vision and vocation of kingdom-bringing."[93] On the one hand, there is a continuity between the Old Testament Israel and the restored Israel that Jesus envisioned. On the other hand, Israel was profoundly redefined as the restored Israel became centered not on the law, but on Jesus.

The view of Jesus as the new center of the holiness of the disciples is supported at least by the following evidence: (1) the centrality of Jesus's teaching in the life and mission of the disciples, (2) the shift of the location of the presence of God from the temple to Jesus, (3) Jesus as the true revealer of God, (4) Jesus as *the* new center of Israel's missionary vocation, and (5) the missionary vocation of Israel *radicalized* through Jesus.

The Centrality of Jesus's Teaching in the Life and Mission of the Disciples

In the Gospel of Matthew, Jesus is presented not only as a new Moses, the lawgiver, but as greater than Moses. The formula, "You have heard that it was said . . . But I say to you . . . ," proves the authority of Jesus as greater than Moses. Snodgrass articulates, "Jesus is the authoritative interpreter of the law, but Matthew does not now suggest that we merely follow Rabbi Jesus. The law is no longer the center of gravity; *Jesus is*."[94] The holiness of the disciples is no longer measured by the law but by his teaching and his own person. In the Great Commission in Matthew 28:20, the eschatological people of God, of which the community of the disciples is a prototype, were called not specifically to obey the law, but everything that *Jesus* commanded them. Hagner points out, "the obedience of discipleship is now centered not upon the commandments, but upon Jesus and his teaching. . . . Although

---

"love your enemies and pray for those who persecute you, that you may be children of your Father in heaven" (Matt 5:44–45a). Jews longed for the days that God would vindicate them, but Jesus did not vindicate Israel in his ministry. Rather, Jesus called Israel to repent and gave her a warning about God's judgment (e.g., Matt 11:20–24; 23:1–39; Luke 10:13–14). The most obvious evidence is the fact that Jesus did not conflict with the Roman governor, but with the Jewish leaders. While the crucifixion of Jesus was permitted by the Roman governor Pontius Pilate, it was the Jews who asked him to crucify Jesus (Mark 15:11–15; John 19:1–16).

93. Wright, *Jesus and the Victory*, 592.

94. Snodgrass, "Matthew and the Law," 126. Emphasis added.

the righteousness of the Torah is still in view, the call is not to obey the commandments *per se*, but to obey the teaching of Jesus."[95]

Jesus as the New Locale of the Presence of God

Another biblical witness that indicates the shift of the center of the disciples' holiness is that the location of the presence of God, the original source of holiness, was shifted from the Temple to Jesus. Stephen C. Barton calls this shift "dislocation and relocation of holiness."[96] He states, "In early Christianity, the claim is made that God is to be found somewhere new, though not in an unanticipated place. God is present in the person of the Son of God, himself the One in whom dwells the Holy Spirit of God."[97]

In the four Gospels, the theme of the presence of God continues in such a way that God was present among the people of Israel *in and through Jesus*. The presence of God was no longer primarily in a place but in a person. The opening chapter of the Gospel of John presents Jesus as the divine presence dwelling among the people of Israel by introducing him as the Word who "was with God," "was God" (John 1:1), and "became flesh and lived among us" (John 1:14). Jesus as the "self-expression" of God, and "an extension . . . of his own identity and deity,"[98] came down to and stayed among the people of Israel. Commenting on John 1:1, Köstenberger states, "In the beginning the God of Israel created the world through the Word: now, in Christ, that same God took on flesh, made his residence among his people and revealed his glory."[99] The Gospel of Matthew introduces Jesus with the name "Emmanuel," which means "God is with us" (Matt 1:23). As Robert H. Smith comments on this name of Jesus, "The presence of Jesus is the presence of God."[100] France states, "Matthew's overt interpretation of 'Immanuel' . . . takes him close to an explicit doctrine of the incarnation such as is expressed in John 1:14."[101] In his analysis of the motif of divine presence in the story of Jesus's birth of Matthew 1–2, David D. Kupp articulates that God continues to be present with his people through the birth of Jesus when he states, "God's past presence with his people provides the foundation for

---

95. Hagner, "Holiness and Ecclesiology," 46.
96. Barton, "Dislocating and Relocating Holiness," 197.
97. Barton, "Dislocating and Relocating Holiness," 197.
98. Köstenberger, *Theology of John's Gospel and Letters*, 179.
99. Köstenberger, *Theology of John's Gospel and Letters*, 179.
100. Smith, *Matthew*, 38.
101. France, *Gospel of Matthew*, 49.

a new era of divine presence in Jesus's birth."[102] Thus, as Kupp states, the presence of Jesus represents "the restoration of YHWH's presence" and "the immanence of the transcendent YHWH."[103]

As the meaning of Emmanuel, "God with Us," implies, Jesus in the Gospels represents God who was with Israel. In the Old Testament, God was depicted as the God of and with Israel. The people of Israel were called to be a people with God in their midst. This identity of Israel continued with the disciples because God is present in their midst *in and through Jesus*. In Mark 3:14, one of the reasons that Jesus chose his disciples was for them "to be with him." In his analysis of the Gospel of Mark, Brower states, "The most significant point . . . is that these disciples are now 'with Jesus.'"[104] Thus, like Israel, the disciples were called to be a community with God dwelling in their midst, not by having the temple in their midst, but by being with Jesus.

Jesus as the True Revealer of God

Jesus not only represented the presence of God but revealed God through his earthly ministry. In the Gospel of John, one objective of Jesus's earthly ministry was *to reveal God*. Rudolf K. Bultmann views Jesus's whole ministry as revealing God.[105] This point is given clear expression in John 1:18 (NIV), which reads, "No one has ever seen God, but the one and only Son . . . has made him known." In John 14:9, Jesus says, "Whoever has seen me has seen the Father." One primary factor that enabled Jesus to fully reveal the Father was the unity of the Father and Jesus (John 10:30). Connecting Jesus's ministry of revealing God with his unity with God, Köstenberger states, "what is at stake here is nothing less than Jesus's ability to provide firsthand revelation of God," and he adds, "the revelation mediated by Jesus exceeds that provided though Moses in the Law."[106] Jesus was sent to bear the true "witness" of God the Father.[107] Likewise, the disciples' identity as witnesses of Jesus was nothing less than as witnesses of God who was authentically and fully revealed in and through Jesus.

---

102. Kupp, *Matthew's Emmanuel*, 235.
103. Kupp, *Matthew's Emmanuel*, 240–41.
104. Brower, "Holy One and His Disciples," 65.
105. Bultmann, *Theology of the New Testament*, 54.
106. Köstenberger, *Encountering John*, 153.
107. Köstenberger, *Missions of Jesus and the Disciples*, 109.

Jesus as the *New Center of Israel's Missionary Vocation*

The biblical evidence examined above shows that the center of the disciples' holiness changed from the law to Jesus, but the essence of the disciples' mission remained the same as that of Israel's mission. The change in the disciples' mission is not the matter of *what* but of *how*. They are still called to be holy, but their holiness is not measured by the law, but by the teaching of Jesus. They are still a people with God, the original source of holiness, in their midst, but God is with them as Jesus is with them. They are still called to make God known to the world, but, because God is fully revealed by Jesus, they can make God known to the world by making Jesus known to the world. The disciples' missionary vocation is theocentric by being Christocentric. Now they are called to bear an image of God by bearing an image of Jesus. In his scripturally keen analysis of the mission of Jesus's disciples, Köstenberger states, "The role of Jesus's followers is . . . presented as that of being *representatives, messengers, and witnesses to their sender, Jesus*."[108] Their *Christocentric* mission has a *theocentric* goal. Integrating all these, the mission of the disciples can be defined this way: with Jesus as the new center of their lives, they are called to be a contrast people who embody and present the holiness of God—the presence and character of God—to the world by being witnesses of Jesus in the world.

Jesus's love commandment in John 13:34–35 and his prayer in John 17:1 together clearly show the interrelationship between theocentric goal and Christocentric focus in the disciples' mission. The life of the disciples is profoundly shaped by the way that he loved them. Their distinctiveness shaped by Jesus's love for them leads the world to see the one whom they follow, namely, Jesus. However, their mission ends up with the glorification not of Jesus, but, ultimately, of the Father, as signified in John 17:1, in which he prayed to the Father, "glorify your Son so that the Son may glorify you." The disciples' mission became thoroughly Christocentric but the goal of their mission is ultimately theocentric.

The Missionary Vocation of Israel Radicalized *through Jesus*[109]

As noted above, Israel's missionary vocation continued with the disciples. However, her missionary vocation did not merely continue with the

---

108. Köstenberger, "Challenge of a Systematized Biblical Theology of Mission," 454. Emphasis added. For Köstenberger, the term incarnation stands for Jesus's own ontological uniqueness, and, thus, it is improper in a biblical sense to use the term as a way of Christian mission.

109. The basic meaning of the word *radical* is derived from the Latin word *radix*,

disciples, but was radicalized by being *brought into God's original intent* throughout Jesus's earthly ministry. This aspect of Jesus's earthly ministry is clearly indicated in Jesus's *radical* interpretation of the law, which was the center of Israel's vocation in the Old Testament. This point is clearly indicated in the antitheses of Matthew 5:21–48. The formulation of "You have heard that it was said . . . But I say to you . . . " in the antitheses in Matthew 5:21–48 does not mean that Jesus broke the law of Moses or replaced it with a new law. In his final analysis on whether Jesus broke the written law (not the oral law) in the Gospel of Matthew, Snodgrass concludes, "Matthew did not think that Jesus abrogated the law."[110] James D. G. Dunn states, "Jesus sets himself against not the law as such, but rather against the traditions that had gathered round the law."[111] Thus, as Dunn remarks, Jesus's attitude to the law in the antitheses is "not best described in terms of Jesus setting himself over against Moses and the Torah . . . or of Jesus' 'sovereign liberty' . . . in relation to the Mosaic law."[112]

Rather, the point that Jesus makes in the antitheses is that, as Dale C. Allison Jr. states, "the tension between Jesus' teaching and the Mosaic law is not that those who accept the former will transgress the latter; rather is it that they will achieve far more than they would if the Torah were their sole guide."[113] In this sense, what Jesus attempts to reveal through the antitheses is *the divine intent of the law*. In other words, Jesus brought the law into its "divinely intended . . . meaning."[114] Thus, as Driver notes, "[Jesus] gave [the law] its fullest meaning by taking as his point of departure its root in the intention

---

which means "root." Reflecting this Latin origin, in the Merriam-Wester Dictionary, the word *radical* is defined as "of, relating to, or proceeding from a root." Similarly, the Oxford Dictionary defines the word as "relating to or affecting the fundamental nature of something." This study's use of the words *radical* or *radicalize* reflects this basic meaning of the word in order to highlight an original intention, fundamental aspect, or essence of something, particularly God's original intention of what Israel should look like for his mission.

110. Snodgrass, "Matthew and the Law," 123. Also see Segal, "Matthew's Jewish Voice," 7, 22.

111. Dunn, "Law," 514.

112. Dunn, "Law," 514.

113. Allison, *New Moses*, 183.

114. Hagner, *Matthew 1–13*, 106. Hagner interprets the meaning of the verb, "to fulfill" in light of the context of Matt 5:21–48, in which, according to Hagner, "Jesus defines righteousness by expounding the true meaning of the law as opposed to wrong or shallow understandings." Hagner, *Matthew 1–13*, 106.

of God."¹¹⁵ In this regard, as Dunn points out, "several of the antitheses are best seen as a *radicalization,* not an abrogation, of the law."¹¹⁶

In addition to Jesus's antithesis, the conflict between Jesus and Jewish leaders on the law further illustrates the fundamental difference of the interpretation of the law between Jesus and Jewish religious leaders. One particular example is the conflict between Jesus and Jewish leaders on the law concerning the Sabbath. The conflict on the Sabbath law is found in all the four Gospels (Matt 12:1–14; Mark 3:1–6; Luke 13:10–17; John 7:21–24, 9:1–34), in which Jesus's healing on a Sabbath day led to the conflict between Jesus and Jewish religious leaders. In these biblical cases of conflict regarding the Sabbath law, Jesus's critique of Jewish leaders indicates that they did not properly understand God's divine intention for the Sabbath law. This case illustrates the fact that, through his earthly ministry, Jesus brought the divine intent of the law, which Jewish leaders failed to understand and live up to.

In view of the centrality of the law in Israel's missionary vocation, Jesus's *radical* interpretation of the law reveals that Israel's missionary vocation did not merely continue with the disciples, but became *radicalized* through Jesus's earthly ministry. Jews failed to understand and live out *God's original intent* of what Israel was called to be for his mission, but Jesus revealed it as illustrated in his interpretation of the law. It means that the followers of Jesus are no longer subject to an old interpretation of the law, but to a new interpretation of the law as taught and embodied by Jesus.

Summary

What we discussed in this section shows that there is a continuity between what God intended the people of Israel to be in the Old Testament and what Jesus intended his disciples to be. This observation supports the view that one aspect of Jesus's earthly ministry to the people of Israel was the continuity of God's work of shaping them toward their missionary vocation. On the one hand, their missionary vocation—being a contrast people—continued with the disciples. In this sense, if God's work for them at Mt. Sinai was their *original* missional formation, Jesus's ministry can be viewed as a *renewal* of their missional formation. If the former was grounded in the Sinai Covenant, the latter is established in the New Covenant. On the other hand, Israel's missionary vocation was *radicalized* with Jesus as the new center of the disciples' holiness. The disciples were called

---

115. Driver, *Images of the Church in Mission,* 177.
116. Dunn, "Law," 510.

not merely to be a contrast people, but, being centered on Jesus, they were called to be a *radical* contrast people, shaped toward what God originally intended Israel to be for the mission of God. In doing so, Jesus shaped the disciples as a people who present the holiness of God—the presence and character of God—to the world by presenting Jesus as the new center of God's holiness to the world. The discussion in this section shows that the missionary vocation of Israel restored by Jesus was *redefined*, while he reaffirmed the essence of Israel's missionary vocation.

E. Jesus Shapes the Disciples as an *Inclusive* Contrast People

In comparing second-temple Judaism and the Gentile mission of Jesus's followers, Köstenberger and O'Brien state, "*second-temple Judaism was not a missionary religion.*"[117] If this statement is true, one question that needs to be answered is this: *Where did the seeds of the missionary movement of the early church come from?* Senior observes continuity and newness on the nature of mission between the Old and New Testaments. He states, "first century Judaism never experienced a call to mission among Gentiles equivalent to that which swept through early Christianity. While there are deep currents of continuity between Old and New Testaments on the issue of mission (as in so much else), there is also striking development."[118] As the previous section demonstrated, Jesus's earthly ministry was a continuity of God's work of shaping Israel as his missionary people for his mission. However, as discussed earlier, new elements sowed through the earthly ministry of Jesus led to the launching of the Gentile mission by his followers immediately after his death and resurrection.

On the one hand, as Senior states:

> [A] careful look at the biblical data reveals that this missionary impulse did not come from Jesus of Nazareth in the form of an explicit, clean-cut, and immediate missionary program. Jesus, in effect, was not the first missionary to the Gentiles. . . . [T]he connection between the ministry of Jesus and the post-Easter

---

117. Köstenberger and O'Brien, *Salvation to the Ends of the Earth*, 65. Italics in original. For Köstenberger and O'Brien, "while Jews did allow sympathizers and proselytes to participate in their religious practices to a certain extent, their attitude (at least in Palestine) appeared generally to be guided by national or sectarian Jewish considerations, so that it is doubtful whether much of second-temple Judaism even can be said to have engaged in some form of 'passive' mission." Köstenberger and O'Brien, *Salvation to the Ends of the Earth*, 65.

118. Senior and Stuhlmueller, *Biblical Foundations for Mission*, 141.

missionary activity of the church is more subtle, more developmental, more rooted in the dynamics of history.[119]

This new element, which triggered the disciples' Gentile mission, shaped by Jesus's earthly ministry, was not as much explicit as his aim of their restoration of Israel toward her missionary vocation. It is probably because the primary focus of Jesus's ministry was the people of Israel, and because he envisioned the Gentile inclusion into the kingdom of God as a future event.

On the other hand, Jesus's role in this new development is indicated in light of the biblical fact that the Gentile mission of the early church was launched right after his death and resurrection. In other words, such an outward movement of mission, which is strikingly different from Israel's mission in the Old Testament,[120] would not have taken place without the new seeds he planted through his earthly ministry. Senior states, "The catalyst that triggered the missionary consciousness of the early church and shaped its basic message was the person and ministry of Jesus. . . . [I]n him the worldwide perspective of early Christianity finds its source."[121] Thus, this section looks into how Jesus shaped a new dimension of the disciples' mission and demonstrates that another aim of Jesus's earthly ministry was *to lay a foundation for his followers' Gentile mission*, which he made explicitly clear after his death and resurrection.

One new and decisive factor that enabled the followers of Jesus to reach out to Gentiles is related to their *inclusive* nature. Van Engen observes that the early church "was not anything like the exclusivist, introverted, secret mystery religions of the day," but was "a *radically inclusive* religion that aimed to proclaim its message and extend its fellowship to both men and women, slaves and free, Romans, Jews, Greeks, barbarians, and all persons who would receive it."[122] In this regard, one aim of Jesus's work of the disciples' missional formation can be viewed as shaping them as an *inclusive* contrast people. This section looks into ways that Jesus sowed the seeds of

---

119. Senior and Stuhlmueller, *Biblical Foundations for Mission*, 142.

120. The Old Testament prophecy envisioned the salvation of the Gentile nations and their gathering toward God, and indicates Israel's mediatory role between God and Gentiles. However, since a centrifugal aspect of Israel's mission to the Gentile nations was implicitly hinted, it is likely that the Jews hardly entertained the Gentile mission by reaching out to Gentiles. In this regard, as discussed later in chapter 4, Jewish believers' hesitance and reluctance in reaching out to Gentiles is quite understandable. For a fuller discussion on Israel's mission to the nations in the Old Testament prophecy, see Martin-Achard, *Light to the Nations*; Oswalt, "Mission of Israel to the Nations"; Grisanti, "Israel's Mission to the Nations"; Okoye, *Israel and the Nations*, 109–43.

121. Senior and Stuhlmueller, *Biblical Foundations for Mission*, 141–42.

122. Van Engen, "Glocal Church," 165. Emphasis added.

inclusiveness in the disciples, by tracing two characteristics of Jesus's earthly ministry: (1) Jesus's boundary-crossing ministry within Israel, and (2) Jesus's positive attitude toward the Gentiles.

Jesus's Boundary-Crossing Ministry within Israel

One distinctive aspect of Jesus's earthly ministry is that he crossed conventional boundaries of the Jewish tradition. Jesus's boundary-crossing of the Jewish tradition indicates that he envisaged the inclusive character of his followers. Especially, two distinctive aspects of Jesus's earthly ministry to Jews are related to the boundary-crossing characteristic of his ministry: (1) solidarity with the outcasts,[123] and (2) emphasis on moral and internal virtues in interpretation of the law.

Jesus's Solidarity with the Outcasts

One major characteristic of Jesus's earthly ministry to the people of Israel was Jesus's inclusive attitude toward the outcasts. Ferdinand Hahn sums it up as below:

> [T]he conventional boundaries within Israel, as they had been drawn by devout Jews of all shades of opinion, no longer existed for [Jesus]: neither to the sick who were segregated on cultic and ritual grounds, nor to the prostitutes and sinners who were boycotted on moral grounds, nor to the tax-collectors who were excluded on religious and nationalist grounds, did he refuse contact, help, and fellowship. But it is obvious that his claim went still further, for it may have been precisely because of his commission to all Israel that he also turned to the Samaritans and tried to break down the existing prejudices.[124]

---

123. In light of Jesus's Greatest Commandment (Matt 22:35–40; Mark 12:28–34), this aspect of Jesus's ministry can be viewed as part of practicing the commandment of loving neighbors. This commandment is rooted in the Old Testament (Lev 19:18) and God expected Israel to care for the socially marginalized in the Old Testament (Deut 10:17–19). Thus, it can be said that, in his solidarity with the outcasts, Jesus demonstrated a way of life that radically practices this love commandment, which is already part of God's expectation of Israel in the Old Testament. For the Old Testament's teaching about the orphan, the widow, and the poor, see Patterson, "Widow, the Orphan, and the Poor."

124. Hahn, *Mission in the New Testament*, 30.

Jesus's embrace of the marginalized demonstrated, in Senior's word, his "expansive concept of God's people."[125] The eschatological people of God shaped by Jesus's boundary-crossing ministry was not to be sectarian but to welcome all of those who respond to Jesus's invitation into the kingdom of God, *regardless of social class*. The kingdom of God revealed in Jesus's boundary-crossing ministry was by nature *inclusive*. Furthermore, this inclusive nature of the kingdom of God was couched in a clear preference for the socio-economically marginalized.

One major way that Jesus demonstrated his inclusiveness toward the outcasts was *his solidarity with them*.[126] As Senior observes, "The [four] Gospels present Jesus as provocatively associating with those members of Jewish society considered outside the law and, therefore, excluded from participation in the religious and social community of Israel."[127] Among biblical cases of Jesus's solidarity with the marginalized within Israel, the most symbolic and prophetic is *Jesus's table fellowship with sinners and tax collectors*. The Gospels witness to Jesus's ongoing relationship with sinners.[128] Because of his table fellowship with the marginalized such as sinners and tax collectors, Jesus was even called "a glutton and a drunkard, a friend of tax collectors and sinners" (Matt 11:19). In his study on Jesus's table fellowship, Santos Yao notes, "Jesus . . . has exemplified a *radical inclusiveness* through his indiscriminate fraternizing even with the lowly and the outcasts of his society."[129] In this regard, it can be said that, as Richard P. Thompson remarks, Jesus, through his solidarity with the marginalized, "redefined the Jewish concept of holiness," which "distinguished the holy from the unholy, the faithful from the faithless, and the insider from the outsider" and presented "an alternative understanding of holiness defined

---

125. Senior and Stuhlmueller, *Biblical Foundations for Mission*, 154.

126. Byung-Mu Ahn constructs a biblical case of the intimate relationship between Jesus and the marginalized. Ahn developed the so-called "minjung theology," ("minjung" literally means "people"), a Korean liberation theology, by theologically reflecting on Jesus's identification with the marginalized for the Koreans in the sociopolitical context of oppression. For Ahn's thesis, see Ahn, "Jesus and the Minjung in the Gospel of Mark."

127. Senior and Stuhlmueller, *Biblical Foundations for Mission*, 147. Also see Perrin, *Rediscovering the Teaching of Jesus*, 102–8; Senior, *Jesus*, 69–82. For the historical background of this motif, see Jeremias, *New Testament Theology*, 108–21. For the thorough study on Jesus's table fellowship with the outcasts, see McMahan, "Meals as Type-Scenes in the Gospel of Luke," 1.

128. Wright, *Jesus and the Victory*, 149. For example, see Matt 9:10, 11:19; Mark 2:15–17; Luke 7:31–35.

129. Yao, "Table Fellowship," ii. Emphasis added.

by the *inclusive* nature of God's salvific work rather than by the *exclusive* nature of God's people."[130]

Jesus's solidarity with the outcasts, which was epitomized by his table fellowship with sinners, profoundly reveals the inclusive nature of the kingdom of God which should be embodied by the followers of Jesus, while the disciples did not immediately understand or practice this. For the disciples who eye-witnessed Jesus's solidarity with outcasts, the message that Jesus communicated with them is clear: (1) the kingdom of God is open to all who respond to his invitation to it, *regardless of social class*,[131] and, thus, (2) the disciples are called to be an *inclusive* contrast people who present the *inclusive* kingdom of God in the way that Jesus did.

Emphasis on Moral and Inward Virtues in Interpretation of the Law

While implicit, another biblical evidence that vindicates Jesus's boundary-crossing ministry within Israel is the way that Jesus interpreted the law. While he himself was a Jew and committed to the law, his interpretation of it was not focused on religious regulations of the Jewish tradition or Jewishness of the law. Ida Glaser keenly observes this point as below:

> The Sermon on the Mount lays down Matthew's foundation for understanding the kingdom of God. As the Jews expected, the kingdom of God fulfills the Law and the Prophets. What must have surprised Jesus' hearers is what he omits. There is no mention of an ethnic, political or national kingdom, a particular social order or culture, or even particular religious practices. Their absence is especially clear in the Beatitudes.[132]

Rather, his interpretation of the law emphasized moral and inward virtues embodied in the law, such as love, justice, compassion, and integrity. Senior comments, "While Jesus himself was undoubtedly a strict Jew, there are examples where he summons up his own authority and his own experience to place the values of compassion and inner integrity in direct

---

130. Thompson, "Gathered at the Table: Holiness and Ecclesiology in the Gospel of Luke," 92–93. Emphasis added. Craig L. Blomberg calls this inclusive holiness defined by Jesus's table fellowship with outcasts *"contagious holiness"* because impurity and immorality from outcasts, particularly sinners, does not impact Jesus's holiness and rather because Jesus imparts his holiness to them. See Blomberg, *Contagious Holiness*.

131. Schillebeeckx, *Jesus*, 218.

132. Glaser, *Bible and Other Faiths*, 115.

confrontation with his opponents' interpretation of the law."¹³³ Jesus denounced scribes and Pharisees for their failure to live up to such virtues (Matt 23:13–36), and highlighted the value of compassion (Mark 3:1–6). In Mark 7:1–23,¹³⁴ "the purification rituals are relativized in favor of inner cleanliness and integrity," as Senior observes.¹³⁵ Jesus even said that "justice and mercy and faith" are "the weightier matters" compared to the tithing law (Matt 23:23).¹³⁶ This way of interpretation of the law by Jesus implies that the characteristic of the disciples was to be shaped not by Jewish traditions, which failed to embody God's intention of the law, but by the virtues—moral and inward—that God intended in the law.

The Kingdom of God Calls for Costly Commitment

Jesus's ministry of crossing the conventional boundaries within Israel resulted often in conflict with Jewish rulers.¹³⁷ His ministry shows that the kingdom of God is not only inclusive but *countercultural*, in the sense that he critically engaged with dominant Jewish traditions, which fell short of God's intention for Israel. Because of his countercultural ministry, Jesus's life is characterized by conflict with those who advocated and sustained Jewish traditions.¹³⁸ The conflict between Jesus and Jewish religious leaders concludes with the death of Jesus. As Babu Immanuel states, "the cross of Jesus, viewed from [a] human point of view, is the culmination of and an unavoidable finale to the various conflicts Jesus had with the Jewish religious leadership."¹³⁹ In this regard, Jesus's boundary-crossing ministry revealed that the inclusive nature of the kingdom of God is *countercultural* and *costly*. By extension, it also indicates that the disciples' mission, modeled on Jesus's boundary-crossing ministry, calls for *costly commitment*.¹⁴⁰

---

133. Senior and Stuhlmueller, *Biblical Foundations for Mission*, 148.

134. Also see Matt 15:1–20.

135. Senior and Stuhlmueller, *Biblical Foundations for Mission*, 148.

136. Jesus's emphasis on justice, mercy, and faith is consistent with the Old Testament. For example, Jesus quotes Hos 6:6, "I desire mercy, not sacrifice," in Matt 9:13 and 12:7. However, like the people of Israel in the Old Testament, Jews, particularly their religious leaders, failed to understand and practice them in a way that God intended them to do.

137. See Kingsbury, "Developing Conflict"; Immanuel, "Jesus' Cross, Conflicts and the New Testament."

138. For a thorough study of conflict in the four Gospels, see Beck, *Jesus and His Enemies*.

139. Immanuel, "Jesus' Cross, Conflicts and the New Testament," 28.

140. Jesus also explicitly mentioned the costly commitment required to follow him.

In sum, the dual biblical evidence of Jesus's boundary-crossing ministry within Israel shows that the kingdom of God, which Jesus revealed, is *inclusive*. The life that embodies the inclusive kingdom of God is countercultural, critically engaging with a dominant culture, and demands *costly commitment*. The disciples, whose mission is modeled on Jesus's boundary-crossing ministry, were called to be an *inclusive* contrast people who present the *inclusive* nature of the kingdom of God through a *costly* commitment to *critical* engagement with the world.

Jesus's Positive View of Gentiles

In addition to his boundary-crossing ministry within Israel, Jesus's positive attitude toward Gentiles demonstrates his inclusive and expansive view of the kingdom of God beyond the Jewish ethnic boundary. Jesus's positive view of Gentiles can be glimpsed from three observations from his ministry: (1) the multicultural context of his ministry, (2) emphasis on faith above ethnicity and nationality, and (3) anticipation of the trans-ethnic kingdom of God.

The Multicultural Context of Jesus's Ministry

Jesus's openness toward the Gentiles is implicitly seen in his choice of Galilee as a main stage of his earthly ministry. Jesus started his ministry in Galilee and chose his disciples in Galilee. As Paul Hertig observes, "Both Matthew and Mark refer to [Galilee] as [Jesus'] hometown.... It served as a home base for Jesus and his disciples in their itinerant ministry."[141] Jesus established his ministry in Galilee, by choosing his disciples there (Matt 4:18, 21). Galilee was the place where Jesus commissioned his disciples to make disciples of all nations in Matthew 28:16–20. Jesus and his core disciples were Galilean.

At the time of Jesus, Galilee was surrounded by Gentile nations.[142] Because of this geographical location of Galilee, Jews were able to contact Gentiles and to be exposed to different cultures in the region.[143] The link between Galilee and Gentiles is made clear in the phrase "Galilee of

---

For example, see Matt 5:11–12; 16:24. The parables of the hidden treasure and the pearl (Matt 13:44–46), in which those who found treasure and pearls sold everything to get them, also highlight the same point.

141. Hertig, "Galilee Theme," 155.
142. Hennessy, *Galilee of Jesus*, 8; Hertig, "Galilee Theme," 158–59.
143. Hennessy, *Galilee of Jesus*, 8.

Gentiles" (Matt 4:15).[144] Hence, as Howard Clark Kee states, Jesus's ministry arose in a "bilingual, multicultural environment."[145] Richard Gardner views Galilee as a geographic symbol that embraces both the Jews and the Gentiles. He states, "inasmuch as Galilee is a part of the area of Zebulun and Naphtali, it represents God's fidelity to the old land of promise. Inasmuch, however, as Galilee is a land of the Gentiles, a gateway as it were to other nations, it represents God's freedom to expand the boundaries of holy geography and claim new lands for his purposes."[146] Living and doing his earthly ministry in Galilee, Jesus was already with Gentiles, even though he did not intentionally approach them at the time. Galilee implicitly symbolizes Jesus's openness toward Gentiles.

Faith above Ethnicity and Nationality

As already discussed, Jesus did not intentionally approach Gentiles during his time, but they approached him. However, this passive mode of Jesus's relationship with Gentiles in his ministry does not indicate his rejection or negative view of Gentiles. Rather, Jesus revealed his positive attitude toward Gentiles, who approached him, not on the basis of ethnicity or nationality but of their faith. Senior notes, "there is a consistent emphasis on the response of faith and obedience to God as the critical criterion for judgment, a criterion that relativizes race and status."[147] Two representative examples for this case are the stories of a centurion (Matt 8:5–13) and a Gentile woman (Matt 15:21–28; Mark 7:24–30). When they approached Jesus, he granted them what they asked for desperately, based not on their ethnicity but *on their faith*.[148]

In the story of the centurion's faith, Jesus even commended the centurion for his faith as better than the faith of any of the people of Israel (Matt 8:10). As Craig S. Keener comments, the centurion who shows the exemplary faith "functions as a foretaste of the fruits of the Gentile mission

---

144. The phrase "Galilee of Gentiles" is quoted originally from Isa 9:1, but scholars find no biblical warrant for the idea that the phrase "Galilee of Gentiles" in Isa 9:1 and Matt 4:15 foreshadows the Gentile mission. However, in light of the fact that Galilee was politically under the Gentiles in the days of Jesus, Warren Carter interprets the phrase as Galilee "under the Gentiles." For Carter's full argument, see Carter, "Matthew and the Gentiles," 264–66.

145. Kee, "Early Christianity in the Galilee," 19, 22.

146. Gardner, *Matthew*, 7.

147. Senior and Stuhlmueller, *Biblical Foundations for Mission*, 154.

148. Blomberg, *Matthew*, 142; Healy, *Gospel of Mark*, 145; Keener, *Gospel of Matthew*, 270.

yet to come."[149] In the story of the Canaanite women's faith, Jesus's seemingly harsh response to her request to heal her demon-possessed daughter appears as though he showed a negative view of Gentiles. However, even in this case, Jesus ultimately granted a Canaanite woman's desperate request to redeem her demon-possessed daughter, and even commended her faith, saying "Woman, *great is your faith!* Let it be done for you as you wish" (Matt 15:28). The overall conversation between Jesus and the Gentile woman does not lead to the message about the exclusion of the Gentiles from the kingdom of God or the negative view of the Gentiles,[150] but rather, as France comments on Mark 7:24–30, "The whole encounter builds up to the totally positive conclusion of vv. 29–30, while the preceding dialogue serves to underline the radical nature of this new stage in Jesus's ministry."[151] The point that this story communicates is that, as Mark L. Strauss points out, "the presence and power of the kingdom is already available to all who respond in faith—whether Jew or Gentile."[152] Thus, while Jesus's primary focus in his ministry was on Jews, Jesus's emphasis on faith in interacting with the Gentiles who approached him offers a glimpse into the kingdom of God as open to Gentiles who respond with faith.

Anticipation of the Trans-ethnic Character of the Kingdom of God

Jesus's openness to Gentiles also can be seen in the banquet motif of his teaching (Matt 8:11–12; Luke 13:22–30). By using the banquet motif, he envisaged the eschatological ingathering of the Gentile nations. In Matthew 8:11–12, the banquet motif is a part of the story of the Gentile centurion's faith (Matt 8:5–13), indicating that the inclusion of the Gentile nations into the kingdom of God calls for faith.[153] On Jesus's banquet motif

---

149. Keener, *Gospel of Matthew*, 270. Craig L. Blomberg observes the christological and universal aspects of the centurion's faith when he states, "'Such great faith' does not refer to a particular quantity but to a quality of faith, which is both Christological in focus and universal scope." Blomberg, *Matthew*, 142.

150. Biblical scholars interpret that Jesus's hesitant and seemly harsh response to the Canaanite woman's request does not mean the exclusion of Gentiles from the kingdom of God, but a temporal priority of his ministry to Israel, see Edwards, *Gospel According to Mark*, 220; France, *Gospel of Mark*, 296; Boring, *Mark*, 214; Healy, *Gospel of Mark*, 144; Stein, *Mark*, 352–53.

151. France, *Gospel of Mark*, 296.

152. Strauss, *Mark*, 313. According to Mark L. Strauss, it is mostly likely that Jesus is intentionally provocative in order to bring out the woman's faith. In doing so, Jesus was aiming to reveal that the kingdom of God already began to be open to the Gentiles.

153. Most scholars generally agree that one implication brought by the Gentile centurion's faith and the eschatological banquet is that faith or trust in Jesus is the primary

in Matthew 8:11–12, Senior states, "This statement . . . places Gentiles on equal footing with the Israelites in the messianic age."[154] This eschatological banquet with the nations appears as a part of a discourse in Luke 13:22–30, in which many Israelites are excluded from salvation. Furthermore, the Lukan account of the eschatological banquet is located within the larger context of a discourse on entrance into the kingdom of God,[155] implying that the kingdom of God is fully open to Gentiles.[156] The most striking to Jesus's Jewish hearers is that, as in both Matthean and Lukan cases of the banquet motif, Gentiles are included in the eschatological kingdom of God, whereas the people of Israel are excluded. These banquet motifs show that the eschatological people of God that Jesus envisioned as the consequence of his ministry would be defined not by ethnicity or nationality, but be "transnational" and "transethnic."[157] As John T. Carroll comments on the Lukan account of the eschatological banquet, "Israel fulfills its vocation in the world, but its character and composition as a people is undergoing redefinition, as Luke tells the story."[158] The eschatological people of God renewed and gathered by Jesus are to be as *inclusive* so as to embrace all, *regardless of ethnicity or nationality*.[159]

Summary

The discussion on the two aspects of Jesus's ministry—his boundary-crossing ministry within Israel and his positive view of Gentiles—suggests that Jesus presented to his eyewitnesses, particularly the disciples, the *inclusive* nature of the kingdom of God. Shaped by Jesus's boundary-crossing ministry and positive view of Gentiles, the disciples were called to be an *inclusive*

---

key to membership in the kingdom of God. See France, *Gospel According to Matthew*, 155–56; Wilkins, *Matthew*, 343; Witherington, *Matthew*, 184.

154. Senior and Stuhlmueller, *Biblical Foundations for Mission*, 153.

155. Stein, *Luke*, 378.

156. Among scholars, there are different views on the issue of whether those who "will come from east and west, from north and south" in Luke 13:29 are the people of Israel scattered abroad or the Gentiles. However, as R. Alan Culpepper points out, "it is clear that Luke is vitally interested in Israel's rejection of the gospel and the subsequent inclusion of Gentiles." Culpepper, "Luke," 278. Furthermore, this reversal is clearly evidenced in the following narrative in which Jews rejecting Jesus is followed by Gentiles accepting the gospel about Jesus.

157. Trites and Larkin, *Gospel of Luke and Acts*, 206.

158. Carroll, *Luke*, 291.

159. The eschatological ingathering of Gentiles in the Old Testament prophecies already foreshadowed the inclusion of Gentiles into the kingdom of God.

contrast people who present the kingdom of God which is open to all who respond to the invitation into it through repentance, faith, and obedience, regardless of social class, ethnicity, and nationality. While Jesus did not initiate the Gentile mission until his death and resurrection, it can be concluded that one objective of Jesus's earthly ministry was to prepare the disciples for the Gentile mission. Eckhard J. Schnabel states:

> In the beginning was Jesus. Without the person of Jesus of Nazareth, the messianic Son of Man, there would be no Christians. Without the ministry of Jesus there would be no Christian missions. Without Christian missions there would have been no Christian Occident. The first Christian missionary was not Paul, but Peter, and Peter would not have preached a "missionary" sermon at Pentecost if he had not been a student of Jesus for three years.[160]

In order for the disciples to authentically participate in the expansion of the kingdom of God beyond Israel, Jesus sought to shape the disciples not just as a contrast people (a particular kingdom of God), but also an *inclusive* contrast people (an inclusive kingdom of God).

F. The Risen Jesus Rebuilds and Expands the Disciples' Missionary Vocation

Two more remaining christological events, namely Jesus's death and resurrection, further transformed the disciples toward their missionary vocation, the foundation of which Jesus already began to lay down in his pre-Easter ministry. The following two sections of this chapter look at how these two pivotal events shaped the disciples toward their missionary vocation. This section pays attention to the risen Jesus's ministry to the disciples, analyzing biblical narratives in which the risen Jesus shaped the disciples toward their missionary vocation.

Restoration of the Disciples' Relationship with Jesus

As already investigated, the disciples were no longer centered on the law, but Jesus. They were called to follow Jesus, and even left their previous lives behind to follow him (Matt 4:18–22; Luke 15:10–11, 27–28). However, as the four Gospels depict, their behaviors right after the death of Jesus were far from that. The death of Jesus suddenly changed everything on the side

---

160. Schnabel, *Jesus and the Twelve*, 3.

of the disciples. For them, the death of Jesus did not mean victory or hope, but failure and hopelessness. Wright notes, "the crucifixion of Jesus was the end of all their hopes."[161] Craig G. Bartholomew and Michael W. Goheen comment, "Jesus' crucifixion naturally has left his disciples perplexed and despondent. Everything they have hoped for seems lost."[162] The behaviors of Jesus's disciples immediately after his death reveal their loss of faith in and commitment to him,[163] and indicate that the disciples still needed to understand their missionary vocation and be transformed toward it. The disciples of Jesus who witnessed his death proved that they would not be able to fulfill their missionary vocation without Jesus among them. However, due to their encounter with the *risen* Jesus, "all this soon begins to change."[164] Two post-resurrection narratives show that the disciples' encounter with the risen Jesus led to restoration of their faith in and commitment to him: John 21:1–19 and Luke 24:13–35.

Peter's Encounter with the Risen Jesus (John 21:1–19)

The post-resurrection narrative of John 21 pictures the risen Jesus's work of "rehabilitation and commissioning."[165] In John 21, Peter decided to go back to the life of fishing which he had left behind to follow Jesus, and the other disciples who were with Peter joined his decision (John 21:3). There is no mention of why they decide to go fishing,[166] but, as Leon Morris states, "a general impression left is that of man without purpose."[167] One obvious factor that caused their loss of purpose is the fact that "they had lost the presence of Jesus."[168] For them, there was no reason for them to follow Jesus who had died. However, when they met the risen Jesus while fishing, they came to know that Jesus rose from death, and, more importantly that the risen Jesus came back to be with them (John 21:4–6).

---

161. Wright, *Surprised by Hope*, 39.

162. Bartholomew and Goheen, *Drama of Scripture*, 165.

163. For example, Peter who claimed to be willing to die for Jesus, betrayed him three times (Matt 26:69–75). The disciples who left everything to follow Jesus returned to their previous lives (John 21). The hopelessness felt by the disciples is indicated in Luke 24:21, in which one of two disciples on the way from Jerusalem to Emmaus says, "we *had hoped* that he was the one to redeem Israel."

164. Bartholomew and Goheen, *Drama of Scripture*, 165–66.

165. Wright, *Resurrection of the Son of God*, 676.

166. For different views on why they went to fish, see Whitacre, *John*, 489–90.

167. Morris, *Gospel According to John*, 760.

168. Morris, *Gospel According to John*, 760.

The following story of John 21 shows that, as a result of encountering the risen Jesus, Peter's relationship with him was restored, indicated when Peter confessed his love for Jesus in response to Jesus's three questions about whether Peter loves him (John 21:15–17). Furthermore, Jesus called Peter to follow him (John 21:19). The encounter with the risen Jesus led Peter to overcome his past denials of Jesus, to restore his relationship with him, and to resume his commitment to follow him. Wright points out, "The triple question [of Jesus to Peter] and [Peter's] response mirror the triple denial with the affirmation of love, the love of disciple for master. . . . Peter is back on the map of genuine discipleship. This leads to a new commission himself."[169]

Two Disciples and on the Road to Emmaus (Luke 24:13–35)

The post-resurrection narrative of Luke 24, in which two disciples of Jesus encountered the risen Jesus on the way to Emmaus, reveals that they had at least two problems—unbelief about the resurrection of Jesus and failure (or inability) to understand scriptures. When they met the risen Jesus, they overcame these problems. First, they heard from women that Jesus was resurrected, but did not believe it (Luke 24:10–11). Their unbelief left them with despair of hope they had on him (Luke 24:21). Second, they failed to understand the scriptures about Jesus (Luke 25:25). Joel B. Green views their problem as "the need for revelation."[170] They needed an interpreter of scriptures to understand the person and work of Jesus. These two problems they had explain their *inability* to fulfill what Jesus expected them to be.

Nevertheless, when they encountered the risen Jesus, their problems vanished. They finally believed in the resurrection of Jesus, having their eyes opened to recognize him (Luke 24:31); they came to have scriptural understanding of who Jesus is and of what happened to him (Luke 24:27). Furthermore, as a consequence of the restoration of their faith in and commitment to the risen Jesus, they became bold witnesses of the risen Jesus whom they met (Luke 24:33–35).

---

169. Wright, *Resurrection of the Son of God*, 676. Wright also observes the same point in the post-resurrection narrative in the Gospel of Mark. Commenting on Mark 16:7, in which the risen Jesus said to three women who came to his empty tomb, "go, tell his disciples and Peter," Wright states, "The singling out of Peter for special mention seems obviously designed to go with the tragic story of his denial of Jesus in 14.66–72." Wright, *Resurrection of the Son of God*, 629.

170. Green, *Gospel of Luke*, 843–44.

Two Implications

These two post-resurrection narratives, in which the disciples' relationship with Jesus was restored, show that the disciples were *in need of another divine encounter* in order to be what Jesus envisioned them to be. The consequence of the disciples' encounter with the risen Jesus is that their faith in and commitment to him were not only restored (in the case of Peter in John 21) but also became scripturally grounded (in the case of the two disciples on the road to Emmaus in Luke 24). Two aspects of the disciples' missional conversion can be identified from the analysis of the two post-resurrection narratives.

First, the disciples' missional conversion began with *the restoration of their relationship with Jesus*. Since the disciples' lives were centered on Jesus, the disciples' transformation toward their missionary vocation involved the restoration of their relationship with him. This aspect of the disciples' missional conversion is parallel to Israel's missional conversion, which always involved the restoration of her relationship with God. In this sense, Israel's relationship with God is parallel to the disciples' relationship with Jesus. Second, another aspect of the disciples' missional conversion is the significance of *the presence of the risen Jesus* in the midst of the disciples for the fulfillment of their missionary vocation. The disciples' behaviors when Jesus died can be viewed as the consequence of the absence of Jesus among them. On this point, this case is similar to the golden calf story, in which the people of Israel failed what God intended them to be while Moses, who for them represented accessibility to the presence of God, was absent. In both cases, the disciples and Israel failed what they were called to be when they felt the absence of the presence of God. The fact that the disciples' relationship with Jesus was rebuilt, when the risen Jesus came back to them, implies that the disciples needed the presence of Jesus in their midst to fulfill their missionary vocation. In this sense, the presence of the risen Jesus in the midst of the disciples is the *fulfilling* factor of their missionary vocation.

The Gentile Mission Launched with and by the Risen Jesus

In the four Gospels and the book of Acts, it was only after the death and resurrection of Jesus that the Gentile mission was *explicitly* launched. Lucian Legrand states, "the accounts [of the resurrection of Jesus] converge in a single ending: the sending of the disciples forth on a mission to the world. It is the same with Acts 1:8. In the context of such a broad divergency in the choice of the other apparition accounts, this convergence in a conclusion is all the more striking."[171]

The post-resurrection narrative of the Gospel of Matthew explicitly portrays the risen Jesus as one who sends his disciples to all nations with the disciple-making mission (Matt 28:19). Luke's two-volume work shows that the Holy Spirit (or the risen Jesus in and through the Holy Spirit) made the followers of Jesus his witnesses "in Jerusalem, in all Judea and Samaria, and to the ends of the earth" (Luke 24:48; Acts 1:8). The post-resurrection narrative in the Gospel of John shows, as Wright notes, "The mission of Jesus to Israel has . . . been transformed by the Spirit into the mission of the church to the world."[172] The risen Jesus who was sent by the Father becomes the one who is sending his disciples to the world (John 20:21). All the four Gospels, with the long ending of the Gospel of Mark, and the book of Acts, show that the risen Jesus not only restored the disciples' relationship with him, but *directed them to the world*.

The Universal Lordship of the Risen Jesus

In the post-resurrection narratives, the Gentile mission launched by Jesus comes with a new reality of the *universal* lordship of Jesus. Particularly, three post-resurrection narratives—Matthew 28:18–20; John 20:25; and Acts 2:14–36—reveal the nature of the risen Jesus's universal lordship and its implications for the disciples' missionary vocation.

The Present, Universal Lordship of Jesus Declared (Matt 28:18–20)

The Great Commission text in Matthew 28:18–20 connects the universal lordship of Jesus with his resurrection. In Matthew 28:18, the risen Jesus declared to his disciples, "*all authority in heaven and on earth* has been given to me."[173] This verse reveals that, as Keener states, the risen Jesus is "king in the kingdom of God."[174] Jesus's lordship was inaugurated with his resurrection.[175] Furthermore, the resurrection of Jesus not only revealed his lordship

---

171. Legrand, *Unity and Plurality*, 68–69.

172. Wright, *Resurrection of the Son of God*, 676.

173. For Ulrich Luz, the phrase "in heaven and on earth" means "over the whole creation," Luz, *Matthew 21–28*, 623.

174. Keener, *Matthew*, 718.

175. In this study, the two terms, "lordship" and "kingship," are viewed as words with the same meaning. Observing the allusion of Dan 7:14 in Matt 28:18, R. T. France prefers the word "kingship" to the word "lordship" in referring to the new ruling

but also disclosed that the scope of the lordship of Jesus is *universal*. As Bosch comments, "What is new is the *universal extension* of his authority."[176] The universal domain of the risen Jesus's lordship is associated with his resurrection in a way that, as W. D. Davies and Dale C. Allison Jr. state, "through the resurrection Jesus is exalted and made Lord of the cosmos."[177] Thus, while Jesus claimed his authority before his resurrection, "the universality of Jesus's authority is a *new post-Easter fact*."[178] Another point to be made is that, with the promise of his continuous presence with his disciples, Jesus not only announced his lordship over the universe, but *now is exercising* his lordship. Douglas R. A. Hare pointedly articulates, "Jesus is not waiting passively in heaven for his glorious arrival as judge and king but is already exercising his Lordship as God's penitentiary Son. The Great Commission is thus founded on Jesus' *present* Lordship."[179] One implication of the present, universal lordship of the risen Jesus is that, as Legrand states, "Jesus is the one acting, and the disciples are his assistants."[180]

The Deity of the Risen Jesus Confessed (John 20:25)

If the post-resurrection narrative of Matthew 28:18–20 highlights the present, universal lordship of the risen Jesus, the post-resurrection narrative of John 20 reveals the *deity* of the risen Jesus as in the confession of Thomas about the risen Jesus, "My Lord and my God!" (John 20:28). Wright states:

> The so-called 'Doubting Thomas' takes one small verbal step and a giant leap of faith and theology: 'My lord and my god' (20.28). This at last is faith indeed. The disciples, with Thomas (of all

---

position of the risen Jesus, and for France, Jesus's kingship over the universe is the extension of Jesus's inheritance of the Davidic kingship over Jews. For France's point of view, see France, *Gospel of Matthew*, 1112–13. However, in light of the deity of Jesus and his unity with the Father, the kingship of the risen Jesus can go further back to the kingship of God in the Old Testament.

176. Bosch, *Transforming Mission*, 78. Emphasis added. Also see Meier, "Two Disputed Questions," 413; Matthey, "Great Commission," 166.

177. Davies and Allison, *Matthew*, 683. Also see Luz, *Matthew 21–28*, 623. Christological hymns in the New Testament connect the resurrection of Jesus and his universal lordship (e.g., Eph 1:20–23; Phil 2:6–11; Col 1:15–20; 1 Pet 3:18–22).

178. Davies and Allison, *Matthew*, 683n34. Emphasis added. Davies and Allison highlight the continuity of the authority of Jesus between the pre-resurrection period and the post-resurrection period, while admitting this new dimension of the authority of Jesus, Davies and Allison, *Matthew*, 683n34.

179. Hare, *Matthew*, 333.

180. Legrand, *Unity and Plurality*, 81.

people!) as their spokesman, have confessed that the 'flesh' they had known, and now know again in a new way was also in truth *the 'Word' who was one with the father*.[181]

J. Ramsey Michaels observes, "this is the first time anyone (aside from the Gospel writer) has called him 'God,' or 'my God.' Finally, the introduction of Jesus to the reader as 'God' (1:1) or 'God the One and Only' (1:18), is confirmed from within the narrative."[182] Drawing on an *inclusio* structure of the Gospel of John,[183] Edward W. Klink III states, "Thomas's ascription of these two titles to Jesus are a fitting conclusion to the Gospel [of John]. A character in the narrative comes to complete agreement with the opening declaration of the narrator that 'the Word was God' (1:1), forming an *inclusio* between the beginning and end of the Gospel proper."[184]

The use of the two titles of Jesus—Lord and God—together in Thomas's confession reveals the *meaning* of the deity of Jesus: the risen Jesus was *equal to God of Israel* in the eyes of Thomas. This overlapping relation between God and the deity of Jesus is found in the fact that the use of the two titles is an allusion to the way that the people of Israel refer to God in the Old Testament. Gerald Borchert observes:

> The confession of Thomas is not unlike the attribution to 'my God and my Lord' in Ps 34:23 and to a lesser extent is somewhat similar to Pss 29:3 and 86:15. But more pointedly it also touches directly upon the daily Jewish reciting of the Shema, 'Hear, O Israel, the Lord our God, the Lord is one' (Deut 6:4). The early Christians thus claimed for Jesus attributes akin to Yahweh, the God of the Old Testament.[185]

If this is the case, the post-resurrection narrative of John 20 clearly communicates the message that the risen Jesus is not merely the revealer of God but *God himself*. In this view, the presence of the risen Jesus can be viewed as a continuation of the presence of God of Israel.

---

181. Wright, *Resurrection of the Son of God*, 668. Emphasis added.

182. Michaels, *Gospel of John*, 1018.

183. *Inclusio* is a technical term in Latin used in rhetorical criticism. Richard N. Soulen delineates the term *inclusio* as a term for "a passage of Scripture in which the opening phrase or idea is repeated, paraphrased, or otherwise returned to at the close." Soulen, *Handbook of Biblical Criticism*, 94.

184. Klink, *John*, 878. Also see Köstenberger, *John*, 579, 579n9.

185. Borchert, *John 12–21*, 315. Also see Keener, *Gospel of John*, 2:1211.

The Lordship of the Risen Jesus Proclaimed (Acts 2:14–36)

A third biblical post-resurrection narrative, which explicitly reveals the lordship of the risen Jesus, is Peter's first sermon in Acts 2:14–36. Peter concludes his long sermon by proclaiming in Acts 2:36, "Therefore let the entire house of Israel know with certainty that *God has made him both Lord and Messiah, this Jesus* whom you crucified." More importantly, the risen Jesus's accession of two titles—Lord and Messiah—is seen as a result of the resurrection and exaltation of Jesus (Acts 2:32–36). C. K. Barrett states, "the appointment took place when God raised up and thereby vindicated Jesus."[186] Thus, as Barnabas Lindars points out, "The argument of the 'Resurrection speech' can be summarized in v.36: the Resurrection proves that Jesus is both Lord . . . and Christ."[187]

The two titles of the risen Jesus—Lord and Messiah—reveal several aspects of the lordship of the risen Jesus. First, the title "Messiah" is a political term in the sense that the title highlights the *kingship* of the risen Jesus over the people of Israel. Messiah (or Christ in Greek) is the Jewish term, literally meaning the anointed one, and, among Jews, it was usually understood as the title of Israel's king, who would come from the lineage of David to restore Israel.[188] Thus, Peter was certain about the kingship of Jesus and that he is the one who would restore Israel; therefore, Jews who were listening to Peter's sermon were challenged to accept Jesus as "their rightful ruler."[189] The second title "Lord" is a religious and political term. On the one hand, Greeks used the term "lord" to refer to their gods. This religious meaning of this title emphasizes the deity of Jesus. In Barrett's words, Jesus was claimed as "Messiah in the role of a supernatural *kurios* [which is the Greek term for lord]."[190] Darrell L. Bock interprets the meaning of the term "Lord" in light of the Jewish usage of the title "Lord" for Yahweh: "The title 'Lord' was used by Palestinian Jews as a title for Yahweh. . . . The resurrection shows that Jesus's authority is one that God attests to be equal to God's own."[191] This connection between God and Jesus's title "Lord" means that the risen Jesus is not a mere human king of Israel like David, but his lordship is equated

---

186. Barrett, *Acts 1–14*, 151.
187. Lindars, *New Testament Apologetic*, 46.
188. Keener, *Acts*, 1:964–65.
189. Keener, *Acts*, 1:963.
190. Barrett, *Acts 1–14*, 152.
191. Bock, *Acts*, 136. Bock understands the title *Lord* as one who saves, not one who reigns, and thus for Bock, Jesus as Lord means a figure of deliverance like the title of Messiah. However, in his interpretation of the title *Lord*, he fails to see that the lordship of Jesus, equal to the lordship of God, demands a response of obedience.

with the divine lordship of God. On the other hand, the title "Lord" was a title for Caesar in the Roman Empire.[192] Therefore, as William S. Kurz points out, "the Christian confession that Jesus is Lord meant that Jesus alone, and not Caesar, is owed absolute loyalty and submission. Thus this confession of allegiance to a higher authority had cultural and political consequences."[193] With the two titles used together by Peter, he proclaims the *deity* and *lordship* of the risen Jesus.

These three post-resurrection narratives examined above reveal that the disciples are facing *a new reality* brought by the resurrection of Jesus: God made the risen Jesus the lord over the whole universe. The *lordship* of the risen Jesus is *universal, present,* and *divine*. This new reality demands a proper response both from Jews and from Gentiles. Keener articulates, "That Jesus is Messiah (i.e., Israel's king) and that he is lord at God's right hand are truth claims that demand *universal* allegiance; that is, they demand the response of *all humanity*."[194]

In light of the *present, universal, divine* lordship of Jesus, two implications about the nature of the disciples' missionary vocation can be drawn. First, the disciples' Gentile mission was not a mission to be done by their own strength, but was still the mission, in which the risen Jesus exercises his authority and power. The risen Jesus not only initiated the disciples' Gentile mission, but would be present in their midst, guiding and empowering them. Second, the disciples' Gentile mission was not merely a command, but also a *logical, corresponding response* to the reality of the true identity of Jesus. In a sense, the disciples' global mission can be viewed as the consequence of the true identity of the risen Jesus. In his analysis of the Great Commission of Matthew 28, Bosch bluntly makes this point when he states:

> If Jesus is indeed Lord of all, this reality just has to be proclaimed. Nobody who knows of this can remain silent about it. He or she can do only one thing—help others also to acknowledge Jesus' lordship. And this is what mission is all about—"the proclaiming of the lordship of Christ" (Michel 1941:262). . . . *Mission is a logical consequence of Jesus' induction as sovereign Lord of the universe*. In the light of this, the 'Great Commission' enunciates an empowerment rather than a command.[195]

---

192. Kurz, *Acts*, 57.
193. Kurz, *Acts*, 57.
194. Keener, *Acts*, 1:963. Emphasis added.
195. Bosch, *Transforming Mission*, 78. Emphasis added.

The Continuous Presence of the Risen Jesus with the Disciples

In the previous chapter, the presence of God in the midst of Israel was viewed as the *fulfilling* factor of Israel's missional conversion.[196] In the Gospels, the theme of the presence of God continued as God was present in and through Jesus. From the very beginning, the disciples were a community with God as they were with Jesus. Furthermore, the post-resurrection narratives reveal that Jesus, who embodied the presence of God, would continue to be with the disciples in and through the Holy Spirit.

The Continuous Presence of the risen Jesus

The presence of Jesus with his disciples did not end with his death; he promised his disciples even before his death and resurrection that he would continue to be with them (Matt 18:20). One implication of this observation is that the fulfillment of their global mission would not be possible without the continuous presence of Jesus with them. Legrand makes this point clear when he comments on Matthew 28:20 as below:

> The mission to the nations will rest not on human ability, but on the authority of the Risen One. . . . In the face of the immense task assigned them in verses 19–20, the image of confusion and indecision portrayed by the Eleven is tragicomic. But the point is precisely that it is not human beings, but the authority of the Master and *his continuing presence*, that will take the nations in charge.[197]

This point is further emphasized by the biblical witness that *some disciples doubted* in Matthew 28:17.[198] In the Gospel of Matthew, the motif of doubt is linked to the motif of "little faith," as in Matthew 14:22–32 in which Jesus rebuked Peter who doubted.[199] The fulfillment of their missionary vocation requires their faith in Jesus, but the doubting of the disciples indicates lack of faith in Jesus. However, their "little faith" should not suggest that they would not be able to fulfill their mission at all, but it

---

196. For a full discussion of this point in this study, see the section on the presence of Yahweh in chapter 2.

197. Legrand, *Unity and Plurality*, 80. Emphasis added.

198. This point is further supported by the interpretation that the term "some" refers not to some of the eleven disciples who gathered, but to all the eleven disciples. See Luz, *Matthew 21–28*, 623; Talbert, *Matthew*, 312.

199. Luz, *Matthew 21–28*, 623; Nolland, *Gospel of Matthew*, 1263; Turner, *Matthew*, 688; Osborne, *Matthew*, 1077.

highlights that the risen Jesus would be with them in order to help them fulfill their missionary vocation.

The necessity of the continuous presence of the risen Jesus for the fulfillment of the disciples' missionary vocation does not mean that the disciples' role would be merely passive. Rather, the fulfillment of their missionary vocation requires their continuous dependence on and trust in Jesus who would be with them. In other words, in order to fulfill their missionary vocation, the disciples need to respond to Jesus who would be with them in order to empower and guide them.

The Promise of the Presence of the Holy Spirit

The promise of the presence of the Holy Spirit in the Gospels of John and Luke and the book of Acts (John 14:16-17; Luke 12:12; Acts 1:8) is not contradictory to the promise of the continuous presence of the risen Jesus in Matthew 28:20. Rather, the former confirms the latter; the former shows how the latter will be actualized to the disciples: *The risen Jesus will be continuously present with his followers in and through the Holy Spirit.*[200] Commenting on Jesus's promise of his continuous presence in Matthew 28:20, Henry Stob states:

> And now that Spirit has come. And in him Christ is present with us. It is his Spirit, with whom he is so intimately associated and so definitely identified that he could say in literal truth: Lo, I am with you always. It is as if he would say to his troubled and sorrowing disciples: True, you will see me no more. Our walks, our conversations will come to an end. I go presently to my Father. But I will not leave you alone. . . . What I brought you and wrought for you remains. My Spirit I give you; my Spirit will abide with you. You will have not the memory of me merely, nor only my teachings, but myself. I will lead you and guide you, comfort and console you, instruct and succour you, and bring you at last into the presence of my Father.[201]

The analysis of the ministry of Jesus, both before and after his ascension, shows that the theme of the presence of God who dwells in the midst of the Israelites continues in the New Testament, first, in and through Jesus during his earthly ministry, and then in and through the Holy Spirit after his ascension. God who dwelt in the midst of the disciples in and through

---

200. Shore, "Preaching Mission," 328.
201. Stob, "Lo, I Am with You Always," 16.

Jesus would continuously be with them as the risen Jesus would continue to be with the disciples in and through the Holy Spirit. The promise of the continuous presence of Jesus in their midst indicates the significance of the presence of the risen Jesus for the disciples to fulfill their missionary vocation. It implies that the nature and scope of the disciples' missionary vocation require their continuous dependence on the risen Jesus who is present with them in and through the Holy Spirit.

Summary

The analysis of the post-resurrection narratives shows that the risen Jesus continued to shape the disciples toward their missionary vocation by rebuilding and expanding the disciples' missionary vocation. The ways that the risen Jesus shaped the disciples toward their missionary vocation were already observed in the investigation of the ways that God shaped Israel for his mission in the Old Testament.

The post-resurrection narratives, in which the risen Jesus rebuilt the disciples' relationship with Jesus by restoring their faith in and commitment to him, reveal two aspects of the disciples' missional conversion. First, the disciples' missional conversion involved *the restoration of their relationship with him*. Since the disciples' life was centered on Jesus, the disciples' missional conversion involved the restoration of their relationship with him. This point is parallel to the observation that Israel's missional conversion always involved the restoration of her relationship with God. Second, *the presence of Jesus* with the disciples is essential for them to fulfill their missionary vocation. The disciples' immediate response to the death of Jesus can be viewed as the consequence of Jesus's absence among them. This point is parallel to the golden calf story, in which the people of Israel committed a sin against God while Moses, who, for them, represented accessibility to the presence of God, was absent. The presence of the risen Jesus re-centered the disciples on him. It implies, first, that the disciples are unable to fulfill their missionary vocation without the presence of the risen Jesus in their midst, and, second, that they ought to constantly depend on Jesus in order to fulfill their missionary vocation. In this sense, the presence of the risen Jesus in the midst of the disciples is the *fulfilling* factor of their missionary vocation.

These two observations recall one central aspect of how God shaped Israel toward being God's missionary people: Israel's missionary vocation will be fulfilled through Yahweh's faithfulness and her trust in and dependence on him. This point is observed in the analysis of the post-resurrection narratives. On the one hand, the disciples' immediate response to the death of Jesus proved that, as Israel could not fulfill their missionary vocation without God, the disciples could not fulfill their missionary vocation without Jesus. It implies that they ought to constantly depend on Jesus in order to fulfill their missionary vocation. On the other hand, the risen Jesus's work of restoring the disciples reveals that, as God was faithful to shaping Israel for his mission, Jesus was faithful to shaping the disciples toward their missionary vocation.

The risen Jesus not only restored the disciples' relationship with him, but also *expanded* their missionary vocation by sending them to all nations. The resurrection of Jesus served as the trigger of the Gentile mission, since, in the post-resurrection narratives, the risen Jesus is portrayed as the one who explicitly launched the Gentile mission. The Gentile mission, which was mentioned as the future event before his death and resurrection, was announced as inaugurated with and by the risen Jesus. This is a *new* development which was not found in God's missional formation of Israel in the Old Testament. Two findings from the analysis of the post-resurrection narratives explain the nature of the disciples' centrifugal mission to the Gentiles. First, the initiation of the Gentile mission by the risen Jesus comes with *his lordship which is universal, present, and divine.* The expansion of the disciples' missionary vocation can be viewed as the natural, logical, and corresponding response to the new reality about the risen Jesus, who, as a result of his resurrection, is made the king of the whole universe. Because of this new reality about who the risen Jesus truly is, all nations are situated in an eschatological context, in which they are challenged to choose whether or not they will serve the risen Jesus as their new king. Second, *the presence of God* as the *fulfilling* factor of Israel's missionary vocation in the Old Testament continues in the disciples' global mission. The risen Jesus not only re-centered the disciples on him but promises his continuous presence with the disciples in and through the Holy Spirit. The one who sends the disciples to the world is also the one who will continuously be with them in order to constantly empower and guide them in mission. While the global mission is commissioned to the disciples, it is still a mission of the risen Jesus. For the disciples to fulfill their mission in and to the world, they ought to continuously depend on and follow Jesus who would be with them in and through the Holy Spirit.[202]

---

202. The role of the Holy Spirit in fulfilling the missionary vocation of the followers of Jesus will be considerably discussed in chapter 4.

G. The Crucified Jesus Intensifies and Expands the Disciple's Missionary Vocation

On the one hand, the post-resurrection narratives showed that the death of Jesus left the disciples with a feeling of hopelessness and resulted in loss of their relationship with Jesus. On the other hand, through the death of Jesus, God revealed an essential aspect of what the disciples' mission should look like. Interpreting the meaning of the death of Jesus in light of his resurrection, this section proposes that, as an event inseparable from and interrelated with the resurrection of Jesus, the death of Jesus established an essential nature of the disciples' mission of embodying the radical and inclusive nature of the kingdom of God. When the disciples were sent to all nations, they were called to announce that Jesus was not merely the universal lord who was raised from the dead, but the lord who gave himself for all humanity. This point is very clear when Jesus said to the disciples, "This is my body, which is given for you. Do this in remembrance of me" (Luke 22:19) in his last supper. Jesus expected his death to be remembered and reflected in the life and mission of his followers. This section focuses on the *meaning* of the death of Jesus for the nature of the disciples' missionary vocation, and argues that, through his death, God *further radicalized* and *universalized* the kingdom of God and, by extension, the disciples' missionary vocation.

Jesus's Death and the Radical Kingdom of God

As already argued, Israel's missionary vocation not only continued with the disciples, but was radicalized with Jesus as the new center of the disciples' holiness. Jesus's work of radicalizing the kingdom of God reaches the zenith with his death, which provided his disciples with *the* model of the way of life for those who belong to the kingdom of God. Jesus through his death demonstrated the way of life that obeys the Great Commandment (loving God and loving neighbors), by which Jesus summarized the divine intent of the law originally given to Israel in the Old Testament (Matt 22:35–40). By his death, Jesus demonstrated his radical love for God and for neighbors even at the cost of his life. By deciding to lay down his life, he proved that he loved to fulfill the will of God more than to keep his life (Luke 22:42), and that he forgave even those who mocked and killed him (Luke 23:34). He became the example *par excellence* of what Jesus said in Matthew 5:44: "Love your enemies and pray for those who persecute you." In this way, Jesus, who taught the way of life that embodies the kingdom of God, became the one who lived such a life. In their encounter with Jesus who loved God and others even at the cost of his life, the disciples were called into such a life of love and commitment, which characterizes what the *radical* embodiment of the kingdom of God would look like.

This aspect of the disciples' missionary vocation is made clear in John 13:34-35, in which Jesus says to his disciples, "I give you a new commandment, that you love one another. Just as I have loved you, you also should love one another. By this everyone will know that you are my disciples, if you have love for one another." According to these verses, through the way of life demonstrated by his love for his disciples, the ultimate expression of which was his death, Jesus will be known to the world, and the world will be drawn to him.[203] Three implications about the nature of the disciples' missionary vocation can be derived from these verses. First, their missionary vocation is primarily about *being a contrast community* whose inward life is characterized by loving one another. Second, their missionary vocation is *intensified*, being modeled on the way that Jesus radically embodied the kingdom of God. The kingdom of God, which was to be embodied by the disciples were to be as radical as the kind of radical love that Jesus demonstrated through his death. Third, the nature and goal of their missionary vocation is *Christocentric*, centered on Jesus. Not only the distinctiveness of the disciples is shaped by the way that Jesus radically embodied the kingdom of God, but their distinctive life presents Jesus, of whom they are the disciples, to the world.

Jesus's Death and the Inclusive Kingdom of God

The biblical fact that Jesus officially and explicitly initiated the Gentile mission only after his death and resurrection indicates the inseparable relationship between the beginning of the Gentile mission and the death and resurrection of Jesus. As examined in the discussion of the resurrection of Jesus, it has been argued that the disciples' Gentile mission can be viewed as a natural, logical, and corresponding response to this new reality which emerged as a result of the resurrection of Jesus. While it is scripturally true, the full biblical explanation about the origin of the disciples' Gentile mission would be incomplete without the discussion on the death of Jesus. This

---

203. Richard B. Hays argues for the explicit link between Jesus's new commandment and his death, stating, "Indeed as continue to read the farewell discourse material [John 15:12-14, 17], the link between the love commandment and laying down one's life is made explicit.... Thus, Jesus's death is depicted by John ... as an act of self-sacrificial love that establishes the cruciform life as the norm for disciples. Those within the community may be called upon literally to let down their lives for one another." Hays, *Moral Vision of the New Testament*, 144-45.

section argues that, along with the universal lordship of Jesus, his death provides another historical and theological explanation for the reason why the Gentile mission began only in the post-resurrection period.

The point that is made here is that the disciples are called not only to be a community of radical love, in which they love another one as Jesus loved them, but to *mediate* the *universal* love of God, which he demonstrated through the death of Jesus, to all nations. This point is rooted in and derived from *the biblical pattern of the relationship between grace and obedience*.[204] As will be demonstrated, this relationship, referred to as the *grace-obedience pattern* in this section, is characterized by *human obedience as a grateful and joyful response to divine grace*. In light of the pattern, the view of the disciples' mission as mediating God's love to all nations becomes clear with three points as discussed below. First, the death of Jesus demonstrated God's love for all nations. Second, all nations are called to obey as a response to God's love for them. Lastly, therefore, the disciples are called to mediate God's love to all nations both in word and deed so that all nations may have opportunities to respond to God's love for them.

All Nations Called to Respond to God's Love

As argued in chapter 2, the relationship between the Exodus and the Sinai Covenant indicated that the requirement of obedience in the Sinai Covenant was given to the people of Israel as their grateful and joyful response to God's grace which was demonstrated in the Exodus.[205] Commenting on these components—divine grace and human obedience—in the covenant, William Johnson states, "YHWH now summons Israel, hitherto the passive participant in the irresistible divine act, to positive *response*."[206]

This grace-obedience pattern is also found in the context where the risen Jesus sent the disciples to all nations in Matthew 28:18–20. It appears as though the grace-obedience pattern does not exist in the Great Commission because the divine grace for all nations is not mentioned, while obedience is demanded from all nations. However, while not explicitly mentioned in the Great Commission, God's grace for all nations is stated not as a simple

204. The relationship between divine grace and human obedience should be understood within the larger frame of the relationship between biblical indicatives and imperatives. For more discussion of this biblical pattern of the relationship between biblical indicatives and imperatives, see Wright, *Mission of God*, 58–61.

205. For the reason why obedience is not merely a response but a grateful and joyful response, see the discussion on Yahweh's grace in the Sinai Covenant in chapter 2.

206. Johnstone, *Exodus 1–19*, 399. Also see Bailey, *Exodus*, 208. Emphasis added.

statement but *as a narrative* before Jesus demanded obedience from all nations: *the narrative about the death of Jesus*, which was God's once-for-all grace for all nations.[207] As the New Testament writers interpret, the death of Jesus is an expression of God's radical and universal love for *all*. While not mentioned within the Great Commission text, the death of Jesus as God's grace for all nations is followed by Jesus's demand for obedience from all nations. In this sense, the grace-obedience pattern in the Sinai convent continues in the Great Commission of Matthew 28.

If the Exodus was an event in which God introduced himself to the Israelites, the death of Jesus, along with his resurrection, is an event whereby he introduced himself to all nations. If the resurrection of Jesus revealed his universal lordship, his death revealed his gracious character by demonstrating his self-giving love for all nations. Through the death and resurrection of Jesus, God provided all nations with *the* reason to *gratefully* and *joyfully* accept Jesus as their new king to follow, serve, and obey. All nations have a reason to *gratefully* accept Jesus as their king because the death of Jesus demonstrated his radical love for all nations. They have a reason to *joyfully* obey his commandments because his death revealed that he would be a different kind of king and, by extension, that the new world in which Jesus will reign as king will be a different kind of kingdom.[208] As Wright states, "The kingdoms of the world run on violence. The kingdom of God, Jesus declared, runs on love. That is the good news. . . . Jesus *on the cross* was the ultimate good news in person."[209] In this sense, it can be said that, through the mission of the disciples, all nations are called to accept Jesus as their king, neither in a legalistic manner nor in a sense of duty, but as a *grateful* and *joyful* response to the death and resurrection of Jesus.[210]

207. For the universal motif associated with Jesus's death, see Matt 26:28; Mark 10:45, 14:24; John 3:16.

208. As in the discussion on the Sinai Covenant in chapter 2, the Exodus was the event by which God not only proved his lordship over the people of Israel, but also revealed *what kind of a king he would be*: By responding to their cries and redeeming them from the suffering of slavery, he proved that he will be the king who takes care of them with *steadfast love*.

209. Wright, *Simply Good News*, 44. Emphasis added.

210. This view of the death of Jesus in relation to the grace-obedience pattern is consistent with the relationship between redemption and covenant in the Old and New Testaments. In the Old Testament, the people of Israel as the *redeemed* people became the *covenant* people called to obey God as their king. Likewise, in the New Testament, those who are *set free* from the bondage of sin through Jesus's death are to be the *new covenant* people called to obey Jesus as their king. The connection of redemption and covenant is clearly found when Jesus referred to the blood he shed on his death as the "blood of the *covenant* which is poured out for many for the forgiveness of sin" (Matt 26:28). Commenting on the verse, Davies and Allison state that it is the deliverance

The Disciples Called to Mediate God's Love to All Nations

If all nations were called to respond not only to the universal lordship of Jesus but also the universal divine love, which was demonstrated through the death of Jesus, the disciples' mission to all nations was to be profoundly shaped by not only the resurrection of Jesus but also his death. Charles B. Cousar remarks:

> The crucifixion shapes the identity of the people of God and functions as the basis for their communal and individual self-understanding. As the Jews are the people of the Torah, modeled by the story it contains and distinguished from others by the circumcision it demands, so the Christian community is a people of the cross. In the story of Jesus' death preached in their assemblies and celebrated at the Lord's Supper, they announce who they are and discover how they are to live.[211]

The disciples were called to present Jesus as the king to all nations by communicating and demonstrating the love of God in their outward engagement with all nations. The disciples' mission was to be authentic witnesses of God who "so loved the world that he gave his only Son" (John 3:16). In this way, all nations were to know, taste, and, eventually, *respond to* God's love mediated by the disciples. Two aspects of the disciples' missionary vocation are drawn from this point. First, the disciples' missionary message to all nations essentially was to include the universal love of God. Second, the disciples were called to engage with all nations in a way that embodies the love of God. In this sense, the *holistic*[212] aspect of the disciples' mission was rooted in and derived from the love of God demonstrated by Jesus's self-giving death. Thus, as R. C. Padilla defines, the holistic mission of the church is nothing less than proclaiming "the love of God through what it says, does, and is."[213]

---

from sin by the blood Jesus shed for all that becomes "a basis of a new covenant." Davies and Allison, *Matthew*, 473. Also see France, *Gospel According to Matthew*, 369; Blomberg, *Matthew*, 391.

211. Cousar, *Theology of the Cross*, 110.

212. According to the Merriam-Webster Dictionary, the adjective *holistic* is a word derived from the term *holism*, which, in the dictionary, is defined as "a theory that the universe and especially living nature is correctly seen in terms of interacting wholes (as of living organisms) that are more than the mere sum of elementary particles." In this view, as C. R. Padilla states, the phrase *holistic mission* or *mission in a holistic way* is used to "correct a one-sided understanding of mission that majors on either the vertical or the horizontal dimension of mission." Padilla, "Holistic Mission," 157.

213. Padilla, "Holistic Mission," 162.

Summary

The death and resurrection of Jesus show that, through these two christological events, God revealed two universal realities: the universal lordship of Jesus and the universal love of God. The disciples' missionary vocation is nothing less than reflecting what this new reality, revealed by the resurrection and death of Jesus, means to them and all nations. From the discussion of his death, an essential nature of the disciples' missional formation can be identified: The meaning of Jesus's death serves as the *radicalizing* and *universalizing* factor of the disciples' missional formation. The death of Jesus is the *historical* and *theological* basis of the *radical* and *inclusive* nature of the kingdom of God, which the disciples are called to embody. On the one hand, through his death, Jesus further radicalized the disciples' missionary vocation by demonstrating to them the way of life that embodies the kingdom of God which is radically different from the world. The disciples are called to embody the kingdom of God in the way that Jesus not only taught but also demonstrated through his death. On the other hand, through his death, Jesus further universalized the disciples' missionary vocation by revealing to the disciples the universal grace of God through his death. The grace-obedience pattern in Jesus's sending the disciples to all nations indicates that all nations are called to accept Jesus as their king in gratefully and joyfully responding to God's grace for them, demonstrated through the death of Jesus. It implies that the disciples' mission to all nations are to be profoundly shaped by God's grace in such a way that they reflect the divine love in word and deed in their engagement with all nations. This aspect of the disciples' mission to all nations are significant because, in doing so, all nations will have opportunities to genuinely respond to the love of God.

H. Summary and Conclusion of the Chapter

This chapter focused on ways by which, throughout his whole ministry, Jesus shaped (1) the disciples' missionary vocation, and (2) the disciples themselves toward it. Jesus continued God's work of shaping the Israelites toward their missionary vocation. Overall, this chapter identified two observations. First, the discussion on the earthly ministry of Jesus demonstrated that Israel's missionary vocation continued with the disciples, while intensified and expanded by the whole ministry of Jesus. Second, the aspects of God's work of shaping Israel for mission, identified in the previous chapter, is also observed in the analysis of the death and resurrection of Jesus. More specific findings are summarized below.

Jesus in Continuation of God's Work of Israel's Missional Conversion

This chapter demonstrated that Jesus's earthly ministry was a continuation of God's work of shaping Israel as his missionary people. While, in the Old Testament narrative, the people of Israel were unfaithful to their covenant relationship with God, and, by extension, thus failed their missionary vocation, God did not give up on them. Through prophets, God promised that he would restore Israel back to him through the ministry of his Servant of Isaiah. Two findings—(1) Jesus's identification with the Servant, and (2) Jesus's intentional focus on Israel in his ministry—show that God continued to shape the Israelites toward their missionary vocation through the earthly ministry of Jesus. On the one hand, Jesus focused on Israel, but he had a missional intention in shaping the disciples, as indicated in the twofold mission of Isaiah's Servant and the banquet motif that Jesus used to mention the inclusion of all nations into the kingdom of God.

Two Aims of Jesus's Work of Shaping the Disciples

One particular strategy Jesus used in order to restore the whole people of Israel was by creating a community of disciples. Jesus worked with and among them so that with the disciples as a nucleus of the eschatological people of God, the whole people of Israel may be restored. Throughout the earthly ministry of Jesus, two aims of Jesus's work of shaping the disciples toward their missionary vocation was made clearer in light of the in-between context of Jesus's earthly ministry between John the Baptist's ministry, whose aim was to bring the people of Israel back to God, and the Gentile mission, which was launched right after his death and resurrection. On the one hand, Jesus sought to shape the disciples as a community of what the true people of God should look like. On the other hand, he aimed at preparing the disciples for the Gentile mission, which would begin right after his death and resurrection. Jesus's work of bridging Israel's mission and the disciples' Gentile mission was already prophesized by the Old Testament prophets, in which, through the Servant of God, he was to restore Israel back to him by establishing the New Covenant, and was to shape Israel as his witness to all nations. This chapter identified these two aims of Jesus's shaping the disciples as a contrast people who embody the kingdom of God, which is both *radical* and *inclusive*.

Radicalization of the Kingdom of God

The study of Jesus's earthly ministry to Israel shows that Israel's missionary vocation not only continues with the disciples, but also is radicalized with Jesus as the new point of reference of holiness. On the one hand, Jesus envisioned them to fulfill Israel's missionary vocation to embody the kingdom of God. The essence of Israel's mission—embodying the kingdom of God by being a contrast people who reflect the holiness of God and present it to all nations—continued with the disciples. This point is supported by Jesus's relationship with John the Baptist and the biblical images he used for the disciples' identity. On the other hand, Israel's missionary vocation were *radicalized* with Jesus as the new center of holiness, as the teaching, life and death of Jesus *redefined* what the people of God should look like. Being centered on Jesus, the disciples were not merely called to be a contrast people but, with Jesus as the new center of their holiness, to be a *radical* contrast people who present the holiness of God—the presence and character of God—to the world by living the way of life that Jesus revealed in his teaching and demonstrated through his death.

Universalization of the Kingdom of God

The kingdom of God revealed and embodied by Jesus is not only radical but also *inclusive* so that the door into the kingdom of God is open to all who accept the invitation into it, regardless of social class, ethnicity, and nationality. Jesus envisioned his disciples to be not only a radical contrast people but also an *inclusive* contrast people. The inclusive nature of the kingdom of God and of the disciples' missionary vocation is implicitly revealed in the boundary-crossing ministry of Jesus and his positive view of Gentiles. The foundation for the inclusive nature of the kingdom of God was made complete with the death and resurrection of Jesus. On the one hand, with the resurrection of Jesus, as the result of which God made Jesus the lord of the whole universe, the disciples were sent to all nations to present Jesus as a new king to serve. The disciples' Gentile mission is not merely a command but more of a natural, logical, and corresponding *response* to the new reality of the universal, present, and divine lordship of the risen Jesus. On the other hand, the death of Jesus, which represents the once-for-all grace of God for all nations, provided all nations with the reason why all nations should want to choose Jesus as their king to serve. It implies that the disciples authentically present the love of God in their engagement with all nations in word and deed so that all nations may have opportunities to know, taste, and respond to the love of God.

Findings on the Disciples' Missional Conversion

The analysis of the post-resurrection narratives shows that the aspects of Israel's missional conversion, identified in the analysis of God's work of Israel's missional conversion, is also observed in the risen Jesus's work on the disciples' missional conversion.

First, the disciples' missional conversion is primarily a consequence of their *encounter with God* in and through Jesus. As Israel's missional conversion resulted from her encounter with God, the disciples' missional conversion resulted from their encounter with God in and through Jesus. In the teaching, life, death, and resurrection of Jesus, the disciples came to know and experience God. The disciples' identity and vocation were profoundly shaped in this divine-human encounter. This point is clearly indicated by their missionary identity, namely as *witnesses of Jesus*, because this identity indicates that the disciples' missionary vocation was profoundly shaped by what they witnessed in their encounter with Jesus.

Second, the disciples' missional conversion involves *the restoration of their relationship with Jesus*. This point is indicated in the observation that the disciples' missionary vocation is centered on Jesus. The behaviors of the disciples in the immediate context of Jesus's death shows that the disciples cannot fulfill their missionary vocation, without the restoration of their relationship with Jesus. This aspect of the disciples' missional conversion was also identified in the analysis of Israel's missional conversion. God's work of bringing the Israelites back to their missionary vocation always involved the restoration of their relationship with God.

Third, the post-resurrection narratives depict *Jesus's faithfulness* to the disciples' missional conversion. When the disciples betrayed and abandoned their relationship with Jesus, Jesus did not give up on his disciples but appeared to them, re-established his relationship with them, and even commissioned them with a global-sized mission. This point is also observed in God's work of re-establishing Israel's missionary vocation. When Israel turned away from him, he faithfully brought them back to covenant relationship with him.

Fourth, the post-resurrection narratives highlight the significance of *the presence of Jesus* for the fulfillment of the disciples' missionary vocation. When the death of Jesus, which meant to the disciples, the absence of Jesus from them, resulted in their loss of faith in and commitment to Jesus, the presence of the risen Jesus among them re-established and expanded their missionary vocation. Furthermore, Jesus's promise of his continuous presence with the disciples in and through the Holy Spirit (crucially fulfilled at Pentecost) further emphasized the role of his presence among them to fulfill their missionary vocation. It implies that the disciples ought to constantly depend on the presence of Jesus who empowers and guides them in mission in order to fulfill their missionary vocation.

These four findings about the disciples' missional conversion are already observed in the analysis of God's work of shaping Israel toward her missionary vocation in the Old Testament. The way that Jesus shaped the disciples follows, reflects, and projects the way that God shaped Israel, while Israel's mission is redefined throughout the earthly ministry of Jesus.

4

The Earliest Church's Encounter with the Holy Spirit and Its Missional Conversion[1]

THE PREVIOUS CHAPTERS ATTEMPTED to identify the nature of the missional conversion of the people of God by addressing implications from Yahweh's work of shaping the people of Israel in the Old Testament narrative (chapter 2) and Jesus's work of shaping the disciples throughout his earthly ministry (chapter 3). This chapter focuses on the Holy Spirit's work of shaping the missionary nature of the earliest church by analyzing relevant biblical cases found in the book of Acts.

The risen Jesus sent his disciples to all nations with a missionary identity as *his witnesses*, and with a missionary vocation of embodying the kingdom of God in both *their inward life* and *their outward ministry to all nations*. However, the mission entrusted to the disciples was not left as a purely human enterprise. The promises of the continuous presence of Jesus among them (Matt 28:20) and of sending the Holy Spirit to them (John 14:15–16) indicate that Jesus will be always with them in and through the Holy Spirit to empower and guide them so that they may fulfill their missionary vocation.

Like the people of Israel who failed to fulfill their missionary vocation in the Old Testament, the disciples of Jesus demonstrated that they were far from what Jesus intended them to be, while they were not as massively unfaithful as Israel in the Old Testament narrative. The disciples misunderstood Jesus's teachings (e.g., Matt 16:5–12). They fought each other, arguing about who was greatest among them (Mark 9:33–37; Luke 9:46–48). One

---

1. The term "the earliest church" is deliberately used in this chapter in order to refer to the church in the book of Acts or in the apostolic period. Thereby, this term is distinguished from another term "the early church" which, in historical studies, is widely used to refer to the church in a longer period—the period before the Nicene council of 325.

of them even betrayed Jesus, with just thirty pieces of silver. Peter, one of his core disciples, denied his relationship with Jesus as Jesus was arrested. They lost their faith in, commitment to, and expectation in Jesus when he was crucified, as examined in chapter 3. The disciples were far from what Jesus intended them to be. Even after the risen Jesus restored, strengthened, and commissioned them with a global mission, they failed to understand Jesus's teaching about the kingdom of God (Acts 1:1–11), demonstrating that, without Jesus, they could not carry out the mission entrusted to them. Oswalt makes this point when he states:

> How were they to live out the stupendous things that he had taught? How were they to live out the kingdom principles that he had laid down? Their failures were displayed on every hand. They clearly had no understanding of the significance of the cross for kingdom living. Like the children of Israel, they were willing to obey, but they seemed incapable of it. They thought only of themselves and their prerogatives. All of the stories of the disciples which we find in the Gospels after the confession of Peter are stories of failure. Surely if the witness of the kingdom depends on these people after Jesus' ascension, the cause is a lost one.[2]

In this chapter, attention is given to ways that God *in and through the Holy Spirit* transformed the earliest church, particularly the church of Jerusalem. Three cases in the book of Acts will be scrutinized, in each of which the Jerusalem Church encountered the Holy Spirit in one way or another, gradually being transformed into a missionary people of God: the outpouring of the Holy Spirit upon Jewish believers (Acts 1–5), Cornelius's Conversion (Acts 10–11), and the Jerusalem Council (Acts 15).

A. The Triune God Continues to Shape His People for His Mission

The previous chapter argued that Jesus, identified as the servant of God in the book of Isaiah, continued God's work of missional conversion of the people of Israel. In the New Testament narrative, God's work of the missional conversion of Israel did not stop with the ascension of Jesus, but continued with the Holy Spirit as indicated in Jesus's promises of his continuous presence with them and of the coming of the Holy Spirit. This continuity is further evidenced by two more biblical factors: (1) the role of the Holy Spirit

---

2. Oswalt, *Called to be Holy*, 128.

in the New Covenant and (2) the missional purpose of the Holy Spirit's work of shaping the earliest church.

The Promise of the New Covenant Fulfilled through Receiving the Holy Spirit

Along with the ministry of the servant of God, identified as Jesus, God through the Old Testament prophets promised that he would restore the people of Israel by establishing the New Covenant with the people of Israel (Jer 31:31–34; Ezek 36:24–28). God shaped Israel toward her missionary vocation by establishing the Sinai Covenant in the Old Testament, and now he reshapes them for his mission by renewing the old covenant with the New Covenant. Scholars generally relate the establishment of the New Covenant not only to Jesus's ministry but also to the ministry of the Holy Spirit to the followers of Jesus.[3] Jesus established the covenant by becoming the foundation for the New Covenant through his whole ministry, and, on that foundation, the New Covenant began to be fulfilled when the Holy Spirit came upon believers for the first time. Dunn states:

> For once again we stand at a watershed in salvation-history, the beginning of the new age and new covenant, not for Jesus this time, but now for his disciples. What Jordan was to Jesus, *Pentecost* was to the disciples. As Jesus entered the new age and covenant by being baptized in the Spirit at Jordan, so the disciples followed him in like manner at Pentecost. With the wider enjoyment of the messianic age made possible by Jesus' representative death, so at *Pentecost* the new covenant, hitherto confined to the one representative man, was extended to embrace all those who remained faithful to him and tarried at Jerusalem in obedience to his command.[4]

The connection between the New Covenant and the Holy Spirit is indicated by the fact that, according to Jewish tradition, the day of Pentecost was closely associated with the establishment and renewal of the Sinai Covenant.[5] One biblical passage that leads to this connection is 2 Chronicles 15:8–15, in which the whole people in the kingdom of Judah gathered for the covenant renewal ceremony in the third month of the year, which is

---

3. For a thorough biblical study on the Holy Spirit's relationship with the New Covenant, see Pettegrew, *New Covenant Ministry of the Holy Spirit*; Keener, *Acts*, 1:784–87.

4. Dunn, *Baptism in the Holy Spirit*, 40. Emphasis added.

5. See VanderKam, "Covenant and Pentecost."

also the month in which the Pentecost festival took place.[6] Drawing on this connection between the Sinai Covenant and the Pentecost festival, Jacques Dupont views the Pentecost event (in Acts 2) as an event intimately associated with the New Covenant. He articulates:

> The Holy Spirit came upon the apostles on the feast day at which Judaism commemorated the promulgation of the Law and the creation of the Covenant between God and his people gathered in "assembly." . . . The Christian Pentecost which celebrates the Spirit's coming, commemorates a New Covenant, which created a new people of God and constituted them a Church. This Covenant is not based, like the old one, on the regulations of a Law imposed on men from without; it is based on the Spirit, who transforms hearts and inspires a filial attitude toward God.[7]

Scot McKnight also affirms this connection between the New Covenant and the Holy Spirit, in light of scriptural evidence from the book of Acts and the Apostle Paul's writings. McKnight claims that what the New Covenant is expected to fulfill was fulfilled through "*pneumatic* experiences."[8] On the basis of that argument, he contends that the event of Pentecost is the moment when the promise of the New Covenant began to be fulfilled. He states, "the covenant hermeneutic owes its origins to the *pneumatic* experiences of early Jerusalem-based followers of Jesus."[9]

Among the New Testament writers, Paul makes a strong connection between the work of the Holy Spirit and the fulfillment of the promise about the New Covenant. According to the New Covenant prophesied in the Old Testament, the law would be written on the *hearts* of the people of God and the Spirit of God would dwell in their *hearts* when the promise of the New Covenant is fulfilled.[10] According to Paul, this is what the Holy Spirit does in the *hearts* of believers.[11] Thus, Paul's view of the work and presence of the Holy Spirit in the hearts of believers affirms the connection between the Holy Spirit and the New Covenant. Dunn observes this point:

> The already established link between Pentecost, covenant renewal, and the giving of the Law probably prompted the first believers to interpret their experience of *the Spirit* as the

---

6. Thompson, *1, 2 Chronicles*, 271; Tuell, *First and Second Chronicles*, 171.

7. Dupont, *Salvation of the Gentiles*, 58–59. Also see McKnight, "Covenant and Spirit," 47.

8. McKnight, "Covenant and Spirit," 51. Italics in original.

9. McKnight, "Covenant and Spirit," 51. Italics in original.

10. See Jer 31:31–34; Ezek 36:26–27; 37:14.

11. See Rom 2:28–29; 7:6; 2 Cor 3; Gal 3:1—4:7; Phil 3:3; Col 2:11; 1 Thess 4:8.

fulfillment of the promise of a new covenant, as the Law written in their *hearts*. . . . But the implications of this insight for continuing faith and conduct were not recognized and elaborated until Paul.[12]

As already noted, the promise of the New Covenant is about God's reshaping the people of Israel toward their missionary vocation. This connection between the Holy Spirit and the New Covenant indicates that God's work of shaping his people toward their missionary vocation continues in and through the Holy Spirit.

The Missional Purpose of the Holy Spirit's Work of Shaping the Earliest Church

Besides the connection between the New Covenant and the Holy Spirit, the missional intention of the Holy Spirit's dealing with the earliest church also indicates that God's work of the missional conversion of his people continued through the Holy Spirit. In other words, the missionary purpose of Israel in the Old Testament continued with the earliest church in the post-resurrection period as the Holy Spirit transformed the church in order to fulfill the same missionary purpose God had for Israel. Two particular biblical cases in the book of Acts provide a general characterization of the missional purpose of the Holy Spirit's dealing with the earliest church: (1) Jesus's promise about the Holy Spirit in Acts 1:8 and (2) the Holy Spirit enabling early Jewish believers to declare the work of God in every language in Acts 2:4–6.

First, the missional intention of the Holy Spirit's work of transforming the earliest church is clearly found in Acts 1:8, in which Jesus says, "you will receive power when the Holy Spirit has come upon you; and you will be my witnesses in Jerusalem, in all Judea and Samaria, and to the ends of the earth." Closely looked into, two promises, which will be fulfilled at the same time, are mentioned in Acts 1:8: (1) the Holy Spirit's empowerment of believers, and (2) their transformation into witnesses of Jesus. The relationship between the two promises is not clearly specified in the verse itself. However, as discussed later, the witnessing ministry of the earliest church immediately followed Pentecost in the book of Acts. This indicates that the fulfillment of the latter (being witnesses of Jesus) was the *direct* consequence of the fulfillment of the former (the Holy Spirit's empowerment). In other words, the transformation of the earliest church toward being a witness of Jesus was promised to be actualized when the promise

---

12. Dunn, "Pentecost," 213. Emphasis added.

about the empowerment by the Holy Spirit was fulfilled. Furthermore, the witnessing ministry of the earliest church is geographically expanded: "in Jerusalem, in all Judea and Samaria, and to the ends of the earth." This phrase of geographical expansion implies that the church's witnessing ministry is not conditioned by geographical (and ethnical) boundaries. This verse is a promise that, through the earliest church's mission, the gospel about Jesus will begin to reach all nations with the fulfillment of the promise about the Holy Spirit's empowerment.

These observations from Acts 1:8 reveal the missional intention of the Holy Spirit's work of transforming the earliest church. Dupont makes this point when he states, "The economy of the Spirit . . . is characterized by real and effective universality. . . . The essential universality of the Church born of the Spirit implies and imposes a call to missionary activity."[13] As Roland Allen observes, "it is in the revelation of the Holy Spirit as a missionary Spirit that the Acts stands alone in the New Testament."[14] This missional purpose of the Holy Spirit's work of shaping the earliest church, revealed in Acts 1:8, is fulfilled throughout the narrative of the book of Acts, as indicated by the observation that the overall structure of the book of Acts is framed by Acts 1:8.[15] In this sense, as Alfred Wikenhauser suggests, the theme of the book of Acts can be formulated this way: "The universal expansion of Christianity begun in the power of, and effected by, the Holy Spirit."[16]

Second, in addition to Acts 1:8, the missionary nature of the Holy Spirit also surfaces in the universal and missional character of the Pentecost event in Acts 2:4-6. When Jewish believers experienced the outpouring of the Holy Spirit, Jewish believers, filled with the Holy Spirit, were enabled to "speak in other languages" (Acts 2:4). The connection between the empowerment of the Holy Spirit and this extraordinary capability suddenly given to Jewish believers is explicitly mentioned: "the Spirit gave them ability" (Acts 2:4). Devout Jewish diaspora people "from every nation under heaven" who stayed in Jerusalem on the day were "bewildered" because "each one heard them speaking in the native language of each" (Acts 2:5-6). This particular happening at Pentecost is quite universal and missional in character, revealing the missional intention and purpose of the Holy Spirit's empowerment of the early believers. Richard P. Thompson contends that the emphasis in this event is not the fact that they spoke in tongues, but its

---

13. Dupont, *Salvation of the Gentiles*, 59.
14. Allen, "Pentecost and the World," 21.
15. DeSilva, *Introduction to the New Testament*, 356–57.
16. Wikenhauser, *Die Apostelgeschichte Und Ihr Geshictswert*, 15, quoted in Boer, *Pentecost and Missions*, 119.

implication for the missional dimension of the event: "such divinely enabled speaking was for the sake of proclamation and salvation to all. It was for the Jewish Diaspora and, by implication, the rest of the world."[17] As Keener comments, "This empowerment is to speak God's own message . . . across cultural boundaries . . . and hence ultimately to form the church across such boundaries."[18] The Holy Spirit's outpouring at Pentecost revealed the missional purpose of the empowerment of the earliest church by the Holy Spirit. Allen plainly encapsulates this point when he states:

> When the Holy Spirit descended upon the Apostles His first gift was the gift of Tongues. Men, gathered from every nation under heaven, marveled to hear the Apostles speak in their tongues the wonderful works of God. . . . Thus, at His first coming, the Holy Spirit revealed His nature and His work as worldwide, all-embracing. He revealed His nature as a Spirit who desired the salvation of all men of every nation; He revealed His work as enabling those to whom He came to preach Christ to men of every nation."[19]

The Triune God at Work in the book of Acts

The two points made about the work of the Holy Spirit—(1) the Holy Spirit's role in the New Covenant and (2) the missional purpose of the Holy Spirit's work of shaping the earliest church—highlight the role of the Holy Spirit in shaping the earliest church in the book of Acts. While the book of Acts is termed the Acts of the Apostles, the centrality of the Holy Spirit is predominant throughout the book. Some scholars suggest that "the Acts of *the Holy Spirit*" is a more appropriate title for the book than the Acts of the Apostles.[20] In the view of most scholars, the Holy Spirit is the central divine agent in the book of Acts. However, this scriptural emphasis on the Holy Spirit does not support the idea that the Holy Spirit was present and acted in the book of Acts in isolation from God the Father and God the Son. All three persons of the Trinity at work in the book of Acts are indicated by the fact that the New Covenant is trinitarian. As already noted earlier, the covenant was initiated by God to bring his people back

---

17. Thompson, *Acts*, 76.
18. Keener, *Acts*, 1:780.
19. Allen, "Pentecost and the World," 22.
20. For example, Larkin, "Mission in Acts," 175.

to him, established by the person and work of Jesus, and fulfilled by the empowerment of the Holy Spirit.

This point is particularly true in light of what had been *already* established before the ascension of Jesus. As pointed out in the previous chapter, Jesus's promises of his continuous presence with his disciples (Matt 28:20) and those who gathered in his name (Matt 18:20) and of the coming of the Holy Spirit (Luke 24:49; John 15:26; 16:7–15) established the unity of the risen Jesus and the Holy Spirit in shaping the followers of Jesus to fulfill the mission of God. The molding of the people of God into a missionary people in the New Testament period is still Yahweh's work as promised through the Old Testament prophets. God was present and acted in and through Jesus, and now is present and works in the power of the Holy Spirit.[21] At the same time, it is still the work of the risen Jesus as he promised, but in and through the Holy Spirit. Keener states, "Jesus is not only the primary subject of proclamation in the speeches; he remains also a dramatic actor in the second volume's narrative."[22] Therefore, while the presence and role of the Holy Spirit is highlighted throughout the book of Acts, all three members of the Trinity are present in unity and at work corporately in the book of Acts. The risen Jesus continues God's work of shaping the missionary nature of his people in the power of the Holy Spirit. While this chapter views the Holy Spirit as the central divine agent of the earliest church's missional transformation, this chapter also affirms that God the Father and God the Son are present and act in and through the Holy Spirit in the biblical cases analyzed in this chapter.

In summary, Jesus's promises of his continuous presence with them and the coming of the Holy Spirit already indicate the continuation of God's work of shaping his people toward their missionary vocation through the Holy Spirit. This continuation is supported by the role of the Holy Spirit in the New Covenant. Furthermore, this continuation is made clear by the missional purpose of the Holy Spirit's work of transforming the earliest church in light of two pieces of biblical evidence: (1) the transformative role of the Holy Spirit in shaping believers as witnesses of Jesus as promised in Acts 1:8, and (2) the universal and missional character of the Pentecost event in Acts 2:4–6. While there is no denying the central role of the Holy Spirit in the book of Acts, it is the triune God—all three members of the Trinity—who continues to shape the earliest church as a missionary people. In light of these findings,

---

21. This point is supported by Robert L. Mowery, who, in his linguistic analysis of the divine title, God in the book of Acts, observes, "'God' is the numerically dominant title in Acts, occurring 159 times." Mowery, "Lord, God, and Father," 90.

22. Keener, *Acts*, 1:502. For a brief survey of the acts of the risen Jesus in the book of Acts, see Keener, *Acts*, 1:502–3.

God's work of shaping his people for his mission does not end with the ascension of Jesus, but continues through the Holy Spirit.

B. The Holy Spirit Empowers and Transforms the Earliest Church

The beginning stage of the earliest church in Acts 2–5 shows its *dramatic* formation. The general characterization of the earliest church in this stage is given particularly in Acts 2–5 as the consequence of its encounters with the Holy Spirit.[23] At this stage, early believers experienced the outpouring of the Holy Spirit two times, in Acts 2:1–13 and 4:23–31. The following investigation on this formative stage of the earliest church focuses on ways that the Holy Spirit shaped both the *inward life* and *outward ministry* of the earliest church's mission.

The Holy Spirit Shapes the Outward Ministry of the Earliest Church

Before Jesus left the disciples and was taken up to the Father, he told them to stay in Jerusalem and wait for what he promised as "the gift of the Father" (Acts 1:4). After his ascension, the disciples stayed in Jerusalem, constantly praying together (Acts 1:14). On the day of Pentecost, they suddenly, and for the first time, came to have an extraordinary experience of the outpouring of the Holy Spirit and were enabled to speak in other tongues (Acts 2:1–4).

With the outpouring of the Holy Spirit upon believers at Pentecost, what Jesus promised about the empowerment of the Holy Spirit in Acts 1:8 began to be fulfilled.[24] The Holy Spirit, who came down upon those who followed Jesus and gathered in prayer on the day of Pentecost, empowered and drove the gathered people for mission. As will be discussed, the following narratives show that the result was *the birth of a boldly witnessing community*.[25] As earliest noted, scholars generally agree with the direct relationship between the earliest church's experience of the Holy Spirit at

---

23. Twelftree, *People of the Spirit*, 18.

24. Boer, *Pentecost and Missions*, 62; Newbigin, *Open Secret*, 58; Marshall, *New Testament Theology*, 159.

25. In Acts 1:8, "you" refers to the disciples of Jesus, but should not be limited to them; it can be a reference to all believers who are empowered by the Holy Spirit. Keener states, "the witnesses specifically addressed in this verse are the Twelve, but their commission becomes paradigmatic for other, later witnesses. . . . They, too, are empowered by the Spirit, a gift for all believers (Acts 2:38–39)." Keener, *Acts*, 1:689.

Pentecost and its missional formation. Glasser claims, "On that day [of Pentecost] the New Testament expression of the people of God, the church, was formed and empowered *for its worldwide mission*."[26] Harry Boer states, "the descent of the Spirit at Pentecost made the disciples apostles, e.g., missionaries."[27] According to Keener, it was "the *direct* consequence of the Spirit's empowerment," that the earliest church became bold witnesses of Jesus.[28] Since the Pentecost event, the earliest church found itself actively and boldly involved in mission under the empowerment and guidance of the Holy Spirit as "the driving force behind any and all movements of the people of God outward, beyond the frontiers of faith, to share the gospel with those who have not yet heard it."[29] In view of the outward ministry and inward life of the earliest church found in the narrative followed by the Pentecost event, it can be said that the formation of the missionary nature of the earliest church believers into bold witnesses is a result of the earliest church's encounter with the Holy Spirit on that day.

The Disciples' Transformation into Bold Witnesses

What immediately follows the day of Pentecost is Peter's first public speech to Jewish people who made fun of them and said, "They have had too much wine" (Acts 2:13). In spite of their teasing, the disciples did not hide themselves, but Peter stood with the other disciples and proclaimed, "This Jesus God raised up, and of that all of us are *witnesses*" (Acts 2:23). He boldly exhorted to the audience, "Repent, and be baptized every one of you in the name of Jesus Christ so that your sins may be forgiven; and you will receive the gift of the Holy Spirit" (Acts 2:38).

From Luke's account of Peter's first speech, three observations are significant for understanding how Pentecost transformed the disciples. First, the disciples' public behavior differed before and after Pentecost. Graham H. Twelftree argues the disciples' dramatic transformation into confident and powerful witnesses took place not after their experience of meeting the risen Jesus, but after Pentecost.[30] Particularly, a sharp contrast is found in Peter's attitude toward the public. Peter transformed from the one who denied Jesus three times[31] to the one who boldly proclaimed Jesus in public. Second,

---

26. Glasser et al., *Announcing the Kingdom*, 259. Emphasis added.
27. Boer, *Pentecost and Missions*, 62.
28. Keener, *Acts*, 1:689. Italics in original.
29. Glasser et al., *Announcing the Kingdom*, 263.
30. Twelftree, *People of the Spirit*, 80.
31. See Matt 26:69–75; Mark 14:66–72; Luke 24:54–62; John 18:15–27.

Peter's public speech immediately following the Pentecost event indicates the direct impact of Pentecost on the disciples; their experience of the outpouring of the Holy Spirit enabled him to proclaim the gospel of Jesus. Third, Peter's act of bold proclamation was not merely an individual witnessing, but was *corporate*, indicated by the fact that he was "standing with the eleven" (Acts 2:14). D. Zac Niringiye comments on this point:

> It is instructive that even in the case where only Peter addressed Jewish pilgrims, the text says that 'Peter stood up with the eleven' (Acts 2:14). And the response is recorded as addition to the community rather than just people turning to Jesus for their salvation only. Proclamation should not be thought of simply as an individual's task, seeking conversion of individuals. . . . Proclamation is a community task, transforming community.[32]

These three observations from Peter's act of proclamation in Acts 2 shows that the transformation of the disciples into bold witnesses of Jesus was derived from their experience of the outpouring of the Holy Spirit upon them at Pentecost.

Being Bold Witnesses as an Answer to the Church's Prayer

Another biblical case that shows that the believers' transformation into bold witnesses of Jesus is intimately related to their encounter with the Holy Spirit is found in Acts 4, in which the whole church as well as the disciples became bold witnesses as a result of the outpouring of the Holy Spirit. Acts 4:1–22 highlights bold acts of Peter and John to the public. The direct relationship between their public acts and the work of the Holy Spirit in them is indicated in Acts 4:8, in which Peter is "filled with the Holy Spirit" when he was speaking in the council of Jewish rulers and elders. While the council warned them "not to speak or teach at all in the name of Jesus" (Acts 4:18), the response of Peter and John to the council reveals the peak of their boldness: "Peter and John answered them, 'Whether it is right in God's sight to listen to you rather than to God, you must judge; for we cannot keep from speaking about what we have seen and heard'" (Acts 4:19–20). In the following narrative (Acts 4:23–31), the boldness in witnessing reached the whole church. When Peter and John returned, the whole church heard their report and corporately prayed to God; they "raised their voices together to God" (Acts 4:24). The content of their corporate prayer is roughly divided into two categories: an appeal (or report) to God that both Jews and Gentiles are bitterly hostile

---

32. Niringiye, "To Proclaim the Good News of the Kingdom," 18.

against Jesus (Acts 4:24–28) and a request for boldness in witnessing, and signs and wonders (Acts 4:29–30). Then, in the following verse, it is testified that all the believers who were praying "were all filled with the Holy Spirit and spoke the word of God *boldly*" (Acts 4:31).

Three observations, which are parallel to Acts 2, show the role of the Holy Spirit in transforming the earliest church toward becoming a bold witnessing community. First, as in the case of the Pentecost event, believers' boldness in witnessing is directly associated with their experience of being filled with the Holy Spirit. Being filled with the Holy Spirit, Peter spoke in boldness in the council. After their corporate prayer, the whole church was filled with the Holy Spirit and proclaimed the word of God in boldness.[33]

Second, along with their act of bold witnessing, the missionary concern of the earliest church in prayer in Acts 4 reveals the church's missionary nature. They were in the midst of oppression, as indicated in what Peter and John experienced in the council and the content of the church's corporate prayer. However, the early believers did not pray for protection from oppression or judgment against oppressors. Rather, the whole church asked God, "Lord, . . . enable your servants to speak your word with great boldness" (Acts 4:29 NIV). Richard N. Longenecker states:

> Most significant is the fact that these early Christians were praying not for relief from oppression or for judgment on their oppressors, but for enablement from God "to speak your word with great boldness" amid opposition and for God to act in mighty power "through the name of your holy servant Jesus." Their concern was for God's word to go forth and for Christ's name to be glorified—in effect, for the church's witness—while leaving to God their own circumstances."[34]

As William J. Larkin Jr. notes, "With this request we learn the believers' great concern is not for their own safety but for the mission's advance."[35] Furthermore, the early church's missionary commitment can be glimpsed in light of the fact that they prayed for "great" boldness, not just boldness.[36] This adjective, "great," which literally means "complete,"[37] is an indicator of the level of boldness required in order to overcome oppression and, by extension, the strength of the oppression and hostility they faced. The level of threats that

---

33. Gaventa, *Acts of the Apostles*, 98.

34. Longenecker, "Luke," 780. Also see Bock, *Acts*, 202.

35. Larkin, *Acts*, 80.

36. This phrase is translated as "all" as in "all boldness" in other English translations of the Bible such as NRSV and ESV.

37. Larkin, *Acts*, 80.

the church faced was as strong as the threats that Peter and John had faced, and was also as intensive as what Jesus faced. As Gaventa notes, "The threats against Peter and John by the Jewish leaders are the equivalent of the threats against Jesus."[38] In this respect, it can be said that, as John B. Polhill comments, "Just like the threats, plots, and rages against Jesus, the community viewed itself in much the situation he had experienced."[39] The prayer request for such a high level of boldness needed for public proclamation indicates the seriousness of the church's concern for their witnessing ministry. Regarding that request for great boldness, it should be noted that, as David G. Peterson comments, "Such boldness is a divine gift, not a moral virtue to be acquired by repeated exercise."[40] The church "needed to have their courage renewed," but they prayed for the renewal of boldness, indicating that they believed that such a renewal could come only from God.

It seems that the church learned from the Pentecost event that boldness for witnessing was the answer to their prayer because they had prayed constantly (Acts 1:16) before they experienced becoming bold as a consequence of the outpouring of the Holy Spirit in Acts 2. This implies that the missionary nature of the earliest church is juxtaposed with its dependence on God. This point has been established in the previous two chapters of this study: the missional formation of Israel (chapter 2) and the disciples of Jesus (chapter 3) entail their trust in and dependence on God. Given such oppressive context, the fact that the church did not pray for protection or judgment, but rather for being enabled to witness in boldness shows the church's commitment to the missionary task of witnessing. These observations about the missionary character of the church's corporate prayer show the missionary nature of the earliest church in the sense that the church was enthusiastically seeking to witness about Jesus, even in a bitterly oppressive context by depending on and trusting in God.

Third, the earliest church's experience of the Holy Spirit and, by extension, of its transformation toward being a bold witnessing community is closely related to the church's corporate prayer. One common observation in Acts 2 and 4 is that the believers experienced the Holy Spirit when they were praying together. This observation shows that, as in the case of Acts 2, the experience of being filled with the Holy Spirit was not a one-sided event, in which the role of believers was mostly in passive mode, but an event that involved the earliest church's dependence on God as they were committed to prayer. In other words, as Bock comments, the earliest

---

38. Gaventa, *Acts of the Apostles*, 97.
39. Polhill, *Acts*, 149–50.
40. Peterson, *Acts of the Apostles*, 202.

church's corporate prayer was "an expression of complete dependence on God, a recognition of his sovereignty, a call for God's justice and oversight in the midst of opposition."[41] In this sense, their experience of the outpouring of the Holy Spirit in Acts 2 and 4 can be viewed as God's answer to their corporate prayer. The role of prayer in these two cases implies the two-way relationship between God and the church for its missional formation: God empowered the earliest church for mission through the Holy Spirit, as the early church depended on and trusted in God. One consequent implication for the nature of the church's missional conversion is that the missional conversion of the church requires *its dependence on and trust in God*. This aspect of the church's missional conversion already surfaced in God's dealing with the people of Israel in the Old Testament narrative and in Jesus's ministry to the disciples.

The Holy Spirit Shapes the Inward Life of the Earliest Church

When closely looking into the formation of the church in its early stage (Acts 2–5), the characterization of the inward life as well as the outward ministry of the earliest church follows the account of the church's experience of the Holy Spirit. This indicates the causal relationship between the church's experience of the Holy Spirit and the distinctiveness of the church's life. The outpouring of the Holy Spirit onto the earliest church not only shaped its outward mission, but transformed it into a new *social* and *spiritual* community.

The Social *Aspect of the Earliest Church's Life*

Two descriptions of the earliest church's life (Acts 2:44–45; 4:32–37) show that the church, which experienced the outpouring of the Holy Spirit, has become a new social reality in which its members are committed to one another through the practice of (1) selfless sharing and (2) table fellowship. The practice of sharing possessions is first described in Acts 2:44–45 which reads, "All who believed were together and had all things in common; they would sell their possessions and goods and distribute the proceeds to all, as any had need." This selfless-giving practice of the earliest church is described again in Acts 4:32–37 in a more detailed way. The account of sharing possessions in Acts 4 includes the immediate consequence of the practice: "There was not a needy person among them, for

---

41. Bock, *Acts*, 210.

as many as owned lands or houses sold them and brought the proceeds of what was sold" (Acts 4:34). The absence of the needy likely alludes to the Jubilee Year in Deuteronomy 15:4, which reads, "There will . . . be no one in need among you." This allusion implies that the social aspect of the earliest church is in continuation with what God expected from the Israelites in shaping them as a contrast community in the Old Testament.[42] In this respect, it might be possible to say that the community of believers shaped by their experience of the Holy Spirit was beginning to fulfill what God socially expected from the people of Israel in the Old Testament.

From these observations, it seems to be clear that, from its beginning, born out of the outpouring of the Holy Spirit, the earliest church was a new social reality in which its members cared for one another by sharing personal possessions with one another. As Nissen states, "[the earliest church was] a community of common ownership. The first Christians gave until all needs were met - those who had too much gave up their surplus and treated nothing as their own. . . . All this is accomplished in the power of the Spirit."[43] The life of the earliest church was characterized by, in Glasser's words, "the reality of their loving acceptance of one another and their pattern of selfless sharing (*koinonia*)."[44] The members of the church "sensed their calls to participate in the new social reality that the Holy Spirit was sending forth into the world."[45]

The earliest church's practice of sharing possessions was rooted in the life and teaching of Jesus. As Keener points out, the earliest church's selfless sharing "fulfills Jesus's example and teaching regarding possessions. . . . Their commitment was radical, fitting Jesus's demand for disciples in the Gospel."[46] That being said, the work of the Holy Spirit should be viewed not as initiation of something other than what Jesus intended the disciples to be, but as actualization of what Jesus envisioned about what the disciples as a contrast community should look like. Hence, the church that was shaped by its encounter with the Holy Spirit was missionary in its character, not only because of their bold witness to Christ, but also because of their radical alternative lifestyle that reflected the teaching and life of Jesus.

Along with selfless sharing, *the table fellowship*, which was one of the characteristics of the earliest church, also shows another aspect of the

---

42. Barram, *Missional Economics*, 217–18.
43. Nissen, *New Testament and Mission*, 58.
44. Glasser et al., *Announcing the Kingdom*, 265.
45. Glasser et al., *Announcing the Kingdom*, 265.
46. Keener, *Acts*, 1:1012, 1022.

earliest church as a new social reality.[47] The practice of the table fellowship is descriptively mentioned only in Acts 2:46: "they broke bread at home and ate their food with glad and generous hearts." While the earliest church's table fellowship is mentioned only once in Acts 2, this practice shows a significant aspect of the church's social reality. Yao, in his in-depth biblical and missiological study on the theme of table fellowship, states, "Table fellowship, as a symbol of the infiltration of the Kingdom of God, has profound missiological significance in the New Testament."[48] He goes on to state, "The table fellowship of the Jerusalem Church is uniquely inclusive. Sinners, tax collectors, and all marginalized people in the periphery of the Jewish society are discovering their unconditional acceptance in the table fellowship of the Church."[49] Furthermore, like the practice of sharing possessions with the needy, this distinctive social practice of table fellowship reflects the ministry of Jesus because, as explored in the chapter about the earthly ministry of Jesus, Jesus already demonstrated and modeled it in his earthly ministry. Thus, early Christians had tasted and learned the inclusive and boundary-crossing practice of table fellowship from the ministry of Jesus before they started to have such a radically inclusive table fellowship. Yao sees the continuity of the practice of table fellowship from Jesus's earthly ministry to the earliest church as he states below:

> Jesus, in particular, has exemplified fraternizing even with the lowly and the outcast of his society. Hence he is accused of being a "glutton and drunkard, and a friend of sinners." The Jerusalem Church, in following the pattern set by Jesus, has similarly learned how table fellowship functions as an inclusive praxis that surmounts the various social boundaries within its Jewish society.[50]

Thus, the two particular social lifestyles—selfless sharing and inclusive table fellowship—vividly portray the early church as a socially-contrast community which reflects the life and teaching of Jesus. This new social reality of the earliest church was not a human invention. Rather, that was already envisioned in God's work of shaping Israel in the Old Testament and in Jesus's earthly ministry. This social distinctiveness of the people of God became reality in the life of the earliest believers through their encounter with the Holy Spirit.

47. For a thorough biblical study on the theme of table fellowship and its missiological implication, see Yao, "Table Fellowship."
48. Yao, "Table Fellowship," ii.
49. Yao, "Table Fellowship," 108.
50. Yao, "Table Fellowship," ii.

The Spiritual Aspect of the Earliest Church's Life

The characterization of the earliest church in Acts 2–5 shows that the church was not only a socially distinctive community but also a profoundly *spiritual* community. The early believers were devoted to the apostles' teaching and testimony and prayer (Acts 2:42), praised God (Acts 2:47), spent some time in the temple (Acts 2:46), experienced the divine presence and work of God among them through signs and wonders done by the apostles (Acts 2:43), and listened to the apostles' powerful testimony about the resurrection of Jesus (Acts 4:33). The spiritual character of the earliest church is found throughout the book of Acts. From the very beginning of the earliest church, the church was, first and foremost, a *spiritual* community, a community that was born out of the outpouring of the Holy Spirit (Acts 2:1–4) and continuously sought the guidance and empowerment of the Holy Spirit (Acts 4:23–31). The church's practice of praise and prayer is mentioned after the narrative that follows Acts 2–5.[51] In light of this scriptural description about the spiritual aspect of the earliest church, it becomes obvious that the church which was shaped by the Holy Spirit was profoundly a spiritual community, deeply committed to God. Furthermore, this spiritual aspect of the church's life is interrelated with the social aspect of the church's life since, as pointed out above, the church's social distinctiveness was shaped by its experience of the Holy Spirit, was nothing less than the actualization of what God had originally expected of his people, and resulted from the church's faithful relationship with God.

The Growth of the Church

One subsequent consequence of the earliest church's distinctive—both social and spiritual—life was "having favor with all the people" (Acts 2:47). This phrase indicates that the earliest church kept a good reputation with people outside the church. Two points can be drawn from the meaning of this phrase. First, this consequence indicates that the earliest church was "not an isolated, private club or a hermetically sealed community."[52] Its lifestyle was visible to and recognizable from the surrounding community. This point is supported by the fact that believers gathered in public places such as "the temple" on a daily basis (Acts 2:46). It seems logically legitimate to say that the visibility of their distinctive lifestyle is closely related to the

---

51. For example, see Acts 6:6; 8:15; 10:46; 11:18; 13:2–3; 20:36; 21:20.
52. Bock, *Acts*, 154.

good reputation they had with people outside.[53] Second, the visibility of the church's distinctiveness resulted in a centripetal mode of the earliest church's mission, as the summary of the church's life is concluded with a note that "the Lord added to their number daily those who were being saved" (Acts 2:47).[54] As Bock comments, "This good reputation apparently impacts their witness."[55] The distinctiveness of the church's lifestyle, shaped by its experience with the outpouring of the Holy Spirit, is missionary by nature, drawing people to the church and leading them to salvation.

The Holy Spirit Deals with Sin in the Earliest Church

On the one hand, as discussed above, the description of the earliest church in Acts 2–5 indicates that the church was radically transformed as the church encountered and was filled with the Holy Spirit. However, the earliest church was *not without problems*, both socially and spiritually, as illustrated in the case of Ananias and Sapphira in Acts 5:1–11.[56] Ananias and Sapphira sold a piece of property but did not bring to the apostles all the money they sold their properties for by keeping a part of the money for themselves (Acts 5:1–2). Their pure motivation in sharing the sold possession with others was quite possibly compromised, as indicated in Peter's words to Ananias: "The property was yours to sell or not sell, as you wished. And after selling it, the money was also yours to give away. How could you do a thing like this?" (Acts 5:4 NLT). The fact that Ananias lied suggests that he pretended to do what he was expected to, but actually he did not. What needs to be noticed is that, in Peter's following words, the act of Ananias and Sapphira was not merely a lie to the apostles but to the Holy Spirit (Acts 5:3) and God (Acts 5:4). Their deceitful act was an act of putting "the Spirit of the Lord to the test" (Acts 5:9). Their compromised heart led them to deceive the apostles by bringing only part of the money. The act of deception culminated with sudden death as a divine judgment by the Holy Spirit.

From this episode, two points significant in understanding the reality of the earliest church and the role of the Holy Spirit are identifiable. First, the earliest church was *not* an ideal community. The case of Ananias and Sapphira possibly was not just one case but illustrates the kind of problems

---

53. The historian Stephen Neill recognizes this aspect of the lives of Christians in the first three and half centuries. See Stephen, *History of Christian Missions*, 36–38.

54. Bock, *Acts*, 134; Keener, *Acts*, 1:1038.

55. Bock, *Acts*, 154. Also see Keener, *Acts*, 1:1038.

56. Another biblical case that shows problems in the church is the neglect of Greek-speaking widows during food distribution in Acts 6:1–6.

that the earliest church faced. This point is supported by the contrast with the short account about Barnabas. Logically speaking, it is unlikely that Barnabas was the only believer who "sold a field that belonged to him, then brought the money, and laid it at the apostles' feet" (Acts 4:36–37). Thus, these two cases—of Barnabas and of Ananias and Sapphira—that stand in contrast show that, while believers shared their possession with one another in a selfless manner (as represented by Barnabas), the earliest church was *not ideal* in reality (as illustrated by Ananias and Sapphira). Furthermore, it should be noted that the deceitful act of Ananias and Sapphira was not merely moral but also spiritual because it was an act deceitful to God. Keener observes, "Ananias and Sapphira wanted to join God's community while also retaining their personal autonomy from God's authority. They thereby risked infiltrating God's church with Satan's agenda."[57] Thus, the matter at issue was a sin against God, epitomizing spiritual problems among believers.

Second, it was the Holy Spirit who dealt with the sin of Ananias and Sapphira, as indicated by their sudden death. A case parallel to this case is found in a previous chapter's section that discussed ways that God dealt with sins among the Israelites during the wilderness period of the Old Testament narrative. When Ananias and Sapphira suddenly died as judgment by God for deceiving and testing him with their possessions, "great fear seized the whole church and all who heard of these things" (Acts 5:11), keeping the earliest church from being corrupted by sin against God, which could have resulted in failing to fulfill the missionary vocation of the church. As Bock states, "such a divine act serves to remind the community of its call to holiness and its loyalty to God."[58] The Holy Spirit's direct act of judgment for purifying his people is not a new one that suddenly developed in the book of Acts.[59] As already looked into in chapter 2, biblical cases similar to this occasion are also found in the Old Testament narrative. From the moment God called the people of Israel, he continued to purify them from sin which ruined their relationship with God. God's concern about sin was significantly related to their missionary vocation because failure in their relationship with God could directly result in failing their missionary vocation.

In conclusion, this biblical episode of Ananias and Sapphira can be viewed as a biblical case that shows, first, that the earliest church was *not* an ideal community but was struggling with social and spiritual sins, and, second, that the inward transformation of early Christians—embodying a

---

57. Keener, *Acts*, 2:1183.
58. Bock, *Acts*, 227.
59. Keener, *Acts*, 2:1193.

social and spiritual reality of the kingdom of God—was intimately related to their *encounter with God in the Holy Spirit*.

Summary

To sum up, the earliest church's missional formation in its early stage was the result of its encounter with the Holy Spirit. The outpouring of the Holy Spirit shaped the inward life and outward ministry of the earliest church. On the one hand, early believers became bold witnesses of Jesus. On the other hand, they were transformed into a new *social* reality, which embodied and practiced the inclusive nature of the kingdom of God that Jesus demonstrated and taught, and a *spiritual* community, which deeply committed to God. The earliest church's distinctiveness in its social and spiritual life impacted the church's mission by earning a good reputation among the people outside the church, and, by extension, resulting in a centripetal force of the church's mission. Hence, the mission of the earliest church, shaped by its encounter with the Holy Spirit, was both centrifugal and centripetal. In this sense, the early stage of the earliest church can be viewed as a biblical case in which, by encountering the Holy Spirit, the missionary character of the church was *holistically* formed.

Another finding from the earliest church's missional formation in its early stage is that the church's transformation by the Holy Spirit was not a one-sided event. The earliest church expressed its dependence on and trust in God through its corporate prayer; the outpouring of the Holy Spirit was God's answer to their prayer. The earliest church was desiring and expecting Jesus's promise to be fulfilled in Acts 2, and explicitly sought to be empowered by the Holy Spirit in prayer in Acts 4. Hence, it can be said that the transformation of the earliest church was not forced to irresistibly happen by the outpouring of the Holy Spirit, but, rather, it entailed the earliest church's complete trust in and full dependence on God.

Finally, the earliest church was far from being a perfect church without problems, as indicated by the case of Ananias and Sapphira. The church struggled with social and spiritual temptations within it. Particularly, the fact that the sin of Ananias and Sapphira was resolved by the Holy Spirit's intervention is parallel to the case of God's dealing with Israel's sin in the Old Testament narrative. Both Israel in the Old Testament and the earliest church in the New Testament show that the fulfillment of what they were called to be would be impossible without God's presence and work among them. This problem of sin in the earliest church, like the case of Ananias and Sapphira, implies that the presence and work of the Holy Spirit in the church is a vital factor to the fulfillment of the church's missionary vocation.

C. The Holy Spirit Shapes the Earliest Church in a *Crosscultural* Context

Since the Day of Pentecost, the earliest church found itself outwardly witnessing about Jesus and inwardly being transformed as a contrast community that embodied the life and teaching of Jesus and was deeply committed to God. However, the earliest church's mission did not go beyond the particularity of Jewish ethnic boundary yet. This section looks into ways that the Holy Spirit guided the earliest church to overcome its cultural captivity in order to have it participate in God's global mission, by exploring the story of Cornelius's conversion (Acts 10) and its transformational impact on the earliest church through Peter's mediatory role (Acts 11).

Cornelius's Conversion, and the Beginning of the Gentile Mission

Before analyzing the story of Cornelius's conversion, it might be helpful to see the place of Acts 10–11 within the larger context of the book of Acts. The place and role of Acts 10–11 in the unfolding narrative of the development of the Gentile mission in the book of Acts provides a clue to the relationship between Cornelius's conversion and the beginning of the earliest church's Gentile mission.

The connection between Cornelius's conversion and the beginning of the Gentile mission in the narrative of the book of Acts is implied in the wider context of Acts 9–11. The book of Acts mentions the first fruits of the Gentile mission, namely the first multicultural church at the city of Antioch (Acts 13), not right after Paul's conversion (Acts 9:1–19), but after another conversion, that is, Cornelius's conversion (Acts 10), which resulted in the church's conversion toward God's global mission (Acts 11:1–18). This observation at least implies that there is a connection between the expansion of the Jerusalem Church's understanding of its missionary vocation and the beginning of the Gentile mission. Harold Dollar states, "Acts 10 makes it clear that the major obstacle to a mission to the Gentiles was not the reluctance of the Gentiles to embrace the gospel but the theological difficulties Jews had to overcome before they could preach to Gentiles."[60] The earliest church, originally rooted in God's election of the people of Israel, renewed and gathered by Jesus, and empowered and guided by the Holy Spirit, came to be challenged to embrace God's global mission. As Van Engen points out, "From this episode [of Acts 10] the entire Gentile mission flows."[61] The following discussion closely look at two consecutive events in Acts 10–11: Cornelius's Conversion (Acts 10) and its impact on the Jerusalem Church (Acts 11).

Peter's Conversion by Cornelius's Conversion[62]

The story of Cornelius's conversion begins with God who prepared and led the whole process of the event in Acts 10. First of all, an angel of God appeared before Cornelius in order to deliberately arrange a meeting with Peter by telling him to send for Peter (Acts 10:1–7). It was the act of God who accepted Cornelius's prayers and alms (Acts 10:4). Then Peter saw a vision, in which he saw all kinds of four-footed animals, including unclean animals, on a sheet which was coming down from heaven and the Holy Spirit told Peter to kill and eat them (Acts 10:11–13).[63] The way that Peter responded to the Holy Spirit in the vision shows that Peter would not have overcome his Jewish ethnic boundary without the Holy Spirit's guidance. Peter refused the Holy Sprit's instruction, because of the law which forbade the people of Israel to eat unclean animals.[64] In light of the whole narrative of Cornelius's conversion, the Holy Spirit's intent for the vision obviously was not about animals but about people, particularly about the Gentiles.[65] Polhill states, "Some scholars feel that Peter's vision dealt more with food laws than with interaction with Gentiles. This is to overlook the fact that

---

60. Dollar, *St. Luke's Missiology*, 171.

61. Van Engen, "Peter's Conversion," 136.

62. This study defines the meaning and scope of conversion broadly insofar as its meaning ranges from religious conversion to Christian faith (as in the case of Cornelius's conversion) to significant transformation in theology and practice of a believer or a community of faith (as in the case of Peter's transformation). For this study's definition of conversion, see the Definition of Key Terms in chapter 1.

63. In Acts 10:13, Peter heard "a voice" and, in Acts 10:19, it was "the Spirit" ("the Holy Spirit" in NLT) who was speaking to Peter. Based on verses 13 and 19, it can be said that the voice Peter heard in verse 13 was the voice of the Holy Spirit.

64. For the law on clean and unclean animals, see Lev 11.

65. While scholars disagree on whether food laws were indeed abrogated by this vision, the focus of this vision was not the food law but the Gentiles, as indicated in Peter's words about the Gentiles he met: "God has shown me that I should not call anyone profane or unclean" (Acts 10:28).

the two are inextricably related. In Leviticus 20:24b–26 the laws of clean and unclean are linked precisely to Israel's separation from the rest of the nations."[66] Thus, as F. F. Bruce points out, "The animals in the vision are parabolic of human beings: Peter is being prepared to accept Cornelius's invitation to visit him."[67] Whether the vision was about food or about Gentiles, Peter could not accept because of the law of separation based on clean and unclean divisions. Peter's response is quite understandable because keeping the law has to do with his Jewish identity. Thus, as Dollar comments, "Peter's refusal to eat these unclean animals should not be interpreted as disobedience on his part. Peter's refusal is based on his commitment to the Mosaic law and is an indication of his orthodoxy."[68] The fact that this vision was repeated three times (Acts 10:16) suggests this point. On the one hand, the threefold repetition of the interaction between the Holy Spirit and Peter "reinforces that God is speaking and is to be believed."[69] On the other hand, it also indicates how difficult it was for Peter to violate the food law. As Richard P. Thompson comments, the repetition accentuates "Peter's misunderstanding and stubborn refusal to heed."[70]

In the following scene, the Holy Spirit continuously plays a deliberate and pivotal role in interactions between Peter and the Gentiles sent by Cornelius. While Peter was "greatly puzzled" about the vision, not able to understand its meaning, three Gentiles sent by Cornelius arrived at Peter's place and looked for him (Acts 10:17–18). At that moment, the Holy Spirit prompted him to meet the Gentiles without doubting because they were sent by the Holy Spirit (Acts 10:19–21). Through the guidance of the Holy Spirit, Peter was brought into contact with the Gentiles beyond the limit that Jewish law allowed (Acts 10:28); he allowed them to enter and stay in his house and even went with them to the house of Cornelius (Acts 10:23). Throughout what he experienced under the guidance of the Holy Spirit, Peter came to learn that God removed the boundary between Jews and Gentiles, as indicated when he said, "God has shown me that I should not call anyone profane or unclean" (Acts 10:28). He came to realize that "God shows no partiality" (Acts 10:34).

Then, in the following narrative of this episode, Peter's encounter with the Holy Spirit in Cornelius's house led him to a *further* theological

---

66. Polhill, *Acts*, 255. Also see Gaventa, *Acts of the Apostles*, 165–66. There has been disagreement on whether Gentiles are part of the purity system of Israel. For different views of this issues, see Miller, "Reading Law as Prophecy," 81n26.

67. Bruce, *Acts of the Apostles*, 256.

68. Dollar, *St. Luke's Missiology*, 82.

69. Bock, *Acts*, 389.

70. Thompson, *Acts*, 206.

paradigm shift in understanding the salvation that God was bringing to the world. While Peter was witnessing about Jesus—his life, death and resurrection to the Gentiles at Cornelius's house (Acts 10:34–43), "the Holy Spirit fell upon on all who heard the word" (Acts10:44) and "even on the Gentiles in Cornelius's house" (Acts 10:45). When Peter and other Jewish believers eye-witnessed the Gentiles "speaking in tongues and extolling God" (Acts 10:46), they were "astounded," indicating that they did not expect that it would happen even to the Gentiles almost in the same way that it happened to Jewish believers on the day of Pentecost.[71] Peter's immediate response was to baptize in the name of Jesus those Gentiles who received the Holy Spirit. Peter was initially not able even to imagine the salvation of Gentiles, but, as indicated in Peter's act of baptizing them, now he came to be fully convinced that God's salvation is not limited to Jews but is open to Gentiles. For Peter, the outpouring of the Holy Spirit upon the Gentiles was God's confirmation that the church should not reject Gentiles, based on ethnical differences, but must embrace them, based on the evidence of the work of the Holy Spirit among them.

Two points significant for understanding the role of the Holy Spirit in shaping the earliest church can be drawn from the analysis of Acts 10. First, what should be noted in this episode is that God is "the dominant actor throughout this episode, not humans."[72] It was a divine instruction from God that the earliest church's mission should not be limited to Jews and that God's salvation should reach out to the Gentiles through the earliest church's mission. As Marshall states, "This was no merely human decision, but that it was the result of God's clear guidance."[73] Second, as Guder states, Peter's understanding of Christ "was deepened, and his own sense of the scope of the gospel was revised – and expanded."[74] While Acts 10 is predominantly known as the story about Cornelius's conversion, the broader context of this event within the book of Acts suggests that God's intention in this episode was to open Peter's eyes to see what God was initiating to fulfill his global mission. Dollar points out:

---

71. The similarity between these two events is undeniable, not least because, in both cases, those who were experiencing the outpouring of the Holy Spirit were enabled to speak in tongues and praised God (Acts 2:4, 10:46, 11:17).

72. Dollar, *St. Luke's Missiology*, 86. While it is true that scriptural evidence shows that it was the Holy Spirit whom Peter encountered, the episode as a whole was planned and initiated by God who accepted and remembered Cornelius's prayers and alms (Acts 10:4, 31). Peter also admitted that it was God who acted behind the whole event of Cornelius's conversion (Acts 10:28, 33, 34).

73. Marshall, *Acts of the Apostles*, 181.

74. Guder, *Continuing Conversion*, 89.

> What happened to Peter here in chapter 10 . . . was perhaps more important, and certainly much more demanding psychologically and intellectually, than what happened to Cornelius. From one standpoint the conversion of the Gentiles was no problem for God; the difficulty was in bringing the Jewish Christians to see that Gentiles did not need to become Jews as they became Christians.[75]

As Van Engen also observes, "The radical transformation and conversion here is ascribed to Peter, not to Cornelius."[76]

The Earliest Church's Conversion by Peter's Conversion

The significance of Peter's theological transformation is found in the following chapter, Acts 11, in which Peter played a pivotal role in the theological transform of the earliest church. The episode of Cornelius's conversion does not end with Peter's paradigm shift on salvation and the church's mission, but also led the leaders of the earliest church to experience the same paradigm shift. As a main character in this episode, Peter represents the earliest church since he was the leader of the church. Thus, it is logical that Peter's view of mission is not different from the earliest church's, considering his leadership position and influence on the church.[77] When apostles and believers in Judea heard what Peter did with the Gentiles, they criticized Peter for his contact with them (Acts 11:1–3). Their reaction to Peter is reminiscent of Peter's refusal to obey the Holy Spirit's command to kill and eat unclean animals in the vision and suggests that, like Peter, they never entertained the idea that salvation was available to the Gentiles. As Köstenberger and O'Brien state, "the early church resisted the idea of Gentiles being evangelized directly or accepted into the Christian fellowship without first becoming Jewish proselytes."[78]

However, Peter's testimony about what the Holy Spirit did to him and to the Gentiles "not only silenced his critics but led to a recognition by the church that salvation was available for the Gentiles."[79] As Wright states, "The conversion of Cornelius astonished Peter and his friends and then the rest of the church. They had to recognize it as nothing less than an act

---

75. Dollar, *St. Luke's Missiology*, 87.

76. Van Engen, "Peter's Conversion," 136.

77. For the relationship between Peter and the Jerusalem Church, see Donfried, "Peter," 253–54.

78. Köstenberger and O'Brien, *Salvation to the Ends of the Earth*, 143.

79. Marshall, *Acts of the Apostles*, 181.

of God."[80] Those who heard his witness said, "So then, even to Gentiles God has granted repentance that leads to life" (Acts 11:18). What they said in this verse indicates that they came to know that their mission is not limited to Jews but is to reach out to Gentiles, because God's salvation is also available to the Gentiles.

As Van Engen states, "For the early Jewish church, the Holy Spirit's coming to Cornelius and his household constituted a radical transforming moment, a major paradigm shift."[81] This analysis of Acts 11 shows that the culmination of the whole event in Acts 10–11 was not just Peter's conversion but also "the [beginning of the] conversion of the church from ethnocentrism to multiculturalism."[82] The ending of this episode shows that the church, whose understanding of salvation was confined by their Jewish ethnic identity, was transformed to accept the fact that God's salvation was already reaching Gentiles. This broadening of the church's understanding of salvation also means that the eyes of the earliest church began to be open to the Gentile mission, being further prepared to participate in God's global mission. The realization that salvation is not limited to Jews reveals that the earliest church's mission would be no longer limited to Jews, but should reach out to Gentiles. In this sense, it can be said that God in this episode aimed at a paradigm shift of the earliest church's understanding of the mission of God and the mission of the church. As Flemming states, "The story of announcing God's acceptance of Gentiles like Cornelius is actually a tale of two conversions: the conversion of Cornelius to faith in Christ and the conversion of Peter (and ultimately the church) to a radically new vision of God's boundless mission."[83] As a result, "the Jerusalem church subsequently accepted the Gentiles' conversion to Jesus the Messiah without insisting that they come via the Jewish route."[84] Ever since, the early church found itself in the midst of God's *trans-ethnic* mission. The three conversions in the story of Cornelius's conversion shows God's concern about *the conversion of the church* toward its missionary vocation.

The three conversions in Acts 10–11 show that God was concerned with *the conversion of the church* toward its missionary vocation as well as the conversion of Gentiles. Guder notes, "Even the disciple of Jesus who was eyewitness to the salvation events needed continuing conversion."[85] It

---

80. Wright, *Knowing Jesus*, 172.
81. Van Engen, "Peter's Conversion," 136.
82. Park, "Hospitality as Context for Evangelism," 388.
83. Flemming, *Recovering the Full Mission of God*, 153.
84. Köstenberger and O'Brien, *Salvation to the Ends of the Earth*, 144.
85. Guder, *Continuing Conversion*, 89. Also see Dollar, *St. Luke's Missiology*, 90.

was God who initiated the Gentile mission, but he did it in cooperation with Peter who was a leader of the earliest church, in order to shape the church to participate in God's global mission. This point is implicitly indicated by the fact that only after this paradigm shift of the earliest church's understanding of its missionary vocation did the narrative in the book of Acts change its focus toward the Gentile mission with a first reference to a church at Antioch, which was theologically and ethnically different from the church of Jerusalem.[86]

Summary

In Acts 10–11, God continued to shape the earliest church toward God's global mission in and through the Holy Spirit. While the earliest church was already a missionary community in its early stage (Acts 2–5), the biblical evidence from Acts 10–11 shows that the earliest church was still bound to their ethnic boundary and could not understand nor embrace the inclusive and universal nature of the kingdom of God. However, in its encounter with the Holy Spirit, the earliest church moved one more step closer toward understanding the universal nature of God's mission in which it was called to participate.

Act 10–11 is the story of a threefold conversion because, as Lesslie Newbigin points out, "this is not of the conversion of Cornelius but also of Peter and of the church."[87] The earliest church's encounter with the Holy Spirit, who was outpoured upon the Gentiles in Acts 10–11, ultimately resulted in its theological transformation, leading it to understand and embrace God's global mission in which salvation is available even to the Gentiles. As Brian S. Rosner states, "In the conversion of Cornelius (9:32—11:18), Luke presents a full historical and theological justification for the universalism of the gospel."[88] The earliest church, which was a witness of Jesus among Jews, came to realize that the church was called to be a witness of Jesus not only to Jews but also to the Gentiles.

Four findings from Acts 10–11 provide implications significant to the nature of the church's missional conversion. First, this episode suggests that the earliest church's paradigm shift in understanding salvation and its mission would not have taken place without *the guidance of God in and through the Holy Spirit*. This finding suggests that this divine intervention

---

86. For more details on this transition of focus in the book of Acts, see the discussion on the context of the Jerusalem Council in the following section.

87. Newbigin, *Open Secret*, 59.

88. Rosner, "Process of the Word," 227.

was indispensable in order for Peter and other leaders of the earliest church to overcome their ethnocentric view of salvation and mission. As Rosner observes, "in the so-called conversion of Peter, we see the lengths to which God went to overcome the reluctance of Jewish Christians to preach the word to Gentiles (visions, trances, angels and the Spirit)."[89] What led the earliest church to the transformation was nothing but revelation from God in and through the Holy Spirit. This point provides one implication for the missional conversion of the church: *The missional conversion of the church involves the church's encounter with God in and through the Holy Spirit.*

Second, while God was the main transforming agent in this episode, *this case should not be viewed as a one-sided event* in which Peter and other leaders of the earliest church were irresistibly forced to accept what the Holy Spirit revealed about its mission to the Gentiles. While the Holy Spirit guided and convinced them about what he would reveal to them, it was their willingness to accept what they learned from the Holy Spirit.

This point becomes clear when this episode is compared with the story of the prophet Jonah. Shawn B. Redford recognizes the similarities between Peter's conversion (Acts 10) and the story of Jonah. Both of the two cases illustrate "God's struggle to involve the Jews in mission."[90] Redford states, "With Peter, each situation is not as brazenly against God's mission as Jonah, but the similarities strikingly demonstrate the longevity and continuity of the obstacles that God faced to involve Israel in mission to the nations."[91] While Redford's observation about the continuity between these two cases is identifiable, the response of Peter (and the earliest church's leaders) to the revelation from God stands in contrast to Jonah's refusal to accept God's mercy to the people of Nineveh. The prophet Jonah rejected God's compassion to the people of Nineveh, being angry at God's forgiveness of them (Jonah 4). On the contrary, in the conclusion of the story of Cornelius's conversion, Peter and other church leaders embraced God's revelation that salvation is available to the Gentiles. Peter said to other leaders of the earliest church, "If then God gave them the same gift that he gave us when we believed in the Lord Jesus Christ, who was I that I could hinder God?" (Acts 11:11). After Peter's critics heard his testimony, they not only "were silenced" but also "praised God" (Acts 11:18). They humbly accepted the fact with awe and joy.[92] Furthermore, for the first

---

89. Rosner, "Process of the Word," 227.
90. Redford, *Missiological Hermeneutics*, 238.
91. Redford, *Missiological Hermeneutics*, 238–39.
92. The Jerusalem Church's joyful response to salvation of Gentiles is also plainly found in Acts 15. When Paul and Barnabas visited the Jerusalem Council, their report of the conversion of the Gentiles "brought great joy to all the believers" of the Jerusalem

time, the Jerusalem Church sent Barnabas as a crosscultural missionary to Antioch and he consolidated the faith of Gentile believers there (Acts 11:22–26). One implication derived from this observation is that the missional conversion of the church is not a one-sided event from God, but requires the church's *willingness* to learn from God.

Third, this case introduces one new aspect of the church's missional conversion: *the missional conversion of the church came from its encounter with the Holy Spirit in a crosscultural context.* This is a new factor that emerged as the church began to engage with Gentiles under the guidance of the Holy Spirit. In his analysis of how Peter came to have a correct understanding of God's missional intention, Redford argues that his missionary experience served as a hermeneutical lens to him when he interpreted God's missional intention. He states:

> Despite the fact that Peter is not flooded with Old Testament understandings of God's mission, *he does correctly interpret God's missionary concern for the Gentiles based ultimately on his missionary experience.* As such, Peter uses his missionary experience as a hermeneutical lens to unknowingly develop an appropriate biblical and missiological interpretation of the existing body of Scripture.[93]

As Redford observes, "The ultimate event in Peter's correct interpretation is his observation of the Holy Spirit being received by the Gentiles in the midst of his missionary experience."[94] The earliest church went through its paradigm shift of understanding its mission as it encountered the Holy Spirit *in a crosscultural context*. Peter witnessed what the Holy Spirit did to Gentiles and learned from it, and the earliest church also learned from Peter's testimony about what the Holy Spirit did to the Gentiles. The story of Acts 10–11 reveals that, as Newbigin comments, "mission changes not only the world but also *the church*."[95]

Lastly, the way that the earliest church went through a paradigm shift is not a direct encounter with the Holy Spirit, but *through Peter's testimony*. The factor that transformed the earliest church in this case is the interaction between Peter and other leaders of the earliest church. On the one hand, this episode is the story of the earliest church's encounter with God in and through the Holy Spirit. However, the earliest church's leaders did not directly encounter the Holy Spirit, but indirectly through Peter's

---

Church (Acts 15:3).

93. Redford, *Missiological Hermeneutics*, 245. Italics in original.
94. Redford, *Missiological Hermeneutics*, 245.
95. Newbigin, *Open Secret*, 59. Emphasis added.

testimony. Peter played a crucial role for the earliest church's transformation by sharing his experience and reflection; the leaders of the earliest church responded to Peter both critically and humbly. In this sense, Peter served as a mediator between the Holy Spirit and the earliest church's leaders. What Peter directly experienced throughout Acts 10 is indirectly experienced by other leaders of the church. One implication that comes from this point is that the way that the church encounters God for its missional conversion is *not* limited to a direct experience. This case shows that *mutual interaction with one another* within the church is also a way that God uses to transform the church toward its missionary vocation.

D. The Holy Spirit Shapes the Earliest Church in an *Intercultural* Context

While the earliest church came to find itself in the midst of God's global mission in Acts 10–11, another moment, in which the earliest church moved another step toward being an instrument of God's global mission, is found in the case of the Jerusalem Council in Acts 15. This section explores the way that the Jerusalem Church experienced another paradigm shift regarding its mission. This study of the Jerusalem Council argues that, because of the *intercultural* nature of the Jerusalem Council, the council can be viewed as a biblical case most relevant to the church in today's globalizing context.

Context: from Crosscultural Context to Intercultural Context[96]

The theological transformation of the Jerusalem Church in Acts 10–11 took place in a *crosscultural* context (from a Jewish believer to Gentiles). The context of this story was crosscultural in a sense that Christian faith has spread by

---

96. The term *crosscultural* refers to or focuses on *crossing* cultural boundaries. For example, crosscultural mission means the *spreading* of Christian faith from one culture to another culture, but crosscultural mission also has an intercultural dimension. Unlike the term *crosscultural*, the term *intercultural* is concerned primarily with *interaction* between different cultures. According to the Merriam-Webster Dictionary, the term *intercultural* means "occurring between or involving two or more cultures." In theology, the term *intercultural* is used to refer to interaction between different local theologies, which are shaped in and by different local contexts (e.g., intercultural theology). Lalsangkima Pachuau views the term *crosscultural* as a "one-way activity" and the term *intercultural* as a "two-way interaction" in a theologizing process. Pachuau, "Gospel and Culture." In this study, the term *intercultural* is used in the same way that it is used in theology.

crossing a cultural boundary. However, as will be explained, the context of the Jerusalem Council (Acts 15) was not crosscultural, but *intercultural*, created by a crosscultural mission to the Gentiles. After the conversion of Cornelius, the gospel began to spread, crossing ethnic-cultural boundaries from Jews to Gentiles (Acts 11–14), and a number of Gentiles "became believers and turned to the Lord" (Acts 11:21). Regarding mission among Gentiles and their conversion in Acts 11–14, two observations are significant for understanding the intercultural context of the Jerusalem Council.

First, as Brian Rapske states, "These mission thrusts are universally assessed by Luke in terms of a *divinely* given success."[97] On the one hand, the conversion of large numbers of Gentiles was the result of witnessing done by Greek-speaking Jewish believers at Antioch (Acts 11:20). On the other hand, Acts 11:21 says, "*The hand of the Lord was with them*, and a great number became believers and turned to the Lord." As Wright notes, "The Gentile mission was an act of *God* before it ever became a strategy of the church" and, "Once again the church *was compelled* to recognize *the hand of God*."[98] This verse alludes to the risen Jesus's promise of his continuous presence with his disciples (Matt 28:20), indicating that, as he promised, the risen Jesus was with his followers in mission.[99] In this regard, the spread of the gospel among Gentiles and the conversion of Gentiles should not be viewed purely as due to human efforts or fruits produced by them, but resulted from the work of God among Gentiles through his human witnesses. One implication derived from this observation is that the theology represented by the reality of Gentile converts was not a theological construction achieved merely by human philosophy, but *reflects the work of God* who was at work among Gentiles through his human witnesses.

97. Rapske, "Opposition to the Plan of God and Persecution," 242.

98. Wright, *Knowing Jesus*, 172.

99. This connection with Matt 28:20 is supported in two ways. First, some scholars view the term "the Lord" as a reference to the risen Jesus. See Twelftree, *People of the Spirit*, 21n44; Thompson, *Acts of the Risen Lord Jesus*, 52. Second, the word "hand" often means "presence" in the Bible. Keener states, "In Luke-Acts, God's 'hand' being with a person can be equivalent to God being 'with' him or her in a positive way." Keener, *Acts*, 2:1842. When these scriptural observations are taken together, the phrase, "the hand of the Lord with them," can mean the presence of the risen Jesus with them. Thus, in Luke's assessment, human agents alone were not the agent of the Gentile mission but it was *God* with them. This point is already established in Acts 10, in which, as discussed above, it was God who opened the door of salvation beyond Jews to Gentiles. God not only initiated but also continued the Gentile mission through his witnesses. As Keener states, "God showed his blessing on this ministry to Gentiles, just as he had shown it with regard to Peter's ministry to a Gentile household (11:15–17)." Keener, *Acts*, 2:1842. When these scriptural observations are taken together, the phrase, "the hand of the Lord with them," can mean the presence of the risen Jesus with them. Keener, *Acts*, 2:1842.

Second, the Gentile mission resulted in *the birth of a new community of believers at Antioch, which are in many ways different from the church of Jerusalem*. The church of Antioch has several unique characteristics. The first characteristic that differentiated the Antioch Church from the Jerusalem Church was ethnic diversity. David G. Peterson observes:

> What is most obvious is the ethnic diversity of the leadership of this church. *Barnabas* was from Cyprus, *Simeon* called *Niger* may have been from Africa (*Niger* is a Latinism, meaning "black"), and *Lucius of Cyrene* certainly came from North Africa . . . Mann is described as having been *brought up with Herod the tetrarch*, the ruler of Galilee when Jesus was born . . ., and *Saul* was from Tarsus.[100]

As Keener comments, "They were . . . from a geographically diverse background, emphasizing the cosmopolitan character of the church God used at the foundation of the Gentile mission."[101]

Another characteristic of the Antioch Church is that believers at Antioch were, for the first time, called Christians (Acts 11:26). As the word "Christian" indicates, this community of believers was a messianic community centered on Jesus. Flemming states, "This new name communicates a new status based not on ethnic or prior religious distinctions, but on faith in Christ."[102] This characteristic can be viewed as deriving from the primary fact that the Antioch Church was multiethnic, and therefore could not be called part of a Jewish sect. Lastly, the Antioch Church was different from the Jerusalem Church regarding ministry, as indicated in Acts 13. Dunn views the description of the Antioch Church in Acts 13:1–3 as "a hint of a very different kind of community structure and ministry in the churches of the Hellenistic mission" and, thus, the Antioch Church "differs from the discipleship of Jesus's earthly ministry."[103] The intercultural context of the Jerusalem Council was formed because of the existence of the Antioch Church, which was in many ways different from the Jerusalem Church. As C. K. Barrett comments on the background of the Jerusalem Council, "all that is necessarily presupposed is the existence in Antioch . . . of a mixed church containing . . . uncircumcised Gentiles as well as Jews."[104]

---

100. Peterson, *Acts of the Apostles*, 374–75. Emphasis added.

101. Keener, *Acts*, 2:1982.

102. Flemming, *Contextualization*, 44. Also see Towner, "Mission Practice and Theology," 422.

103. Dunn, *Unity and Diversity*, 114. Also see Dunn, *Acts of the Apostles*, 172.

104. Barrett, *Acts 15–28*, 697.

The primary cause of the Jerusalem Council was theological difference between the Antioch Church and a group of Jewish believers. Some Jewish believers who came from Judea complained about Gentile believers, saying, "Unless you are circumcised according to the custom of Moses, you cannot be saved" (Acts 15:1). The Antioch Church sent Paul and Barnabas and others to the Jerusalem Church in order to deal with the theological issue. When they arrived at the Jerusalem Church, some Jewish believers who belonged to the sect of the Pharisee claimed against them, "It is necessary for them to be circumcised and ordered to keep the law of Moses" (Acts 15:5). The Jerusalem Council was held in order to discuss two different theological understandings of the gospel about salvation. As Flemming observes, the issue emerged as "an *intercultural* conflict"[105] because it was "genuine theological disagreement within the young church, centered around two competing interpretations of the gospel."[106] In this sense, the issue that caused the Jerusalem Council has emerged in an intercultural context.

Issue: the Gospel and the Church's Identity and Its Mission

In Acts 10–11, the matter at issue was primarily ethnicity, more specifically, ethnical Jewishness, in terms of whether or not Gentiles can be saved. After all, Peter and the Jewish believers came to realize that salvation from God is not only for Jews but also for Gentiles. Thus, the theological legitimization of the Gentile mission already settled down in Acts 10–11.

On the one hand, the issues in Acts 10–11 and the Jerusalem Council in Acts 15 were similar in the sense that both were ethnic issues.[107] As Cornelis Bennema states, the issue at the council was "revisiting the agreement of 11:18."[108] However, as Schnabel points out, "the two meetings deal with different questions."[109] It is because Acts 15 "presumes the admission of Gentiles into the church."[110] This means that the issue at the council was different from the issue at Acts 10–11. As Barrett observes from Acts 15:1, "the Jewish believers who raise the issue do not say: Gentiles cannot be

---

105. Flemming, *Contextualization*, 43.

106. Flemming, *Contextualization*, 45.

107. Richard J. Bauckham identifies five conferences related to ethnical issues. For Bauchham, Acts 11:1–18 is the first of them, Acts 15 is the fifth of them. See Bauckham, "James, Peter and the Gentiles," 137–38.

108. Bennema, "Ethnic Conflict," 762.

109. Schnabel, *Jesus and the Twelve*, 715.

110. Bennema, "Ethnic Conflict," 762.

saved at all. They say: You cannot be saved unless you are circumcised."[111] Thus, the issue was "what constitutes true conversion in the first place."[112] Moreover, one sect of Jewish believers, identified as Pharisaic Jewish believers in Acts 15:5, at Jerusalem claimed, "It is necessary for them to be circumcised and ordered to keep the law of Moses."[113] If Acts 5:1 and Acts 5:15 are put together, the central issue that caused the Jerusalem Council was not whether salvation is available to Gentiles, but the *condition* for salvation of Gentiles. For the group of Pharisaic Jewish believers, the gospel and Jewish tradition were understood as inseparable, if not the same. Flemming helpfully summarizes the issue as below:

> What precipitates the Jerusalem Council is not simply that Gentiles were being evangelized, but more importantly the *conditions* of their membership in the messianic community. Must Gentiles become "naturalized Jews," that is, Jewish proselytes, and live like Jews in order to have a place in the people of God? Today we might put the question in terms of whether Gentile believers had to become culturally Jewish as a condition of their salvation and as part of their obedience to Christ, or whether they could be accepted in all their "Gentile-ness."[114]

The Essence of the Gospel

The issue of the condition for salvation at the Jerusalem Council was fundamentally related to the gospel itself. The issue dealt with at the Jerusalem Council was both ethnic-cultural and theological, dealing with *the essence of the gospel* in relation to ethnic-cultural issues. In Acts 15:1, the Jewish believers insisted on their view of circumcision as the condition for salvation. In Acts 15:5, Pharisaic Jewish believers even demanded that the Gentile believers should follow their Jewish tradition by keeping the law of Moses.[115] What they insisted on regarding Gentile believers was, in

---

111. Barrett, *Acts 15–28*, 699.

112. Wilson, *Luke and the Law*, 72.

113. While, in Acts 15:1, Jewish believers said that circumcision is a condition for salvation, in Acts 15:5 Pharisaic believers did not mention salvation at all. Because of that difference, some scholars argue that Jewish believers in Acts 15:1 and Pharisaic believers in Acts 15:5 are different sects of Jewish believers.

114. Flemming, *Contextualization*, 44–45. Italics in original.

115. There is debate on whether the group of Jewish believers mentioned in Acts 15:1 and the group of Pharisaic Jewish believers mentioned in Acts 15:5 are the same. However, the issues raised by these two groups have the same nature: The necessity of

Larkin's words, "another gospel."[116] This point becomes clearer in light of Galatians 2:1–10, which, among scholars, generally is viewed as a record about Acts 15.[117] In Galatians 2, Paul asserts that a group of Jewish believers who insisted on the requirement of circumcision for salvation attacked the truth of the gospel that he proclaimed among Gentiles (Gal 2:1–10). Thus, as John Stott comments on Acts 15:1:

> They were telling Gentile converts that faith in Jesus was not enough, not sufficient for salvation: they must add to faith circumcision, and to circumcision observance of the law. In other words, they must let Moses complete what Jesus had begun, and let the law supplement the gospel. The issue was immense. The way of salvation was at stake. The gospel was in dispute. The very foundations of the Christian faith were being undermined.[118]

The assertion of the Jewish believers indicates that the Jewish believers confused the gospel with their Jewish tradition. They were not able to distinguish the gospel from their Jewish tradition. They believed that their Jewish tradition was part of the gospel and that, apart from being faithful to their Jewish tradition, the Gentile believers were still not saved and not qualified to join the church. Jewish believers already accepted the universality of the gospel, learning from the story of Cornelius's conversion in Acts 10–11, but this theological dispute about the condition of salvation in Acts 15 implies that, among them, there was confusion about the essence of the gospel which constitutes salvation.

The Church's Identity and Its Mission

Because the gospel is what the church is called to embody and to proclaim, the question about the essence of the gospel is intimately related to the church's identity and mission. First of all, the central issue at the Jerusalem Council was fundamentally about the identity of the church because the gospel is what the church is called to embody in such a way that the church is, in Newbigin's words, "the only hermeneutic of the gospel."[119]

---

following the law of Moses to be saved or to be part of the community of believers. The issue of circumcision in Acts 15:1 is expanded to include the whole law of Moses in Acts 15:5. See Polhill, *Acts*, 324; Bock, *Acts*, 496–97.

116. Larkin, *Acts*, 218.

117. For a general overview of the relationship between Acts 15 and Gal 2, see Keener, *Acts*, 3:2195–2202.

118. Stott, *Spirit, the Church, and the World*, 243.

119. Newbigin, *Gospel in a Pluralist Society*, 227.

Hans Küng states, "It is this Gospel [of Jesus] from which the Church of Jesus Christ took its origin and which in its daily life the Church continues to take its origin."[120] In this sense, the issue that the Jerusalem Council dealt with was closely and inseparably related to the question of what constitutes the church's identity.

This point becomes clear in light of the fact that the issue of the law of Moses, including circumcision, was a matter of identity to Jews. Acts 5:1 and 5:5 show that, among Jewish believers, there was a view that Jewish traditions such as circumcision and the law of Moses were essentially part of the identity of the church as the people of God. Jewish believers who had this opinion insisted that Gentile believers could join the people of God only if they abandoned their Gentile culture and conformed to Jewish traditions. This point is made clearer in view of what circumcision and the law of Moses meant to Jews. The requirement of circumcision which Jewish believers insisted on as the condition for salvation in Acts 15:1 was one of Jews' most important practices, central to Jewish identity.[121] In Acts 15:5, a group of Pharisaic Jewish believers required Gentile believers not only to be circumcised but also to keep the whole law of Moses. Along with circumcision, the law of Moses was what defined Jewish identity.[122] Those who imposed these requirements upon Gentile believers confused Jewish identity with the identity of the church. As David E. Garland comments on Acts 15:1, the issue that Jewish believers raised was "how the church can still regard itself as the true Israel if it disregards the command about circumcision that is linked to God's covenant with Israel."[123] Thus, as Ben Witherington III states, "Luke understands that there had to be a conclusion about what *constituted* the people of God and what *the basis* was for their relationship to God."[124]

Second, because the central issue at the council had to do with the relationship between the gospel and culture, the issue was also about the church's mission. Particularly, the question the council asked and dealt with was closely related to the question of whether or not the church's mission in the global context essentially involves cultural proselytism, which refers to a process in which a person abandons his or her culture in order to be accepted by a community of believers.[125] The Jerusalem Council

---

120. Küng, *Church*, 23.
121. Keener, *Acts*, 3:2215; Thompson, *Acts*, 259.
122. Willimon, *Acts*, 131; Selman, "Law," 511.
123. Garland, *Acts*, 152–53.
124. Witherington, *New Testament History*, 243. Emphasis added.
125. For the meaning of proselytism or proselytes, see Barrett, *Acts 15–28*, 699;

dealt with the issue of whether or not the gospel can be truly universal and transcultural. In this sense, the council faced a missionally critical moment, striving to discuss what the church's mission to non-Jewish people would look like. Thus, the primary agenda at the council was essentially also about the mission of the church.

The intimate relationship between salvation and mission makes this point plain. The theological issue at the council was directly about the *nature of salvation* (Acts 15:1), a doctrine central to the mission of the church. Bosch states, "For Christians, the conviction that God has decisively wrought salvation for all in and through Jesus Christ stands at the very center of their lives."[126] In this sense, Christian mission can be seen as, in Bosch's words, "mediating salvation" to all.[127] That is why the missiologist Johannes Verkuyl defines missiology on a soteriological basis: "Missiology is the study of the salvation activities of Father, Son, and Holy Spirit throughout the world geared toward bringing the kingdom of God into existence."[128] In a similar way, J. D. Gort states, "the motif of soteriology is . . . . the beating heart of the study of mission."[129] Therefore, how the church understands salvation profoundly impacts the church's understanding and practices of mission. In light of the considerations made above, the central issue that the Jerusalem Council dealt with is also closely related to how the church should understand and participate in the mission of God.

Final Statement: Twofold Consensus

Since the council dealt with what constitutes the identity and mission of the church, the final statement of the church council was the council's answer to the issues. The final statement of the Jerusalem Council was twofold: (1) the theological validation of the inclusion of the Gentile believers into the eschatological people of God without following Jewish traditions and (2) the first explicit initiation of fellowship between the Jewish and Gentile believers.[130] James was the most influential in reaching such a final decision

---

Walls, *Missionary Movement in Christian History*, 51–53.

126. Bosch, *Transforming Mission*, 393.

127. Bosch, *Transforming Mission*, 393.

128. Verkuyl, *Contemporary Missiology*, 5.

129. Gort, "Human Distress, Salvation, and Mediation of Salvation," 195.

130. Kurz, *Acts*, 232. Both of them are significant in understanding the nature of missional conversion of the church from both biblical and historical perspectives, as will be discussed later.

and in forming the council's final statement regarding the issues at stake. James's words are found in Acts 15:19–21:

> Therefore I have reached the decision that we should not trouble those Gentiles who are turning to God, but we should write to them to abstain only from things polluted by idols and from fornication and from whatever has been strangled and from blood. For in every city, for generations past, Moses has had those who proclaim him, for he has been read aloud every sabbath in the synagogues.

The council adopted James's suggestions and the whole Jerusalem church sent the council's decision in a form of a letter to the church at Antioch (Acts 15:22–30). When we closely look into James's final decision, we find that he was concerned about not one but two issues. Bruce Chilton identifies these two issues when he states, "what appears as a single meeting in Acts 15 addresses two distinct issues. The first issue was whether non-Jews might be baptized without being circumcised. . . . The second issue was whether such baptized Gentiles could be embraced in a single fellowship with Jews who had been baptized."[131] As far as the first issue, which is a condition for the inclusion of the Gentiles into the eschatological people of God, is concerned, James in verse 19 states, "we should not trouble those Gentiles who are turning to God." On this decision adopted by the council, Flemming states, "the church emphatically rejects the added requirements of circumcision and Torah keeping for Gentiles."[132] Thus, "the Jerusalem Council decisively settles the question for the church that Gentiles could be evangelized without prior conditions and within their own culture."[133] As Bennema states, the council approved the idea that "Gentile believers belonged to the eschatological people of God *as Gentiles*."[134] The unique contribution of the Jerusalem Council within the context of the whole book of Acts is that, as Flemming points out, "What began with an Ethiopian eunuch, what was symbolized by the centurion Cornelius, is now *formalized* by the church."[135]

While James was the one who facilitated a consensus, Peter provided the very theological basis for the inclusion of Gentile believers into the eschatological people of God. Martin Hengel recognizes the significance of Peter's role as he states, "the legitimation of the mission to the Gentiles

---

131. Children, "Purity and Impurity," 993.
132. Flemming, *Contextualization*, 49.
133. Flemming, *Contextualization*, 52.
134. Bennema, "Ethnic Conflict," 760. Italics in original.
135. Flemming, *Contextualization*, 52. Italics in original.

is virtually Peter's last work."¹³⁶ In Acts 15:7–11, Peter reminded those who gathered at the council of the very lesson they learned from the story of Cornelius's conversion, and the conclusion of his testimony is found in Acts 15:11: "we believe that we will be saved through *the grace of the Lord Jesus*, just as they will." The theological basis for salvation of both Jews and Gentiles is *solemnly christological*. As Dunn states, "At all events, 15.11 puts the emphasis back on the central point: That the grace of the Lord Jesus is both the necessary and the sufficient means of salvation for Jew and Gentile."¹³⁷ This verse confirms that, as already established in the discussion about Jesus's earthly ministry in the previous chapter of this study, the identity and mission of the church is rooted in and centered on *Jesus*, not Jewish tradition.

The second immediate outcome of the council, which is practical and context-sensitive, was the council's initiative for fellowship between the Jewish and Gentile believers. This outcome is found in verses 20–21, in which James suggested that the Gentile believers be burdened with no more than four items to avoid—"to abstain only from things polluted by idols and from fornication and from whatever has been strangled and from blood (Acts 15:20)."¹³⁸ There has been a debate on the background and meaning of the four requirements among New Testament scholars,¹³⁹ but the four prohibitions were not related to the central issue—a condition to be part of the eschatological people of God—which caused the Council to take place, but were, in Flemming' words, "nonessential issues for the sake of unity and fellowship."¹⁴⁰ As Flemming points out, "Although these prohibitions have scriptural precedent, it seems best to view them as temporary and context-specific measures designed to avoid unnecessarily offending the Jews, thereby opening the door to full fellowship between Jewish and Gentile Christians."¹⁴¹ Similarly, Longenecker comments on the four prohibitions, but, for him, this instruction is not only "concessions to

---

136. Hengel, *Acts and the History of Earliest Christianity*, 125.

137. Dunn, *Acts*, 219.

138. These four requirements in Acts 15:20 are a little bit altered in Acts 15:29 and 21:25.

139. The different views of the four requirements will not be discussed in this section because they are not necessarily related to the focus of this section.

140. Flemming, *Contextualization*, 50.

141. Flemming, *Contextualization*, 50. This context-sensitivity of the four prohibitions are supported by Paul's way of dealing with Gentile Christians. Flemming states, "When he is mainly dealing with Gentile Christians who live in an intensely pagan environment in Corinth, he can take a more liberal position than the Jerusalem Council: under certain conditions he allows Christians to eat food that has been offered to idols (e.g., 1 Cor 10:25–27)." Flemming, *Contextualization*, 50.

the scruples of others for the sake of harmony within the church" but also of "the continuance of the Jewish-Christian mission."[142] Thus, this second statement of James can be viewed not as the central theological issue that the council wrestled with.

The final statement of the council was the earliest church's theological conformity on the essence of the gospel, the church's identity, and its mission. The council confirmed that the gospel the earliest church is called to proclaim should not be confused with Jewish traditions. The council affirmed that the identity of the church is not conditioned or confined by Jewish identity, which was centered on the Mosaic law, but is based on the work of Jesus.[143] The council prevented the church's mission from cultural proselytism. In a nutshell, the council can be viewed as an event that laid the theological foundation for the *transcultural* nature of the gospel and the church's identity and its mission *for the first time*.[144]

The Jerusalem Council's Impact on the Jerusalem Church

On the surface, the Jerusalem Council seems to impact *only* Gentile believers by formally affirming that they can be saved and join the eschatological people of God *as Gentiles*, but, at another level, the whole of the Jerusalem Council, including its context, process, and outcome, also had a far-reaching transformative impact on the Jerusalem Church.[145]

First, the expansion of the earliest church challenged the Jerusalem Church to recognize a need to embrace Gentile believers as part of the eschatological people of God. As discussed above, the Jerusalem Council took place in an intercultural context, which was consequentially created by the crosscultural spread of the gospel among Gentiles. This intercultural context brought about a new issue that Jewish believers had never faced before. They knew about the eschatological vision of the ingathering of the

---

142. Longenecker, "Luke," 949.

143. This christological basis of the church's identity in Peter's conclusive statement corresponds to the previous chapter about Jesus's earthly ministry, which demonstrated that the disciples had become no longer centered on the law but on Jesus throughout his earthly ministry.

144. The result of the council did not direct the church of Jerusalem to abandon its distinctiveness shaped by its Jewish background. What the council affirmed is that any particular cultural distinctiveness must not function as normative in defining the essence of the gospel and the theological foundation of the church's identity and mission.

145. Most of, if not all, studies on the Jerusalem Council in Acts 15 recognize the council's impact on the Gentile mission, but fail to see the council's impact on the Jerusalem Church.

nations, which had been foretold by the Old Testament prophets and had been affirmed and envisaged by Jesus. They heard about the story of an individual Gentile's conversion in Peter's testimony. However, they were not clear about what the ingathering of the nations would look like in reality; they could not think of a way other than their way of being followers of Jesus *as Jews*. Probably, the only model that the Jewish believers could think of at best for inclusion of the Gentile believers was proselytism, not least because they had seen Gentiles proselytized as God-fearers. Larkin states, "such a 'proselyte model' of Gentile conversion was natural to Jews."[146]

Now they were facing a reality that they did not and could not imagine. From this point of view, the assertion by the Pharisaic believers on the requirement of circumcision for salvation is understandable. As Flemming points out:

> The Pharisees could appeal to both Scripture (e.g., Gen 17:9–14) and a long precedent of tradition in support of their theological position. *For them, circumcision was not simply an optional cultural form; it was a matter of religious life and death*—the indispensable symbol of the covenant relationship. If Jewish cultural distinctives, including law observance and the Jewish way of life, were divinely sanctioned, how could they possibly be negotiable?[147]

However, being impacted by the process and result of the Jerusalem Council, the Jewish believers for the first time seriously began to perceive that the gospel, the church's identity, and its mission must not be limited to their Jewish particularity and that *the church is by nature universal* or, in Bennema's words, *"trans-ethnic."*[148] The Jerusalem Council was an event, which was caused by the emergence of the transcultural character of the eschatological people of God and theologically and practically dealt with it. The council led Jewish believers to find themselves more or less as part of the eschatological people of God who are bigger than they thought.

The Jerusalem Council is not merely a historical event, but is relevant and paradigmatic to the church today precisely because of the *intercultural* context in which the church today finds itself.[149] The biblical case of the council provides a biblical model or at least some biblical insights for how churches today can overcome their cultural captivity through intercultural engagement with one another. Flemming puts it this way: "For Luke, the

---

146. Larkin, *Acts*, 219.
147. Flemming, *Contextualization*, 45. Emphasis added.
148. Bennema, "Ethnic Conflict," 756.
149. See Strong and Strong, "Globalizing Hermeneutic."

story of the Jerusalem Council is a paradigmatic narrative. In it we see a pattern of God's people articulating their faith within an *intercultural* context, which carries implications for the church in any generation."[150]

Second, the final decision made by the Jerusalem Council led the Jewish believers to a new understanding of salvation in light of God's work among Gentiles. The decision that Gentile believers do not have to follow Jewish traditions was theologically based on Acts 15:11, in which Peter, reminding the Jewish believers of the lesson that they had already learned from the story of Cornelius's conversion, boldly claimed, "we believe that we will be saved through the grace of the Lord Jesus, just as they will." Peter's argument on salvation is drawn in light of God's mission among Gentiles which he witnessed. The point is that Peter challenged Jewish believers to learn from what God was already doing among Gentiles, as indicated in Acts 15:11: "we believe that we will be saved through the grace of the Lord Jesus, *just as they will.*" Thompson keenly observes this point from this verse: "Surprisingly, Peter does not compare the Gentiles' salvation to that of the Jewish believers. Instead, Peter reverses the order and underscores the *Gentiles'* salvation to disclose the basis of the *Jewish believers'* salvation."[151] As Witherington points out, "Peter's conclusion is that if God accepts them without obedience to the law, how can the church require it of them?"[152] From this point of view, it is clear that the new understanding of salvation was drawn in reflecting God's mission at work among Gentiles. It is in light of God's mission to Gentiles that the Jewish believers' view of salvation, contextualized by their Jewish traditions, was decisively rejected. Once again, they had to admit that their ethnocentric view of salvation was *theologically wrong*.

The council's decision about salvation affirms the transcultural nature of the gospel, but it does not mean that the gospel should not be embodied in a cultural form. Obviously, the council affirmed that Gentile believers can keep their cultural identity. As David Seccombe states, "One of the great strengths of Christianity . . . in every age has been its adaptability to any culture, the basis of which was hammered out at the Jerusalem Council."[153] Likewise, the Jewishness of the Jerusalem Church was not banished completely, as indicated in Acts 21:17–26, which mentions that there were many Jewish believers who "are all zealous for the law" (Acts 21:20). The council did not suggest the *uniformity* of the church, but

---

150. Flemming, *Contextualization*, 48.
151. Thompson, *Acts*, 263. Italics in original.
152. Witherington, *New Testament History*, 245.
153. Seccombe, "New People of God," 366.

affirmed the *diversity* of the church, as both Jewish and Gentiles believers were called to accept each other.

Third, the new understanding of salvation led to a new understanding of the identity of the church in such a way that the whole church came to experience a paradigm shift from an ethnocentric view of the church to a *culturally inclusive* one. As Flemming keenly notes, "the process of doing theology at the council serves to shape and redefine that community."[154] The inclusive nature of the church was discovered, drawing from the transcultural nature of salvation, and this inclusiveness was demonstrated in the process of the Jerusalem Council. Flemming observes the ways the identity of the church was redefined through the council:

> The Jerusalem Council refuses to see the church as an exclusive sect, nor even as an enlarged Israel. Instead, Acts 15 describes a church on a journey to a deeper understanding of its identity as the one people of God comprised of two distinct cultural groups who believe in Jesus.... Acts 15 promotes *a vision of a new people of God potentially inclusive of all peoples*, in which every nation and culture can stand on equal footing before the cross."[155]

Similarly, Bennema states, "The critical factor in the formation of early Christian identity [by the council] was that it was no longer attached to a particular ethno-religious identity."[156] As Dollar points out, one consequence of the council is that "[t]he church has taken a quantum leap in understanding her self-identity."[157] Thus, the council firmly affirmed the transcultural nature of the gospel and of the identity of the church once and for all, and, based on that, the *inclusive, universal* nature of the church was claimed. This theological understanding of the identity of the church was a corrective to the Jewish believers whose view of the church failed to go beyond their traditions. Thus, the Jerusalem Council was *more transformative to the Jewish believers* than Gentile believers. Flemming puts it this way:

> [T]he result of the church's adapting the gospel to new circumstances is *the transformation of individuals and of the community*.... The apostles' testimony confronts and capsizes the ethnocentric worldview of those who thought God's election had endowed them with a permanent "most-favored-nation"

---

154. Flemming, *Contextualization*, 52.
155. Flemming, *Contextualization*, 52. Emphasis added.
156. Bennema, "Ethnic Conflict," 762–63.
157. Dollar, *St. Luke's Missiology*, 170.

status. Luke's attention to the unanimity of the decision (Acts 15:22, 25) implies *a change among the believing Pharisees.*[158]

Fourth, the inclusive view of the church had a tremendous impact on the Jerusalem Church's mission in such a way that *the Gentile mission is no longer hindered but rather stimulated by the Jerusalem Church*, as the narrative of the book of Acts after the Jerusalem Council attests. This point is even clearer in the relationship between the Jerusalem Council (Acts 15) and the Gentile mission by Paul and Silas (Acts 16–20). The whole Jerusalem Church, missionally transformed by the Jerusalem Council, stimulated the spread of the gospel to Gentiles through the work of the Jerusalem Church's representatives, Paul and Silas, among Christians in other places. Bennema states, "With the backing of the Jerusalem decree, Paul carried through this program of a trans-ethnic Christianity effectively (Acts 16–20; Rom 15:18–19)."[159] The following narrative after the Jerusalem Council shows the impact of the council's decision and the delegates sent by the Jerusalem Church to churches in different places. The decision was an encouraging and joyful message to the Antioch Church (Act 15:30). Along with delivering the council's decision, the delegates from Jerusalem strengthened believers in other local areas, resulting in an increased number of believers in those areas (Acts 15:32, 41; 16:5).

The Jerusalem Church's support of the Gentile mission is further indicated by the fact that the biblical narrative of the book of Acts after the Jerusalem Council shifts its focus to the Gentile mission. Thus, the Gentile mission of the church became full-fledged by the Jerusalem Council. As Charles H. Talbert observes, "the extension of the gospel to the Gentiles is followed by an episode of Jerusalem approval."[160] Thus, as Ernst Haenchen notes, "chapter 15 is . . . a turning-point. Not only has the focus shifted from Jerusalem. Not even her daughter congregation in Antioch will now be the stage or protagonist of the action. Macedonia, Athens, Corinth, Ephesus: these will be the new landmarks in the history of the mission."[161] On the one hand, the primary focus in the narrative after the Jerusalem Council, turns to Paul and his Gentile mission. On the other hand, Paul's mission to the Gentiles was not purely independent from the Jerusalem Church, but was carried out with the support of the whole Jerusalem Church not least because he was a missionary sent by the church and because the church theologically endorsed the Gentile mission.

158. Flemming, *Contextualization*, 53. Emphasis added.
159. Bennema, "Ethnic Conflict," 756.
160. Talbert, *Reading Acts*, 136.
161. Haenchen, *Acts*, 462.

Thus, if, as noted earlier, the narrative of the book of Acts was structured by Acts 1:8, the Jerusalem Council can be viewed as an event that proves that God was fulfilling Acts 1:8, in which the whole church is called to be witnesses of Jesus "to the ends of the earth." Through the Jerusalem Council, the Jerusalem Church then found itself more clearly participating in God's global mission. God did not abandon the church when it still struggled with the Gentile mission because of its ethnocentrism. Rather, he equipped the church as an instrument of God's global mission. With the deepened and broadened understanding of the identity and mission of the church, the Jerusalem Church was then ready to better serve as God's missionary people to participate in God's global mission.

The Church's Missional Conversion and Intercultural Engagement

Some scholars attempted to view the Jerusalem Council as a biblical model of contextualization.[162] For example, Flemming states that Acts 15 "offers perhaps the fullest and most significant narrative in the New Testament of the process of doing *contextual* theology by the church."[163] According to Mbachu Hilary, "none of the above biblical '*inculturation* texts' surpasses the inculturation text of Acts 15."[164] On the one hand, the issue that, as mentioned above, the council wrestled with was the relationship between the gospel and culture.[165] However, the Jerusalem Council wrestled not with contextualization itself, but with the transcultural nature or translatability of the gospel, which can be viewed as a foundation of contextualization. The final outcome of the council affirms the transcultural nature of the gospel. The gospel is transcultural because it is translatable to any particular culture. In this sense, the council did not contextualize the gospel, either for the Jewish believers or the Gentile believers. The issue was not how the gospel is relevant to a particular culture, but whether the gospel is transcultural. Thus, what the council actually did was to approve the gospel already contextualized by Gentile believers and corrected the gospel already contextualized by Pharisaic Jewish believers. In this sense, the very issue at the council was

---

162. For instance, see Hilary, *Inculturation Theology*; Strong, "Jerusalem Council."

163. Flemming, *Contextualization*, 43. Emphasis added. While Flemming views the Jerusalem Council—along with the story of Cornelius's conversion—as a biblical case for contextualization, the implications he draws from the Council is more of intercultural dynamics in the church's theologizing rather than of contextualization.

164. Hilary, *Inculturation Theology*, 75.

165. Flemming, *Contextualization*, 44–45.

whether or not the church should affirm the cultural translatability of the gospel. In this regard, the Jerusalem Council does not seem to fit as a biblical case for contextualization.

Rather, the context, outcome, and process of the Jerusalem Council were *intercultural* in character. Both Jewish and Gentile believers had already contextualized theologies. As Flemming comments on this theological tension at the council, "Luke's narrative [in Acts 15] exposes genuine theological disagreement within the young church, centered around two competing interpretations of the gospel."[166] One group contextualized the gospel in light of *Jewish tradition*, but for the other group, the gospel was not held to be necessarily clothed with the Jewish practice of circumcision, taking *faith in Christ* as their very theological basis on which they believed to be saved and to join the eschatological people of God. Thus, the theological conflict here is not a matter of contextualization. What really and actually happened at the council was that the Jewish believers' theology was *theologically* challenged by the indigenous expression of the Gentile believers.

Thus, it might be more appropriate or accurate to say that the result of the Jerusalem Council was *re*-contextualization of the gospel particularly on the side of the Jewish believers. They realized that their view of the gospel mixed with Jewish tradition and, thus, was theologically and missionally inappropriate in light of both Scripture and testimonies about God's mission among Gentiles. C. Peter Wagner bluntly calls the theological argument of the Jewish believers "the most blatant example of *faulty* contextualization recorded in the New Testament."[167] While the decision produced at the Jerusalem Council was primarily for the Gentile believers, it was also surprisingly transformative to the Jewish believers, shaping their view of the gospel to be more appropriate for authentic participation in God's mission. Based on this correction of understanding the gospel, the group of Jewish believers overcame their culturally-bound view of the gospel and came to have an appropriate understanding of the church's identity and mission.[168] This intercultural character of the context and process of the council suggests the intercultural dynamic of the missional transformation of the church: the council's final consensus, which had a far-reaching, transformative effect on the Jerusalem Church, was the culmination of intercultural engagement.

---

166. Flemming, *Contextualization*, 45.
167. Wagner, *Acts*, 350. Emphasis added.
168. Flemming, *Contextualization*, 53.

Process: Two Resources and Critical Openness

Along with the context, issue, and result of the Jerusalem Council, the process of decision-making at the Jerusalem Council shows another aspect of the council as a biblical case of the church's missional conversion. In the process of discernment, two crucial factors played a decisive role toward the outcome of the council: *the Holy Spirit* and *Scripture*.

The Holy Spirit

One crucial factor that led to a consensus at the council was the Holy Spirit. While the council itself was not an event in which delegates directly encountered the Holy Spirit, they struggled with the theological implications of the work of the Holy Spirit among Gentiles, which were reported by Peter, and then by Paul and Barnabas. Among the testimonies, most crucial was Peter's testimony to the work of the Holy Spirit at the house of a Gentile named Cornelius and its theological implications (Acts 15:7-9). As Lloyd J. Ogilvie points out, "The significant contribution of Peter was to call the assembly back to what the Lord did through the Holy Spirit."[169] Peter not only reminded delegates of what the Holy Spirit did at Cornelius's house but also drew theological implications from it. Peter viewed the outpouring of the Holy Spirit among Gentiles as *God's divine confirmation* of (1) God's acceptance of the Gentiles (Acts 15:8), (2) no distinction between Jewish believers and Gentile believers (Acts 15:9), (3) no need for keeping the law of Moses (Acts 15:10), and (4) salvation given through the grace of Jesus Christ (Acts 15:11). Thus, as Michael Mullins comments, "The central theme of his speech now is what God (not Peter) has done for the salvation of the Gentiles," and the major point of his speech was that "God, not Peter himself, was the agent of Gentile justification and purification."[170] Peter's speech silenced the Jewish believers who insisted on the necessity of circumcision and the law of Moses (Acts 15:12).

In both of the two events which resulted in the Jerusalem Church's theological transformation—(1) the story of Cornelius's conversion in Acts 10-11 and (2) the Jerusalem Council in Acts 15—Peter's witness about the work of the Holy Spirit at Cornelius's house and its theological implications served as the divine factor that corrected Jewish believers' theological myopia in understanding of the gospel, and, by extension, of the church's identity and mission. Peter's speech was further supported by another testimony of Paul

---

169. Ogilvie, *Acts*, 239.
170. Mullins, *Acts of the Apostles*, 157.

and Barnabas about "all the signs and wonders that God had done through them among the Gentiles" (Acts 15:12). Then, James admitted the Holy Spirit's work among Gentiles as the undeniable divine proof that God was already fulfilling the eschatological ingathering of all nations, as promised in Amos 9 (Acts 15:15-18), and the council reached its final consensus with James's statement, which reads, "Therefore I have reached the decision that we should not trouble those Gentiles who are turning to God" (Acts 15:19). In this sense, those who gathered at the council encountered God in and through the Holy Spirit as they heard the testimonies of Peter, Paul, and Barnabas, and the theological dispute at issue settled down on the basis of what God was already doing among Gentiles in and through the Holy Spirit.

As in the case of Cornelius's conversion in Acts 10-11, the Jerusalem Council revealed that the church's missional transformation requires its capability to perceive and respond to the guidance of God in and through the Holy Spirit. As the Jerusalem Church accepted and followed the guidance of the Holy Spirit in mission, the Jerusalem Church *gradually* found itself in the midst of God's unfolding mission among Gentiles. These two biblical cases in the book of Acts show that the authenticity of the church's mission is shaped as it learns from the Holy Spirit in mission. On this dimension of the church's missional conversion, Newbigin points out, "[the church's] mission will not only be a matter of preaching and teaching but also of learning. When he sends them out on their mission, Jesus tells the disciples that there is much for them yet to learn, and he promises that the Spirit who will convict the world will also lead them into the truth in its fullness (John 16:12-15)."[171] The unfolding narrative of God's mission in the book of Acts demonstrates (1) that the church's faithful and authentic participation in the mission of God requires that the church itself be changed first and (2) that such change takes place as the church learns from God in and through the Holy Spirit.

Scripture

The leaders and elders at the Jerusalem Council seriously took the challenge shaped by Gentile believers, but did not hurry to condemn it or to embrace it. Instead, "there had been much debate" (Acts 15:7). They approached the issue in a careful manner and with a long discussion, striving to reach a statement agreed by all the delegates. Because different theological interpretations of salvation were in tension, the council needed discernment regarding whether Gentile believers' view of salvation should be accepted.

---

171. Newbigin, *Gospel in a Pluralist Society*, 118.

The discernment made at the council was not a purely experiential discernment, but a theological one which involved both missionary experience and scriptural basis.[172] The two major resources used for theological discernment was Scripture and Peter's testimony about the Holy Spirit's work among the Gentiles.[173] Then, what was the hermeneutical dynamic between the roles of Scripture and the testimony?

Some scholars highlight James's role in the use of Scripture. For example, Bauckham claims that the testimonies were not "the finally decisive one," and, thus, after all, "the matter under discussion is one of halakhah (15.5), which could only be decided from Scripture."[174] Drawing on Bauckham's argument, David K. Strong and Cynthia A. Strong highlight the priority of the role of Scripture over testimony at the council when they state, "James . . . evaluated Peter's testimony in light of Scripture, stating that his experience accorded with the words of the prophets."[175] In this view, Scripture is not interpreted in light of the Holy Spirit's acts which Peter witnessed to, but, rather, the acts of the Holy Spirit should be examined in light of Scripture. The problem with this stand is that Bauckham's article focuses not on the primary issue (the inclusion of the Gentiles), but on a practical, context-sensitive issue (the fellowship between Jewish and Gentile believers), namely the four prohibitions. In fact, Bauckham's article does not discuss the relationship between Peter's testimony and James's interpretation of the Old Testament prophecy.

On the other hand, scholars, who seriously analyze the relationship between Peter's testimony and James's interpretation of Scripture, admit the acts of the Holy Spirit as having served as a hermeneutic lens for James's interpretation of Scripture. Luke Timothy Johnson views the Jerusalem council as "a process of *discernment* of God's activity," and observes the priority of the experience of God's act in the discernment process. He articulates, "It is the experience of God revealed through narrative which is given priority in this hermeneutical process: the text of Scripture does not dictate how God should act. Rather, God's action dictates how we should understand the text of Scripture."[176] For Johnson, the hermeneutical process between

---

172. Shawn B. Redford approaches the issue of missiological discernment in terms of hermeneutical process, tracing clues on how biblical characters came to understand the missional intent of God within Scripture. For Redford's full construction of missiological hermeneutics, see Redford, *Missiological Hermeneutics*.

173. Kurz, *Acts*, 232.

174. Bauckham, "James and the Gentiles," 154.

175. Strong and Strong, "Globalizing Hermeneutic," 129.

176. Johnson, *Acts of the Apostles*, 271.

the testimony and Scripture was not the interpretation of the Holy Spirit's work but "the reinterpretation of the Scripture."[177] Johnson points out:

> What is striking about James' citation of Amos 9:11–12 is not simply the dependence on the LXX version ... the way in which that version enables James to perceive a mission to the Gentiles after the 'restoration' of David's tent, but the way in which James puts the case. He says that 'the prophets agree with this' rather than that 'this agrees with the prophets' (15:15).[178]

Thus, what happened to the Jerusalem Council was not Scripture evaluating God's activity, but rather, as James Shelton puts, "The Scripture James quotes is interpreted in the light of the God event that has occurred in the apostolic end-time community."[179] Thus, as Shelton concludes, the process of discernment at the council "shows that the acts of God interpreted by the Holy Spirit-led apostles.... were the key to the resolution of issues in the early Church."[180]

However, the discernment process of the Jerusalem Council does not show that Scripture is always a secondary source in the process of discernment. Rather, the discernment process at the council demonstrates that God's act supports what Scripture says and, therefore, gives the authority to Scripture. God is not a God who is against his word, but a God who fulfills it. The council came into a new revelation not only with experience but with Scripture.[181] The leaders and elders at the council did not bypass Scripture in approaching their final agreement. Their consensus was solidly confirmed by Scripture. Therefore, the hermeneutic dynamic between Scripture and testimony was not one-way, but two-way. One did not rule out the other, but these two resources harmoniously resonated with each other. On the one hand, the testimony about the work of the Holy Spirit served as an interpretive key to Scripture, leading to a proper interpretation of Scripture. On the other hand, Scripture supported Peter's testimony, confirming that God was already fulfilling the promise about the salvation of Gentiles through the Holy Spirit.

---

177. Johnson, *Acts of the Apostles*, 271.
178. Johnson, *Acts of the Apostles*, 271.
179. Shelton, "Epistemology and Authority," 243.
180. Shelton, "Epistemology and Authority," 245.
181. Willimon, *Acts*, 130.

Summary

The Jerusalem Council served as a turning point of the Jerusalem Church's mission, from its culturally-bound theology toward the transcultural understanding of its identity and mission. A missiological implication to be drawn out of this biblical case is that the church's full and authentic participation in God's mission requires not only "a radical change in the messengers"[182] but also *what* the change is, one toward a fuller understanding of the mission of God and the missionary vocation of the church. Along with two biblical cases—(1) the outpouring of the Holy Spirit in the early stage of the Jerusalem Church and (2) Cornelius's conversion—examined in this chapter, the Jerusalem Council shows that, in encountering the Holy Spirit, the Jerusalem Church moved one step toward its missionary identity and call. Reflecting on Acts 10–11 and Acts 15, Dollar makes a concluding remark:

> One of Luke's major points in the two key passages on evangelizing Gentiles (Acts 10–11 and 15) is that the theological barriers to a mission to the Gentiles had been removed by *divine intervention*. After the messengers had grasped God's intentions, then the universal nature of the gospel was clearly understood and the mission to the Gentiles was launched.[183]

The analysis of the Jerusalem Council revealed two facts about the Jerusalem Church. On the one hand, even though it had learned from and had been shaped by multiple encounters with the Holy Spirit, the Jerusalem Church still struggled with its cultural captivity, and did not fully understand the mission of God and the mission of the church. However, through intercultural engagement with one another at the council, the Jerusalem Church went through a theological transformation toward a proper understanding of its identity and mission. The discernment process at the council showed that two resources—the Holy Spirit and Scripture—served as the theological foundation of the final consensus of the council, leading to the church's new understanding of the mission of God and the identity and mission of the church. Thus, the three biblical cases together show that the missional transformation of the earliest church took place as the church constantly encountered the Holy Spirit.

The Jerusalem Council provides two aspects of the church's missional conversion, which did not surface in the other biblical cases examined so far. First, the process of the church's missional conversion is stimulated by *intercultural engagement*. The Jerusalem Council was caused by its intercultural

---

182. Dollar, *St. Luke's Missiology*, 171.
183. Dollar, *St. Luke's Missiology*, 170. Emphasis added.

context, in which two different groups of believers, each of whom represented a local community of faith shaped in a particular cultural context, recognized their theological difference. The two groups engaged with each other interculturally for theological discernment. As a result, the Jerusalem Church's understanding of its identity and mission was deepened and broadened. This aspect of the church's missional conversion is significant particularly for the churches in the globalizing context today because the intercultural context of the Jerusalem Council is parallel to the globalizing context of the church today. In the globalizing context of today, churches all over the world are not only culturally different, but also theologically diverse, as in the intercultural context of the Jerusalem Council. Churches today are not isolated from one another, but interconnected as the intercultural context of the Jerusalem Council.

Second, the process of the church's missional conversion is both *inclusive* and *critical*. On the one hand, the process is inclusive because the church needs to have an open mind in learning from what God was doing among the Gentiles in and through the Holy Spirit. The process is critical because the church seeks to discern God's message with Scripture. The Jerusalem Council did not reject the theology reflected by Gentile believers quickly nor embraced it uncritically. The council went through a theological discernment process which involved both critical and inclusive attitudes to the reports about Gentile believers. On the one hand, Peter's testimony about the Holy Spirit's work at Cornelius's house was enough to silence those who complained about Gentile believers. On the other hand, Peter's view of Gentile believers as authentically and truly saved by God was not uncritically accepted, but was discerned with Scripture. The work of the Holy Spirit did not stand in contrast with, but resonated with Scripture. The discernment process of the Jerusalem Council shows that the church's mission conversion entails an *inclusive* and *critical* discernment process in understanding and fulfilling its missionary vocation.

E. Summary and Conclusion of the Chapter

This chapter delved into three biblical cases in the book of Acts in order to identity ways that the Holy Spirit shaped the missionary nature of the earliest church, demonstrating that the triune God continued to shape his people through the Holy Spirit. All three cases closely examined in this chapter demonstrated that the missional formation of the earliest church primarily resulted from its encounter with the Holy Spirit, while ways that the earliest church encountered the Holy Spirit varied. Through the empowerment and guidance of the Holy Spirit, the earliest church was gradually transformed toward being a witness of Jesus to Gentiles as well as Jews. The analysis of ways that the Holy Spirit shaped the earliest church for mission provides implications for the nature of the church's missional conversion, as summarized below.

Encounter with God in and through the Holy Spirit

All the cases of the earliest church's missional conversion were consequences of its encounter with the Holy Spirit. At the beginning stage of the earliest church, the outpouring of the Holy Spirit transformed the church as a witnessing community which testifies about Jesus in both its inward life and outward ministry. In the cases of Cornelius's conversion and the Jerusalem Council, the earliest church gradually came to know that its mission was not limited to Jews but that the scope of its mission was universal. These two cases crucial to the establishment of the validity of the church's Gentile mission would not have happened without the guidance of the Holy Spirit. In these two cases, the Jerusalem Church was able to overcome its ethnocentrism and took steps toward its missionary vocation as the church encountered the Holy Spirit.

Holistic Transformation

The Holy Spirit shaped the missionary nature of the earliest church's identity and vocation holistically, shaping both the *inward* life and *outward* ministry of the earliest church. While emphasis in the Holy Spirit's mission in the book of Acts is given to believers' outward witnessing, the earliest church was also inwardly transformed. On the one hand, through the experience of the outpouring of the Holy Spirit, the earliest church was transformed toward a bold witness of Jesus since the very beginning. In the following two cases—Cornelius's conversion and the Jerusalem Council—the earliest church was able to overcome its Jewish ethnic boundary to reach out to Gentiles under the guidance of the Holy Spirit. On the other hand, the Holy Spirit transformed the earliest church as a social community who embodied the teaching and life of Jesus and a spiritual community which was devoted to God.

The Church's Missional Conversion as a Two-Way Process

The earliest church's transformation was the consequence of its encounter with the Holy Spirit. However, in all the three cases, early believers were not merely passive receivers who irresistibly followed the lead of the Holy Spirit. Rather, they actively sought the empowerment and guidance of the Holy Spirit. They depended on and trusted in God for their mission through their constant prayer. When the Holy Spirit opened their eyes to see what God was doing in the world, they humbly accepted, embraced, and rejoiced with the new revelation bought by the Holy Spirit. They were willing to be corrected by the Holy Spirit. The earliest church's paradigm shift involved divine-human interaction. This finding implies that the church's missional conversion was not a one-way but a two-way process. For its missional conversion, the church must depend on and trust in God, seek the empowerment and guidance of God, and, most importantly, be willing to be corrected by God.

The Communal Aspect of the Church's Missional Conversion

One unique finding about the earliest church's missional conversion is that the earliest church encountered the Holy Spirit in ways different from a direct encounter with the Holy Spirit. One way that the earliest church indirectly encountered the Holy Spirit was through believers' interaction with one another as in the cases of Cornelius's conversion in Acts 10–11 and the Jerusalem Council in Acts 15. This finding suggests *the communal aspect of the church's missional conversion*. The way that the church encounters God for its missional conversion is not limited to a direct experience. A mutual interaction with one another within the church is also a way that God leads the church to be transformed for his mission.

Crosscultural Mission Experience as a Resource for the Church's Missional Conversion

This chapter identified Act 10–11 as a case in which the earliest church's transformation by the Holy Spirit took place in a crosscultural context. In the case of Cornelius's conversion, the earliest church encountered the Holy Spirit in a crosscultural context. This is a new factor that emerged as the earliest church began to engage with Gentiles under the guidance of the Holy Spirit. The new understanding of the earliest church's identity and mission were established as the church witnessed what the Holy Spirit does through its crosscultural mission. This finding reveals one new aspect of the church's missional conversion: *the church's missional conversion takes place as the church participates in crosscultural mission.*

The Intercultural Aspect of the Church's Missional Conversion

The context where the earliest church experienced its missional conversion was not limited to a crosscultural context, but, as in the case of the Jerusalem Council, the earliest church was moved one more step toward its missionary vocation through intercultural interaction. The whole process of the Jerusalem Council was intercultural in character. The intercultural interaction at the council involved the discernment process characterized by critical openness. The council did not reject or accept the reality of Gentile believers in an uncritical manner. Rather, the council critically examined it with two resources—the Holy Spirit and Scripture. The intercultural character of the council implies that intercultural engagement can and should be viewed as a way for the church to continuously be transformed toward being a missionary community which authentically participates in God's mission. This intercultural aspect of the church's missional conversion is significant and relevant particularly to today's globalizing context which enables churches all over the world to interculturally engage with one another.

5

Conclusion

THIS CHAPTER CONCLUDES THIS biblical-theological study on the theme of the church's missional conversion by integrating and highlighting all the research findings. The findings serve as the basis for drawing theological, theoretical, and practical implications for the church's continuous transformation toward its missionary vocation in order for it to authentically and constantly participate in God's mission.

A. Main Thesis

The main thesis demonstrated throughout this study is, first, that, in Scripture, the missional conversion of God's people was primarily the consequence of their continuous encounter with the triune God, and, second, that this divine-human encounter for the missional conversion of God's people was necessary in view of the ongoing tension between the missional faithfulness of God in fulfilling the missionary vocation of his people, on the one hand, and the missional failure (or missional unfaithfulness) of God's people to their missionary vocation, on the other hand. This thesis is biblically undergirded by the three main chapters (chapters 2, 3, and 4) of this study. Chapter 2 demonstrated that Yahweh was faithful in shaping the people of Israel toward being a contrast people for his mission, while they repeatedly failed their vocation. As addressed in chapter 3, the faithfulness of God continued with the earthly ministry of Jesus, which primarily focused on the people of Israel, who failed their missionary vocation. One aim of Jesus was to restore the people of Israel back to God and prepare them for God's global mission. While the disciples, a nucleus to renew and gather the whole people of Israel, were left purposeless and hopeless upon the death of Jesus, he did not give up on them. Rather, the risen Jesus restored and renewed them by giving them the missionary vocation of being his witnesses to the ends of the earth. Chapter 4 looked into the role of the Holy Spirit in shaping the earliest church into a missionary community which witnessed about Jesus to both Jews and Gentiles. The earliest church began to be transformed as believers experienced the outpouring of the Holy Spirit. Through the deliberate guidance of the Holy Spirit, the earliest church came to overcome its parochialism in understanding the mission of God and the mission of the church and to embrace and participate in God's global mission. In summary, the discussion in these three main chapters of the study demonstrated that the transformation of God's people toward their missionary vocation resulted from their continuous encounter with God. God was unceasingly and unchangingly faithful and committed to having them fulfill their missionary vocation, despite their repeated failure or unfaithfulness to what they were called to be for God's mission.

B. Four Foundational Components of the Church's Missional Conversion

Drawing on the main thesis of this study, the study identified four foundational components that establish what the church's transformation toward its missionary vocation would look like: (1) the missional potentiality of the church, (2) the missional vulnerability of the church, (3) the missional faithfulness of God, and (4) the church's missional conversion through its encounter with God. These components were recurrently observed in each of three main chapters (chapters 2, 3, and 4) of this study. First, the church is *missionally potential*. The church's potentiality to become a missionary people of God is grounded in God's intention and expectation of the missionary nature of the church. In other words, this missional potentiality of the church is derived from God's missional vision for the church. As this study discussed, God in the biblical narrative had a missional purpose for his chosen people, called them to be his missionary people to the world, and expected them to participate in God's mission. The missional potentiality of the church is further indicated by the research finding that, while they often failed their missionary vocation, God finally succeeded in shaping their missionary vocation through his continuous commitment to their missional formation. Drawing on this biblical finding, this study contends that the church is missionally potential to fulfill its missionary vocation.

Second, the church is *missionally vulnerable*. In other words, the church is not able to fulfill its missionary vocation on its own. As this study demonstrated, the people of God in Scripture were chosen with a missionary vocation given to them, but they repeatedly failed to fulfill their missionary vocation. At one level, the people of God repeatedly demonstrated their *missional unfaithfulness* by failing to be faithful to what they were called to be for God's mission. At another level, the people of God fell into their *missional parochialism* in that even their best efforts to be faithful to their missionary vocation failed to fully understand and live out what they were called to be for the mission of God. Bosch admits the church's myopia in understanding and practicing its mission: "Every branch of theology—including missiology—remains piecework, fragile, and preliminary. There is no such thing as missiology, period. There is only *missiology in draft*."[1] Drawing on this research finding, this study asserts that the church as the people of God is *unable* to fulfill its missionary vocation on its own in a constant and authentic manner. By implication, this point indicates that the church should always critically examine its missional status if the church seeks to fulfill its missionary vocation. Thus, the missional conversion of the church should necessarily involve the church's critical evaluation of the way that the church participates in God's mission.

Third, the church's missional conversion lies within the context of *the missional faithfulness of God*. In other words, the church's missional conversion is made possible because of God's unceasing commitment to fulfilling the church's missionary vocation. This study demonstrated that God in the biblical narrative was faithful in fulfilling the missionary vocation of God's people. The biblical cases analyzed in this study testify about the faithfulness of God who continuously shaped his people toward fulfilling their missionary vocation. While the people of God repeatedly failed their missionary vocation, God did not give up on them. Rather, he renewed and reshaped them toward what God intended them to be for his mission. This research finding suggests that, while the church as the people of God is not able to fulfill its missionary vocation on its own, its failure to fulfill its missionary vocation can be overcome by the unceasing and unchanging faithfulness of God since he is continuously committed to shaping his people toward their missionary vocation.

Lastly, the church's missional conversion is primarily the consequence of *its encounter with the triune God*. The first three components mentioned above already indicate this point. As this study explored, whenever the people of God failed their missionary vocation, the missional faithfulness of God was demonstrated through his divine initiative to have them encounter him in order to bring them back to what they are called to be for his mission. This study demonstrated that this divine-human encounter resulted in restoring, deepening, and broadening the way that the people of God understand and practice their missionary vocation. These research findings show that the first three components—the missional potentiality of the church, the missional

---

1. Bosch, *Transforming Mission*, 498.

vulnerability of the church, and the missional faithfulness of God—come to interplay through the church's encounter with God, giving the church opportunities to critically self-examine the understanding and practice of its missionary vocation. In this sense, the church's missional conversion is primarily the consequence of its encounter with God.

In summary, the research findings of this study suggest that the overall contours of the church's missional conversion are constructed by these four components (see Figure 3 below). The church has a missional potential, as God intends and expects the church to be the missionary people of God. However, the church is missionally vulnerable. In other words, the church cannot fulfill its missionary vocation on its own as the church often fails to fulfill what God intended the church to be for his mission either because of its missional unfaithfulness or its missional parochialism. However, the church's missional vulnerability is overcome by the unceasing, unchanging faithfulness of God who is continuously committed to shaping the church toward being his missionary people. These three points come to interplay through the church's continuous encounter with God. In this divine-human encounter, the church has an opportunity to critically self-examine its current missional status (both the understanding and practice of the church's missionary vocation) so that the church can move toward *authentically* and *continuously* fulfilling its missionary vocation.

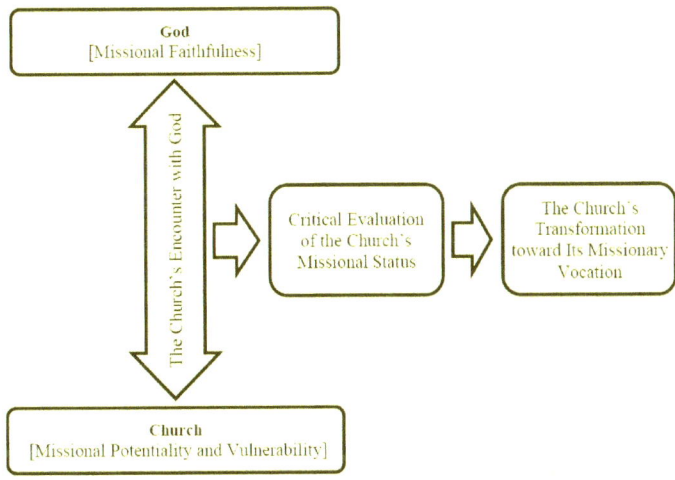

Figure 3. The overall contours of the church's missional conversion.

C. The Trinitarian Aspect of the Church's Missional Conversion

The nature and process of the missional conversion of the church is profoundly trinitarian. In Scripture, the triune God continuously and faithfully shaped his people toward their missionary vocation in order to fulfill his mission. Thus, it is suggested that the missional conversion of the church has a triune foundation, as explained below.

The Church's Missional Conversion Is Theo-Derived

This study shows that God is the origin and source of the missionary nature of God's people. This means that the missionary nature of God's people is fundamentally shaped by and derived from their constant relationship with God. In other words, their missionary nature is neither self-generating nor self-sustaining. This point is clearly demonstrated by two research findings. First, the missionary nature of God's people is derived from their relationship with God. In chapter 2, the analysis of the three identity-defining phrases—my treasured possession, a kingdom of priests, and a holy nation—in the Sinai Covenant showed that Israel's relationships with God and with the nations were interrelated in such a way that her relationship with God determined her relationship with the nations. The missionary role of Israel among the nations was fundamentally grounded in her obedience to God, her privilege to be near the presence of God, and her relationship with the holiness of God. In the period after the establishment of the Sinai Covenant, failure of Israel's relationship with God resulted in the loss of her missional distinctives, which had enabled her to present God to the nations. Thus, for Israel to fulfill her missionary vocation, Israel indispensably required her constant relationship with God.

Second, the presence of God among God's people served as the fulfilling factor for the missionary vocation of God's people. The absence of God from them therefore immediately resulted in failure of their missionary vocation, but the presence of God among them sustained, restored, and renewed their missionary vocation. They were not able to faithfully live out their missionary nature without God who dwells among them.

These two findings of the missional conversion of Israel are also found in the disciples' relationship with Jesus (chapter 3) and the earliest church's relationship with the Holy Spirit (chapter 4). These research findings show that God is the origin and source of the missionary nature of the church and thus that the missional conversion of the church is fundamentally *theo*-derived.

The *theo*-derived aspect of the church's missional conversion explains why the church's missional conversion is primarily the consequence of the church's encounter with God. The church needs to constantly encounter God for its missional conversion because God is the origin and source of the church's missionary nature and because the church's missionary nature is derived from its constant relationship with God. This continuous divine encounter is essential for the church's missional conversion in that the church's missional relationship with the world depends on its relationship with God.

This aspect of the church's missional conversion suggests at least two practical implications. First, the church which seeks its missional conversion should critically evaluate its relationship with God in its life and ministry. The church needs to carefully investigate whether its life and ministry are shaped by its relationship with God, and whether its life and ministry help deepen its relationship with God. Second, the church which seeks its missional conversion must put more trust in God than in sociologically based strategies for congregational change. There are many sociological theories that can be useful for the church to change. They might be effective for the church's change, renewal, or transformation. However, as this study suggests, what fundamentally shapes the church toward its missionary vocation is not those sociologically based strategies, but its constant relationship with God who is the origin and source of the church's missionary vocation.

The Church's Missional Conversion Is Christocentric

This study shows that the missionary nature of God's people became *Christocentric* throughout the earthly ministry of Jesus. As discussed in chapter 2, Israel's missionary vocation was primarily theocentric, being called to embody the kingdom of God by being a contrast community which presents the holiness of God—the presence and character of God—to the nations by living a life that reflects the holiness of God. Israel's life was centered on the law which was given as the practical way to fulfill this theocentric missionary vocation.

As demonstrated in chapter 3, the holiness of God continued with Jesus, who became the new point of reference for holiness. On the one hand, the essence of Israel's missionary vocation continued with the disciples as indicated in Jesus's relationship with John the Baptist and the three identity-defining images in Matthew 5. On the other hand, Israel's missionary vocation was redefined as the identity, life, and ministry of the disciples were centered not on the law but on Jesus, who came to fulfill the law. They were called to embody the *radical* and *inclusive* nature of the kingdom of God, which Jesus revealed throughout his earthly ministry. As the culmination of Jesus's whole earthly ministry, they received a Christocentric missionary vocation, namely, being witnesses of Jesus. Like Israel, the disciples were called to embody the kingdom of God, but they were called to do that not by keeping the law, but by holistically being *witnesses of Jesus* in their inward life and outward ministry. The kingdom of God that the church is called to embody is *fundamentally theocentric,* but *thoroughly Christocentric.*

As demonstrated in chapter 4, the earliest church is radically transformed into witnesses of Jesus both in their inward life and outward ministry through the empowerment and guidance of the Holy Spirit. These research findings show that the missional conversion of the church is thoroughly Christocentric. In other words, through its missional conversion, the church becomes a messianic community which holistically witnesses to Jesus in its inward life and outward ministry.

One practical implication derived from this aspect of the church's missional conversion is that the way that the church reflects Jesus in its theology, life, and ministry can serve as an indicator which points to whether the church is fulfilling its missionary vocation, which is thoroughly Christocentric. The church which seeks its missional conversion needs a critical self-examination by asking questions such as: whether or not the church is holistically reflecting and presenting the presence and character of Jesus in its theology, inward life, and outward ministry; and whether or not the way that the church engages with the world is constantly shaped by a comprehensive christological framework which consists of the birth, life, death and resurrection of Jesus.[2] The consequence of the church's missional conversion should be its radical identification with Jesus, being shaped by the *totus Christus.*

The Church's Missional Conversion Is Pneuma-Driven

This study identifies that, if the church's missionary vocation is Christocentric, the process that transforms the church toward being holistically centered on Jesus is *pneuma*-driven. As examined in chapter 4, the promise about the transformation of the earliest church into witnesses of Jesus began to

---

2. For Bosch, a comprehensive christological framework includes parousia, but in this study, whether or not the mission of the church is shaped by parousia is not clear, so this study does not include parousia in the comprehensive christological framework. See Bosch, *Transforming Mission,* 399.

be fulfilled *through the empowerment and guidance of the Holy Spirit.* At the early stages of the earliest church, the outpouring of the Holy Spirit dramatically and radically transformed the earliest church into a contrast community whose life reflected the teaching and life of Jesus and which boldly witnessed about Jesus to Jews. The earliest church, particularly the Jerusalem Church, gradually came to understand, embrace, and participate in God's global mission under the guidance of the Holy Spirit. Thus, the earliest church's missional conversion was led by the Holy Spirit. These research findings show the *pneuma*-driven process of the church's missional conversion.

The view of the Holy Spirit as the divine agent who shapes the life and ministry of the church has already been affirmed among scholars.[3] Jürgen Moltmann points out, "In the power of the Holy Spirit the church experiences itself as the messianic fellowship of service for the kingdom of God in the world."[4] Craig Van Gelder views the Holy Spirit as the one who "calls, gathers, and sends the church into the world to participate in God's mission."[5] Thus, Van Gelder views the mission of the church as Spirit-led. He states, "It is in the power of the Spirit that the church receives this mandate [to be the sign, witness and foretaste of the kingdom of God], and it is only through the indwelling of the Spirit that the church engages in the ministry of the kingdom."[6] Therefore, the role of the Holy Spirit is vital to the church's missional conversion, and, in this sense, such transformation can be viewed a *pneumatic* experience.

The *pneuma*-driven aspect of the church's missional conversion suggests two practical implications for the church's missional conversion. The central task of the church in seeking the empowerment and guidance of the Holy Spirit for its missional mission is twofold: (1) seeking to be filled with the Holy Spirit and (2) discerning the guidance of the Holy Spirit. The church which seeks to be constantly transformed toward fulfilling its missionary vocation must seek to be filled with the Holy Spirit in its total life and ministry. In doing so, the church does not merely acknowledge the presence of the Holy Spirit in the church, but the church should be led by the Holy Spirit.

---

3. For some biblical-theological treatments of the role of the Holy Spirit in shaping the church, see Moltmann, *Church in the Power of the Spirit*; Van Gelder, *Ministry of the Missional Church*.

4. Moltmann, *Church in the Power of the Spirit*, 289. Moltmann emphasizes the church's experience of the Holy Spirit for becoming a messianic community and a community of the kingdom of God when he states, "Its fellowship with Christ is founded on the experience of the Spirit which manifests Christ, unites us with him and glorifies him in men. Its fellowship in the kingdom of God is founded on the power of the Spirit, which leads it into truth and freedom." Moltmann, *Church in the Power of the Spirit*, 197.

5. Van Gelder, *Ministry of the Missional Church*, 18.

6. Van Gelder, *Ministry of the Missional Church*, 11.

Furthermore, it is equally important for the church to discern the guidance of the Holy Spirit. While the church should be fully open to the work of the Holy Spirit, the church can be misled, failing to be what the Holy Sprit guides it toward. This means that the church needs to learn ways to discern the Holy Spirit among other misleading factors that possibly influence the way that the church participates in God's mission.

In order for these two practical implications—(1) seeking to be filled with the Holy Spirit and (2) discerning the guidance of the Holy Spirit—to work in the church's life and ministry, the church's theology of the Holy Spirit should be able to admit the role of the Holy Spirit in the church's missional conversion, and should neither hinder nor limit the work of the Holy Spirit. Rather, the church should be prepared to be surprised by the Holy Spirit who transforms the church toward its authentic participation in God's mission.

The Church's Missional Conversion Is Fundamentally and Profoundly Trinitarian

Structurally, this study used a trinitarian approach and, thereby, each of three main chapters—chapters 2, 3, and 4—focused on the work of each of God the Father (chapter 2), Jesus (chapter 3), and the Holy Spirit (chapter 4), examining how each of the three members of the Trinity worked to shape the people of God toward their missionary vocation. Because of that, the trinitarian approach taken in these three chapters reflected an economic trinity, which is related to the history of salvation and focuses on the sending activities of God the Father, God the Son, and the Holy Spirit in mission, rather than an ontological trinity (or immanent trinity), which emphasizes the inner aspect of trinity characterized by oneness and the communal nature of the three persons of the Trinity.

However, this study does not view the economic trinity as contradictory to the immanent trinity. Rather, the theological disposition that this study takes is that these two views of the Trinity support and embrace each other. More specifically, this theological position means that the predominant presence of God the Father in the Old Testament narrative does not mean isolation of God the Son and the Holy Spirit from God the Father in the Old Testament narrative. Oneness and corporation in the redemptive acts of the three persons of the Trinity become explicit in the New Testament. In his whole earthly ministry, Jesus was with God the Father in unity and ministered in the power of the Holy Spirit. In the post-resurrection period after the ascension of Jesus, the Holy Spirit became the central divine agent of God's mission, but God the Father and God the Son were also at work in and through the Holy Spirit.

In this sense, this study concludes that the church's missional conversion is fundamentally and profoundly trinitarian. On the one hand, as the three main chapters (chapters 2 to 4) demonstrated, Yahweh's mission to his people continues with Jesus through his earthly ministry and with the Holy Spirit in the post-resurrection period. The people of God were transformed toward their missionary vocation as they encountered Yahweh in the Old Testament narrative, Jesus in the context of the four Gospels, and the Holy Spirit in the post-resurrection period after the ascension of Jesus. God the Father, God the Son, and the Holy Spirit were committed to continuously shaping the people of God for the mission of God. Each member of the Trinity made unique contributions in leading the people of God to fulfill their missionary vocation, as identified above. On the other hand, the missional transformation of God's people should be viewed as the consequence of the triune God since the God whom they encountered is the triune God. In this respect, the church's missional conversion is not only *theo*-derived, but also *trinity*-driven, not only *Christo*centric, but also *trinity*-centered, and not only *pneuma*-driven, but also *trinity*-driven. Taking these two sides of the triune aspect of the missional conversion of God's people, this study concludes that the missional conversion of the church is fundamentally and profoundly *trinitarian*.

D. Other Aspects of the Church's Missional Conversion

Along with its four foundational components and its trinitarian aspect, three more aspects of the church's missional conversion of the church are identifiable from the research findings of this study, and these findings also provide a general characterization of the nature of the church's missional conversion.

The Church's Missional Conversion Is a Continuing Process

This study demonstrates that the church's missional conversion is not a one-time event, but a *continuing process*. As the analyzed biblical cases demonstrated, the people of God were called to be God's missionary people from the very beginning. However, the biblical cases revealed that their missionary nature was shaped as they *continuously* encounter the triune God. As discussed in chapter 2, the people of Israel *repeatedly* failed her missionary vocation as they failed to be faithful to covenant relationship with God. However, in spite of their missional unfaithfulness, God continuously restored, renewed, and re-shaped their missionary nature. As chapter 3 demonstrated, God continued to restore them and shape them toward their missionary vocation through the earthly ministry of Jesus. Jesus created a community of the disciples, as a prototype of the people of God, with which the restoration of Israel began. However, like Israel in the Old Testament, the disciples proved that they were not able to fulfill their missionary vocation on their own, as indicated in their immediate response to the death of Jesus. Nevertheless, when he was risen, he came to them, rebuilt and expanded their missionary vocation. The analysis of the biblical cases in chapter 4 demonstrated that the earliest church *gradually* came to understand that their mission was not confined to their ethnicity and culture. These research findings show that the church's missional conversion should not be viewed as a one-time event but as a continuing process. The church is called to be missionary in nature and purpose, but always *is becoming* missionary in reality. Bosch puts it this way:

> We know today—what many of our spiritual forebears would have found difficult to accept —that the empirical church will always be imperfect. Every church member who loves the church will also be deeply pained by it. This does not, however, call for discarding the church, but *for reforming and renewing it*. The church is itself an object of the *missio Dei*, in constant need of repentance and conversion.[7]

Thus, as Van Engen points out, the reality of the missionary church is always "emerging reality."[8] On the one hand, "The missionary Church is *becoming* what it is."[9] On the other hand, "The missionary church *is* what it is becoming."[10]

The Church's Missional Conversion Is Holistic

This study shows that the church's mission becomes holistic as a consequence of its *continuous* missional conversion. In other words, the missional consequence of the church's encounter with God shapes its holistic mission in both *being* (inward life) and *doing* (outward ministry).[11] This

---

7. Bosch, *Transforming Mission*, 386–87. Emphasis added.
8. Van Engen, *God's Missionary People*, 41.
9. Van Engen, *God's Missionary People*, 44. Italics in original.
10. Van Engen, *God's Missionary People*, 44. Italics in original.
11. In this study, the two terms *being* and *doing* are used to refer to two ways of

point does not mean that the church's holistic mission is a quick, sudden corollary of its missional conversion in a short period of time. Rather, it suggests that the church's missional conversion *constantly* shapes its mission toward being holistic.[12] This study demonstrates that God shaped his people as a contrast people who holistically present the presence and character of God to the world in both *being* and *doing*. As discussed in chapter 2, in the Old Testament narrative, God called the Israelites to be a contrast people who were to embody the kingdom of God primarily in *being* rather than *doing*—by *being a contrast people* whose lives were to reflect the holiness of God. As demonstrated in chapter 3, in the New Testament, Jesus intensified and expanded their missionary vocation throughout his earthly ministry, revealing the *radical* and *inclusive* nature of the kingdom of God. The disciples were called to embody the kingdom of God by being a *radical* and *inclusive* contrast people in both *being* and *doing*. The discussion in chapter 4 shows that, through the empowerment and guidance of the Holy Spirit, the holistic mission of the earliest church emerged not only as a socially distinctive and spiritually devoted community (*being*), and but also as a boldly witnessing community (*doing*).

These research findings attest that, through its missional conversion, the church is transformed not only as a *radical* contrast people whose lifestyle is profoundly shaped by the life and teaching of Jesus, and also as an *inclusive* contrast people who engage with the world by sharing and demonstrating the gospel about Jesus. The missional conversion of the church leads the church to engage with *the whole creation*[13] in its *being* and *doing*. In this sense, the missional conversion of the church is a transformative process by

---

embodying the kingdom of God. *Being* means an inward aspect of a community. *Doing* means a community's outward engagement with the world. Flemming divides the mission of the church into three parts: *being*, *doing*, and *telling*. However, in this study, *telling* is viewed as part of *doing* in order to give more clarity to the understanding of the mission of the people of God. For Dean Flemming's threefold view of the church's mission, see Flemming, *Recovering the Full Mission of God*.

12. In history, often there has been a recovery of mission that is *not* holistic; only partial, not complete.

13. This study did not deliberately deal with the ecological dimension of mission, but affirms that the comprehensive scope of mission includes not only humanity but also the whole creation. The ecological dimension of mission was briefly discussed in relation to the Noahic Covenant in the Theological Framework section of chapter 1 and in the discussion of the law and the comprehensive scope of Israel's sin in chapter 2. This Old Testament indication about the ecological mission was not discussed in chapters 3 and 4, but these two chapters attest that the essence of Israel's mission continued with the disciples and the earliest church, implying that Israel's relationship with the land continued in the missionary vocation of the disciples and the earliest church.

which the church's mission is intensified and expanded by *holistically* embodying the kingdom of God in both *being* and *doing*.

This holistic characteristic of the church's missional conversion practically suggests that the church which seeks its missional conversion should identify factors that hinder or stimulate the holistic mission of the church. In this diagnosis process, the church also can find a way to overcome the negative factors or foster the positive factors so that the church can be constantly shaped toward holistic participation in God's mission. More importantly, the church should be able to relate these factors to its relationship with God since the church's missional conversion involves its relationship with God.

The Church's Missional Conversion Is Ecclesio-Responsive

While the church's missional conversion is pneuma-driven, the role of the church for its missional conversion is not merely passive. In other words, the church's missional conversion is not a one-way process in which the church plays no role, but is a *two-way* process in which the church's active role is essential for its missional conversion. This aspect of the church's missional conversion is indicated in the research finding that the people of God in the biblical narrative were not merely receivers of God's transformative work among them, but, with their own wills, hearts, and minds, they responded to what their encounter with God revealed to them. The church's missional conversion involved its active response to what its encounter with God revealed to it. In the biblical cases examined in this study, when God encountered his people in order to shape them for mission, their role in this encounter was not merely passive, but they actively responded to that divine encounter. As noted in chapter 2, the fulfillment of Israel's missionary vocation entailed her obedience to, trust in, and dependence on God. Likewise, as discussed in chapter 3, the missional formation of the disciples required their faith in and commitment to Jesus. The biblical cases in chapter 4 clearly describe the active role of the earliest church in seeking and responding to the empowerment and guidance of God in and through the Holy Spirit.

This aspect of the missional conversion of the church is further supported by the research finding that God was not a God who forced his people to serve him for his mission, but a God who provides the church with a *reason* to *joyfully* and *gratefully* accept his invitation to be his missionary people. In chapter 2, the establishment of the Sinai Covenant, which led to the missional formation of the people of Israel, was their joyful and grateful response to God's grace for them. In chapter 3, Jesus invited the disciples to participate in God's global mission, by demonstrating his self-sacrificing *love* and universal *lordship*. Their Gentile mission was, on the one hand, to be their *logical, corresponding* response to this new reality of the universal lordship of the risen Jesus and, on the other hand, to be their *joyful* and *grateful* response to God's universal love as demonstrated by the death of Jesus. This research finding suggests that, in encountering God, the church always has a choice—either to accept what God calls it to be or to reject his call—but the church's missional conversion involves its active response to what God reveals to it in its encounter with him. In this sense, the missional conversion of the church is *ecclesio*-responsive.

Two particular practical implications are suggested from this aspect of the church's missional conversion. First, the church must be prepared and ready to accept and follow the lead of the Holy Spirit wherever he guides the church to. J. Robertson McQuilkin states, "Until we have an obedient and believing mindset or heart orientation, the deal is off. The Holy Spirit doesn't force his way on us. But if we meet that simple condition—the same faith response that connected us to him in the first place—we are poised to let the power flow."[14] The missional conversion of the church requires the church to be willing to follow the Holy Spirit. Second, the church needs to trust in and depend on the Holy Spirit. The church should constantly seek the guidance of the Holy Spirit, and be willing to embrace what the Holy Spirit reveals to it. This implication indicates that there is always a cost for the church to pay because the church should be *willing* to be changed to what the Holy Spirit empowers and guides it into.

E. Contributive Factors for the Church's Missional Conversion

This study identified three practical factors that can stimulate the missional conversion of the church. These contributing factors are more practical in nature than the general aspects of the church's missional conversion addressed above.

The Church's Missional Conversion through Communal Life

The communal aspect of the church's life can foster the church's missional conversion because one significant way that the church encounters God for its missional conversion is its individual members' mutual interaction with one another. This practical factor for the church's missional

---

14. McQuilkin, "Role of the Holy Spirit in Mission," 31.

conversion is drawn from the case of Cornelius's conversion examined in chapter 4. An individual Peter's witnessing of the act of the Holy Spirit among Gentiles and the lesson he learned from it resulted in broadening the earliest church's understanding of salvation and its missionary vocation. The transformation of the early church would not have taken place if Peter and the leaders of the church did not interact with one another. This biblical case implies that the church's missional conversion involves believers' mutual interaction with one another. Through mutual interaction, the members of the church theologically and practically impact one another, shaping the church toward its missionary vocation. In this way, not only individuals but also the whole community of faith can be shaped toward its authentic participation in God's mission. Therefore, the communal nature of the church's life is a contributing factor that stimulates its missional conversion, and, conversely, individualism in the life of the church hinders the church's missional conversion.[15]

The Church's Missional Conversion through Crosscultural Mission

The church's active participation in a crosscultural mission positively contributes to the church's missional conversion because the church can learn from what God is doing or wants the church to do in different contexts. This point is clearly presented and illustrated by the cases of Cornelius's conversion and of the Jerusalem Council. Both cases are shaped by early believers' involvement in crosscultural mission. Because of the lessons that they learned from their involvement in crosscultural mission, the earliest church was able to move further toward participating in God's global mission. This research finding indicates that the church's active participation in crosscultural mission can be a contributing factor that stimulates the church's missional conversion in a significant way. This point implies that the church's participation in crosscultural mission and the church's missional conversion

---

15. Along with Acts 9–10, the concept of a corporative identity of the Old Testament supports this point. In God's judgment, a sin committed by an individual Israelite was often viewed as a sin committed by the whole people of Israel. One example of it was the case of Achan whose sin resulted in the Israelites' defeat by Ai (Josh 7). God's judgment was upon the whole people of Israel. God removed his judgment upon them only after Achan's sin was dealt with. One individual's failure was viewed as the whole Israelites' failure. Likewise, the restoration of the Israelite's missionary vocation involved God's dealing with the individual's sin. Thus, the concept of a corporate identity in the Old Testament was assumed in the way that they fulfilled their missionary vocation. For Achan's sin and the Israel's corporate identity, see Howard, *Joshua*, 193–94.

are not in isolation from each other, but they influence one another. On the one hand, what the church experiences in its crosscultural mission impacts the church's understanding of its missionary vocation. On the other hand, the church's missional conversion leads the church to more authentically participate in God's global mission. As the church is constantly and intentionally involved in crosscultural mission, the church is constantly shaped, renewed, reformed, and equipped toward authentic participation in God's global mission. In other words, the church's involvement in crosscultural mission not only impacts the world but also changes the church itself.[16]

The Church's Missional Conversion through Intercultural Engagement

This study indicates that an intercultural engagement of culturally different churches plays a significant role in shaping these communities toward authentic participation in God's mission. In other words, one significant way that a church encounters God for its missional conversion is its intercultural engagement with other churches which are culturally different. This practical factor for the church's missional conversion is drawn from the case of the Jerusalem Council in Acts 15. The council was a result of the intercultural context of the earliest church, and dealt through intercultural engagement with theological issues fundamentally related to the church's missionary vocation. The result impacted both the Jerusalem Church and the Antioch Church. For the Jerusalem Church, the council helped Jewish believers overcome their ethnocentricity and understand God's global mission. For the Antioch Church, the church was able to continue its mission among Gentiles with a firm theological foundation for the transcultural nature of salvation, the gospel, and the church's identity and mission.

The analysis of the Jerusalem Council in Acts 15 shows that churches can encounter God through intercultural engagement with one another; the encounter, by extension, results in their transformation toward more authentic participation in God's mission as they overcome theological shortcomings shaped by their local contexts. Newbigin recognizes the transformative aspect of intercultural engagement. He strongly proposes that "the only way in which the gospel can challenge our culturally conditioned interpretations of it is through the witness of those who read the Bible with minds shaped by other cultures. *We have to listen to others.* This mutual correction is

---

16. Shawn B. Redford explores the role of mission proxies in missiological hermeneutics and affirms the significant role of missionary experience in biblical interpretation. See Redford, *Missiological Hermeneutics*, 232–89.

sometimes unwelcome, but it is necessary and it is fruitful."[17] This aspect of the church's missional conversion presupposes the presence and work of God in a community of faith. The church is not merely a social community but also a spiritual community profoundly shaped by God who dwells in it in and through the Holy Spirit. This spiritual dimension of the church establishes the pneumatological basis of churches' encounter with God through intercultural engagement with one another. In this regard, churches' intercultural engagement with one another should be viewed as a way by which churches encounter God who dwells in each of them in and through the Holy Spirit, and thereby they learn from God for their missional conversion.

F. Four Primary Resources for the Church's Missional Conversion

This study identifies four essential resources which the church should engage with for its missional conversion: The Bible, culture, the church, and theology. For its missional conversion, the church encounters God *in the Bible, in a particular culture, in the church,* and *through theological engagement.*

The Bible: Encountering God in the Bible

The Bible should be viewed as an essential resource for the church's missional conversion. The church encounters God as the church reads, reflects, and studies the Bible because the Bible witnesses about God. The Bible is a source in light of which the church can critically examine its missional status by reflecting on who God is and what he intends the church to be in the world. Thus, the church can be transformed toward its missionary vocation as the church engages with Scripture.

The church engages with Scripture for its missional conversion not in a purely intellectual way, but with the Holy Spirit. The Jerusalem Council serves as a biblical case that shows the role of the Holy Spirit in interpreting Scripture. Those who gathered at the council were able to understand God's global mission revealed in Scripture in light of the work of the Holy Spirit among Gentiles. Peter's witness to the outpouring of the Holy Spirit among Gentiles served as a hermeneutical key for the passage that James viewed as crucial for the missiological problem at issue. The case of the Jerusalem Council shows how the interpretive role of the Holy Spirit impacted the church's missional conversion, indicating the significance of *pneumatological*

---

17. Newbigin, *Gospel in a Pluralist Society*, 196–97. Emphasis added.

hermeneutics for the church's missional conversion.[18] The teaching role of the Holy Spirit that Jesus mentioned in John 14:26 indicates the Holy Spirit's role in the process of scriptural interpretation: "the Advocate, the Holy Spirit, whom the Father will send in my name, will teach you everything, and remind you of all that I have said to you." The Apostle Paul affirms the role of the Holy Spirit in revealing God's intention, when he states, "as it is written, 'What no eye has seen, nor ear heard, nor the human heart conceived, what God has prepared for those who love him'—these things God has revealed to us through the Spirit; for the Spirit searches everything, even the depths of God" (1 Cor 2:6–16). Thus, the church should seek the illuminating guidance of the Holy Spirit in reading, studying, and reflecting on Scripture for its missional conversion. The recognition of the importance of the hermeneutical role of the Holy Spirit should not mean neglecting other methods for studying Scripture, but suggests that the church seek the guidance of the Holy Spirit whenever it uses Bible study tools and methods.

This practical suggestion is more than mere recognition of the role of the Holy Spirit in human efforts to interpret Scripture. On the one hand, as Anthony C. Thiselton states, the Holy Spirit is "operating through the processes of human enquiry."[19] On the other hand, the church, which seeks to encounter God in the Bible for its missional conversion, should acknowledge the proactive role of the Holy Spirit in scriptural interpretation by intentionally looking to the Holy Spirit as a teacher and interpreter in reading and studying Scripture.

Culture: Encountering God in a Particular Culture

Another resource the church should engage with for its missional conversion is culture. The church's missional conversion takes place in a particular culture as the church encounters God *in a particular culture*. In the biblical

---

18. The majority of contemporary scholars do not recognize the significant and essential role of the Holy Spirit in the process of interpretation. However, some scholars recognize the importance of the role of the Holy Spirit. For some excellent studies of the role of the Holy Spirit in biblical hermeneutics, see Wyckoff, *Pneuma and Logos*; Keener, *Spirit Hermeneutics*.

19. One hermeneutical model that affirms the significance of the role of the Holy Spirit as a guide in biblical interpretation is John W. Wyckoff's "facilitator paradigm," where "the endeavor of understanding Scripture would be seen as a cooperative task in which the Holy Spirit's participation is essential." In this model, "The reader would be like the student who relies upon the teacher for insights because 'the teacher possesses greater knowledge and has had more experience.' The reader would look to the Holy Spirit because, like the teacher, the Holy Spirit is 'in a position of being a guide in territory through which he has already passed.'" Wyckoff, *Pneuma and Logos*, 112.

narratives explored in this study, God was a God in history who revealed himself in a particular time and a particular place. He continuously shaped his people through encountering them in particular cultures.

This study shows that the role of culture is significant for the church's missional conversion. This point is illustrated in the earliest church's missional conversion initiated by Cornelius's conversion. While its missional conversion was not influenced by culture, the church encountered the Holy Spirit *in a particular culture,* and learned from what God was doing in a particular culture. In their analysis of the book of Acts, Bevans and Schroeder recognize this dynamic: "The church's missionary nature only emerges as the community engages with *particular contexts*, under the direction of *the Spirit*."[20] As they observe in the book of Acts, "The Jewish identity of the community is transformed into the church as the community recognizes the Spirit among the Samaritans, in the Ethiopian eunuch, in Cornelius and his household, and in the community of Antioch."[21] The church can apply this point in two practical ways, as mentioned above: (1) involvement in crosscultural mission and (2) intercultural engagement with other churches.

The Church: Encountering God Dwelling in the Church

The third resource that the church should engage with for its missional conversion is the church itself. The church encounters God who dwells in it in and through the Holy Spirit. The church is not merely a group of religious people, but a people with whom God is. As this study demonstrated, the presence of God is the fulfilling factor of the missionary vocation of God's people. God is a God who determined to be with his people as early as when he called them in the Old Testament. The missional formation of the Israelites was completed with the construction of the tabernacle which represented the presence of God and was a place where God would meet them. God provided a way that they could encounter God through the tabernacle on a regular basis. In the New Testament, the presence of God in the midst of the Israelites continued in and through Jesus who came to Jews and stayed with his disciples. When the risen Jesus ascended to the Father, God continued to be present with early believers in and through the Holy Spirit as the Holy Spirit came to and dwelt in the earliest church. This point is made explicit in Paul's writings. For example, Paul states, "God's temple is holy, and you are that temple" (1 Cor 3:17). Gordon D. Fee states, "For Paul the Spirit is how God presently dwells in his holy temple.

---

20. Bevans and Schroeder, *Constants in Context*, 13. Emphasis added.
21. Bevans and Schroeder, *Constants in Context*, 13.

Significantly, such dwelling takes place both in the gathered community . . . and especially in the heart of the individual believer."[22] This aspect of the church's missional conversion practically suggests that the church which seeks its missional conversion needs to plan and conduct its whole ministry with *the sense of the presence of the Holy Spirit in it*, and with the humble readiness to be led by and learn from the Holy Spirit.

The view of the church as the temple of God (or the temple of the Holy Spirit) is not limited to a local church but is also applied to the global church because the local church belongs to the global church. Thus, when local churches engage with one another, they should do so with humility and boldness. They should be humble in learning from God who dwells in churches. They should be bold in sharing what God has done through them. They should be willing to be open to one another, while they seek to discern the truth that God reveals to them in and through the Holy Spirit.

Theology: Encountering God through Theological Engagement

Lastly, theology is an important resource that the church should engage with for its missional conversion. If theology is a task or product of seeking to understand God, engagement with a theology can lead the church to a new understanding of God. Thus, the church can encounter God through theological engagement, and, in turn, be transformed toward its missionary vocation. As demonstrated in this study, the way that the earliest church participated in God's mission was profoundly influenced by its theology. The early church's missional conversion involved the church's theological transformation. The church's participation in God's mission expanded when the church embraced what God in and through the Holy Spirit revealed about theological themes, such as the gospel, salvation, and mission. The Jerusalem Council can be viewed as an event, which was caused by and dealt with a theological conflict between two different theologies. In the council, a group of Jewish believers encountered the God of the Gentiles as they engaged with the Gentile believers' theological viewpoint of salvation that God brought to Gentiles. This divine encounter through theological engagement led the Jewish believers to a new theological understanding of God, the gospel, salvation, and mission. Thus, theology is a significant resource through which the church can encounter God for its missional conversion.

---

22. Fee, *Paul, the Spirit, and the People of God*, 15. Also see Moltmann, *Church in the Power of the Spirit*, 294.

To summarize, this study demonstrates that the church's missional conversion is primarily a consequence of its continuous encounter with the triune God. This main thesis is grounded in four foundational components which led the church's transformation toward its missionary vocation: (1) the missional potentiality of the church, (2) the missional vulnerability of the church, (3) the missional faithfulness of God, and (4) the church's encounter with the triune God. Furthermore, this study suggests that the missional conversion of the church is profoundly and fundamentally trinitarian—*theo*-derived, *Christocentric,* and *pneuma*-driven—and that the missional conversion of the church is essentially a continuous process, holistic, and *ecclesio*-responsive. Furthermore, this study identifies three contributive factors that stimulate the missional conversion of the church: the church's communal life, its participation in crosscultural mission, and its intercultural engagement with culturally different Christian communities. Lastly, this study suggests four resources that the church should engage for its missional conversion: Scripture, culture, the church, and theology.

Bibliography

Ahn, Byung-Mu. "Jesus and the Minjung in the Gospel of Mark." In *Voices from the Margin*, edited by R. S. Sugirtharajah, 85–103. Maryknoll, NY: Orbis, 1991.

Alexander, T. Desmond. *Exodus*. Grand Rapids: Baker, 2016.

Allen, Roland. "Pentecost and the World: The Revelation of the Holy Spirit in the 'Acts of the Apostles.'" In *The Ministry of the Spirit: Selected Writings*, edited by David M. Paton, 1–61. London: World Dominion, 1960.

Allison, Dale, Jr. *The New Moses: A Matthean Typology*. Minneapolis: Fortress, 1993.

Averbeck, Richard E. "Priest, Priesthood." In *Evangelical Dictionary of Biblical Theology*, edited by Walter A. Elwell, 632–38. Grand Rapids: Baker, 1996.

———. "Tabernacle." In *Dictionary of the Old Testament: Pentateuch*, edited by T. Desmond Alexander and David W. Baker, 807–27. Downers Grove, IL; Leicester, England: InterVarsity, 2002.

Bailey, Randall C. *Exodus*. Joplin, MO: College, 2007.

Baker, David L. *The Decalogue: Living as the People of God*. Downers Grove, IL: InterVarsity, 2017.

Barram, Michael D. *Missional Economics: Biblical Justice and Christian Formation*. Grand Rapids: Eerdmans, 2018.

Barrett, C. K. *A Critical and Exegetical Commentary on the Acts of the Apostles: Introduction and Commentary on Acts 15–28*. Edinburgh: T. & T. Clark, 1994.

———. *A Critical and Exegetical Commentary on the Acts of the Apostles: Preliminary Introduction and Commentary on Acts 1–14*. Edinburgh: T. & T. Clark, 1994.

Bartholomew, Craig G., and Michael W. Goheen. *The Drama of Scripture: Finding Our Place in the Biblical Story*. Grand Rapids: Baker, 2004.

Barton, Stephen C. "Dislocating and Relocating Holiness: A New Testament Study." In *Holiness: Past and Present*, edited by Stephen C. Barton, 193–213. London; New York: T. & T. Clark, 2003.

Bauckham, Richard J. *Bible and Mission: Christian Witness in a Postmodern World*. Grand Rapids: Baker, 2003.

———. "James and the Gentiles (Acts 15.13–21)." In *History, Literature, and Society in the Book of Acts*, edited by Ben Witherington III, 154–84. Cambridge: Cambridge University Press, 1996.

———. "James, Peter and the Gentiles." In *The Missions of James, Peter, and Paul: Tensions in Early Christianity*, edited by Bruce Chilton and Craig Evans, 91–142. Leiden: Brill, 2005.

Beale, Gregory K. *The Temple and the Church's Mission: A Biblical Theology of the Dwelling Place of God*. Leicester: Apollos, 2005.

Beasley-Murray, George R. *Jesus and the Kingdom of God*. Grand Rapids: Eerdmans, 1985.

Beck, Robert R. *Jesus and His Enemies: Narrative Conflict in the Four Gospels*. Maryknoll, NY: Orbis, 2017.

Bennema, Cornelis. "The Ethnic Conflict in Early Christianity: An Appraisal of Bauckham's Proposal on the Antioch Crisis and the Jerusalem Council." *Journal of the Evangelical Theological Society* 56 (2013) 753–63.

Bevans, Stephen B., and Roger Schroeder. *Constants in Context: A Theology of Mission for Today*. Maryknoll, NY: Orbis, 2004.

Biddle, Mark E. *Deuteronomy*. Macon, GA: Smyth & Helwys, 2003.

Bird, Michael F. *Jesus and the Origins of the Gentile Mission*. London: T. & T. Clark, 2006.

Blackburn, W. Ross. *The God Who Makes Himself Known: The Missionary Heart of the Book of Exodus*. Downers Grove, IL: InterVarsity, 2012.

Blauw, Johannes. "The Mission of the People of God." In *The Missionary Church in East and West*, edited by Charles West and David M. Paton, 91–100. London: SCM, 1959.

———. *The Missionary Nature of the Church: A Survey of the Biblical Theology of Mission*. London: Lutterworth, 1962.

Blomberg, Craig L. *Contagious Holiness: Jesus' Meals with Sinners*. Downers Grove, IL: InterVarsity, 2005.

———. *Matthew*. Nashville: Broadman, 1992.

Bock, Darrell L. *Acts*. Grand Rapids: Baker Academic, 2007.

Boda, Mark J. "Prophets." In *T. & T. Clark Companion to the Doctrine of Sin*, edited by Keith L. Johnson and David Lauber, 27–43. London; New York: Bloomsbury T. & T. Clark, 2016.

Boer, Harry R. *Pentecost and Missions*. Grand Rapids: Eerdmans, 1961.

Booth, Susan Maxwell. *The Tabernacling Presence of God: Mission and Gospel Witness*. Eugene, OR: Wipf & Stock, 2015.

Borchert, Gerald L. *John 12–21*. Nashville: Broadman & Holman, 2002.

Boring, M. Eugene. *Mark: A Commentary*. Louisville, KY: Westminster John Knox, 2006.

Bosch, David J. *Transforming Mission: Paradigm Shifts in Theology of Mission*. Maryknoll, NY: Orbis, 1991.

Breck, John. *The Shape of Biblical Language: Chiasmus in the Scriptures and Beyond*. Crestwood, NY: St. Vladimir's Seminary Press, 1994.

Bright, John. *Covenant and Promise: The Prophetic Understanding of the Future in Pre-Exilic Israel*. Philadelphia: Westminster, 1976.

———. *The Kingdom of God: The Biblical Concept and Its Meaning for the Church*. Nashville: Abingdon, 1953.

Brower, Kent E. "The Holy One and His Disciples: Holiness and Ecclesiology in Mark." In *Holiness and Ecclesiology in the New Testament*, edited by Kent E. Brower and Andy Johnson, 57–75. Grand Rapids: Eerdmans, 2007.

Bruce, F. F. *The Acts of the Apostles: The Greek Text with Introduction and Commentary*. Eugene, OR: Wipf & Stock, 2000.

Brueggemann, Walter. "The Crisis and Promise of Presence in Israel." *Horizons in Biblical Theology* 1 (1979) 47–86.

———. *Theology of the Old Testament: Testimony, Dispute, Advocacy*. Minneapolis: Fortress, 1997.

Brunner, Emil. *The Christian Doctrine of God*. Philadelphia: Westminster, 1950.

Buber, Martin. *Kingship of God*. Translated by Richard Scheimann. 3rd ed. Atlantic Highlands, NJ: Humanities, 1990.

Bultmann, Rudolf K. *Theology of the New Testament*. Vol. 2. New York: Charles Scribner's Sons, 1955.

Carroll, John T. *Luke: A Commentary*. Louisville, KY: Westminster John Knox, 2012.

Carter, Warren. "Matthew and the Gentiles: Individual Conversion and/or Systemic Transformation?" *Journal for the Study of the New Testament* 26 (2004) 259–82.

Caudill, Norah Whipple. "The Presence of God in the Exodus Narrative: Purposes, Means and Implications." PhD diss., Fuller Theological Seminary, 2006.

Children, Bruce. "Purity and Impurity." In *Dictionary of the Later New Testament and Its Developments*, edited by Ralph P. Martin and Peter H. Davids, 988–96. Downers Grove, IL: InterVarsity, 1997.

Childs, Brevard S. *The Book of Exodus: A Critical, Theological Commentary*. Philadelphia: Westminster, 1974.

Chisholm, Robert B., Jr. "The Christological Fulfillment of Isaiah's Servant Songs." *Bibliotheca Sacra* 163 (2006) 387–404.

Cho, Banseok. "The Nature of the Church's Mission in Light of the Biblical Origin of Social Holiness." *The Asbury Journal* 73 (2018) 104–33.

Choi, Hyung-Keun. "Missional Conversion and Transformation in the Context of the Korean Protestant Church." *Mission Studies* 34 (2017) 53–77.

Christian, C. W. *Covenant and Commandment: A Study of the Ten Commandments in the Context of Grace*. Macon, GA: Smyth & Helwys, 2004.

Clements, Ronald. *God and Temple*. Philadelphia: Fortress, 1965.

Clements, Ronald E. *Prophecy and Covenant*. London: SCM, 1965.

Clifford, Catherine E. "Pope Francis' Call for the Conversion of the Church in Our Time." *Australian eJournal of Theology* 22 (2015) 33–55.

Cole, R. Alan. *Exodus*. Downers Grove, IL: InterVarsity, 1973.

Cole, R. Dennis. *Numbers*. Nashville: Broadman & Holman, 2000.

Coleman, Robert E. *The Master Plan of Evangelism*. Grand Rapids: F. H. Revell, 1993.

Collins, Raymon F. "Twelve, the." In *The Anchor Bible Dictionary*, edited by David Noel Freedman, 6:670–71. New York: Doubleday, 1992.

Cook, Joan E. *Hear O Heavens and Listen O Earth: An Introduction to the Prophets*. Collegeville, MN: Liturgical, 2006.

Cook, Stephen L. "Prophets and Prophecy." In *The Oxford Encyclopedia of the Bible and Theology*, edited by Samuel E. Balentine, 2:201–11. New York: Oxford University Press, 2015.

Coppedge, Allan. *Portraits of God: A Biblical Theology of Holiness*. Downers Grove, IL: InterVarsity, 2001.

Cousar, Charles B. *A Theology of the Cross: The Death of Jesus in the Pauline Letters*. Minneapolis: Fortress, 1993.

Culpepper, R. Alan. "Luke." In *The New Interpreter's Bible*, 9:1–490. Nashville: Abingdon, 1995.

Dahood, Mitchell Joseph. "Ugaritic-Hebrew Parallel Pairs." In *Ras Shamra Parallels: the Texts from Ugarit and the Hebrew Bible*, edited by Loren R. Fisher, 2:71–382. Roma: Pontificium Institutum Biblicum, 1972.

Davies, John A. "A Royal Priesthood: Literary and Intertextual Perspectives on an Image of Israel in Exodus 19:6." *Tyndale Bulletin* 53 (2002) 157–59.

———. *A Royal Priesthood: Literary and Intertextual Perspectives on an Image of Israel in Exodus 19.6*. London; New York: T. & T. Clark, 2004.

Davies, W. D., and Dale C. Allison, Jr. *A Critical and Exegetical Commentary on the Gospel According to Matthew*. Vol. 3. Edinburgh: T. & T. Clark, 1988.

Deist, Ferdinand. "The Exodus Motif in the Old Testament and the Theology of Liberation." *Missionalia* 5 (1977) 58–69.

DeSilva, David A. *An Introduction to the New Testament: Contexts, Methods & Ministry Formation*. Downers Grove, IL; Leicester, England: InterVarsity; Apollos, 2004.

Dollar, Harold. *St. Luke's Missiology: A Cross-Cultural Challenge*. Pasadena, CA: William Carey Library, 1996.

Donfried, Karl P. "Peter." In *The Anchor Bible Dictionary*, edited by David Noel Freedman, 5:251–63. New York: Doubleday, 1992.

Driver, John. *Images of the Church in Mission*. Scottdale, PA; Waterloo, ON: Herald, 1997.

Duke, R. K. "Priests, Priesthood." In *Dictionary of the Old Testament: Pentateuch*, edited by T. Desmond Alexander and David W. Baker, 646–55. Downers Grove, IL: InterVarsity, 2003.

Dumbrell, William J. "The Prospect of Unconditionality in the Sinaitic Covenant." In *Israel's Apostasy and Restoration: Essays in Honor of Roland K. Harrison*, edited by Avraham Gileadi, 141–55. Grand Rapids: Baker, 1988.

Dunbar, Paul James, and Anthony L. Blair. *Leading Missional Change: Move Your Congregation from Resistant to Re-Energized*. Eugene, OR: Wipf & Stock, 2013.

Dunn, James D. G. *The Acts of the Apostles*. Peterborough, UK: Epworth, 1996.

———. *The Acts of the Apostles*. Grand Rapids: Eerdmans, 2016.

———. *Baptism in the Holy Spirit: A Re-Examination of the New Testament Teaching on the Gift of the Spirit in Relation to Pentecostalism Today*. Philadelphia: Westminster, 1970.

———. "Law." In *Dictionary of Jesus and the Gospels*, edited by Joel B. Green et al., 505–15. Downers Grove, IL: InterVarsity, 2013.

———. "Pentecost." In *The Christ and the Spirit: Collected Essays of James D. G. Dunn. Pneumatology*, edited by James D. G. Dunn, 2:210–15. Grand Rapids: Eerdmans, 1998.

———. *Unity and Diversity in the New Testament: An Inquiry into the Character of Earliest Christianity*. 3rd ed. London, UK; Philadelphia: SCM; Trinity Press International, 1990.

Dupont, Jacques. *The Salvation of the Gentiles: Essays on the Acts of Apostles*. New York: Paulist, 1979.

Durham, John. *Exodus*. Waco, TX: Word, 1987.

Edwards, James R. *The Gospel According to Mark*. Grand Rapids; Leicester, England: Eerdmans; Apollos, 2002.

Eichrodt, Walther. *Theology of the Old Testament*. Vol. 1. Translated by J. A. Baker. Philadelphia: Westminster, 1961.

Escobar, Samuel. *The New Global Mission: The Gospel from Everywhere to Everyone*. Downers Grove, IL: InterVarsity, 2003.

Evans, Craig A. "A Light to the Nations: Isaiah and Mission in Luke." In *Christian Mission: Old Testament Foundations and New Testament Developments,* edited by Stanley E. Porter and Cynthia Long Westfall, 93–107. Eugene, OR: Pickwick, 2010.

Fee, Gordon D. *Paul, the Spirit, and the People of God.* Peabody, MA: Hendrickson, 1996.

Ferebee, Randolph C. *Cultivating the Missional Church: New Soil for Growing Vestries and Leaders.* Harrisburg, PA: Morehouse, 2012.

Flemming, Dean. *Contextualization in the New Testament: Patterns for Theology and Mission.* Westmont, IL: InterVarsity, 2009.

———. *Recovering the Full Mission of God: A Biblical Perspective on Being, Doing and Telling.* Downers Grove, IL: IVP Academic, 2013.

Flett, John G. *The Witness of God: The Trinity, Missio Dei, Karl Barth, and the Nature of Christian Community.* Grand Rapids: Eerdmans, 2010.

Frame, John M. *The Doctrine of God.* Phillipsburg, NJ: Presbyterian & Reformed, 2002.

France, R. T. *The Gospel According to Matthew: An Introduction and Commentary.* Leicester, England; Grand Rapids: InterVarsity; Eerdmans, 1985.

———. *The Gospel of Mark: A Commentary on the Greek Text.* Grand Rapids; Carlisle, UK: Eerdmans; Paternoster, 2002.

———. *The Gospel of Matthew.* Grand Rapids: Eerdmans, 2007.

Francis. *The Joy of the Gospel: Evangelii Gaudium.* Washington, DC: United States Conference of Catholic Bishops, 2013.

Fredrickson, Kurt Norman. "An Ecclesial Ecology for Denominational Futures Nurturing Organic Structures for Missional Engagement." PhD diss., Fuller Theological Seminary, 2009.

Fretheim, Terence E. *Exodus.* Louisville, KY: John Knox, 1991.

Gardner, Richard B. *Matthew.* Scottdale, PA: Herald, 1991.

Garland, David E. *Acts.* Grand Rapids: Baker, 2017.

———. *Reading Matthew: A Literary and Theological Commentary on the First Gospel.* New York: Crossroad, 1993.

Garrett, Duane A. *A Commentary on Exodus.* Grand Rapids: Kregel Academic, 2014.

Gaventa, Beverly Roberts. *The Acts of the Apostles.* Nashville: Abingdon, 2003.

———. *From Darkness to Light: Aspects of Conversion in the New Testament.* Philadelphia: Fortress, 1986.

Gentry, Peter John, and Stephen J. Wellum. *Kingdom through Covenant: A Biblical-Theological Understanding of the Covenants.* Wheaton, IL: Crossway, 2012.

Gibbs, Eddie, and Ryan K. Bolger. *Emerging Churches: Creating Christian Community in Postmodern Cultures.* Grand Rapids: Baker Academic, 2005.

Glaser, Ida. *The Bible and Other Faiths: Christian Responsibility in a World of Religions.* Downers Grove, IL: InterVarsity, 2005.

Glasser, Arthur F., et al. *Announcing the Kingdom: The Story of God's Mission in the Bible.* Grand Rapids: Baker Academic, 2003.

Goheen, Michael W. *A Light to the Nations: The Missional Church and the Biblical Story.* Grand Rapids: Baker Academic, 2011.

Goldingay, John. *A Critical and Exegetical Commentary on Isaiah 56–66.* London: Bloomsbury, 2014.

———. *Israel's Gospel.* Downers Grove, IL: InterVarsity, 2003.

Gort, J. D. "Human Distress, Salvation, and Mediation of Salvation." In *Missiology: An Ecumenical Introduction. Texts and Contexts of Global Christianity*, edited by F. J. Verstraelen et al., 194–210. Grand Rapids: Eerdmans, 1995.

Green, Joel B. *The Gospel of Luke*. Grand Rapids: Eerdmans, 1997.

Grisanti, Michael A. "Israel's Mission to the Nations in Isaiah 40–55: An Update." *The Master's Seminary Journal* 9 (1998) 39–61.

Guder, Darrell L. *The Continuing Conversion of the Church*. Grand Rapids: Eerdmans, 2000.

———. "*Missio Dei*: Integrating Theological Formation for Apostolic Vocation: Presidential Address." *Missiology* 37 (2009) 63–74.

———. "Missional Theology for a Missionary Church." *Journal for Preachers* 22 (1998) 3–11.

———, ed. *Missional Church: A Vision for the Sending of the Church in North America*. Grand Rapids: Eerdmans, 1998.

Haenchen, Ernst. *The Acts of the Apostles*. Philadelphia: Westminster, 1971.

Hagner, Donald A. "Holiness and Ecclesiology: The Church in Matthew." In *Holiness and Ecclesiology in the New Testament*, edited by Kent E. Brower and Andy Johnson, 40–56. Grand Rapids: Eerdmans, 2007.

———. *Matthew 1–13*. Dallas: Word, 1993.

Hahn, Ferdinand. *Mission in the New Testament*. Naperville, IL: Alec R. Allenson, 1965.

Hamilton, Victor P. *Exodus: An Exegetical Commentary*. Grand Rapids: Baker Academic, 2011.

Hare, Douglas R. A. *Matthew*. Louisville, KY: Westminster John Knox, 2009.

Harrington, Daniel J. *The Gospel of Matthew*. Collegeville, MN: Liturgical, 1991.

Hartley, J. E. "Holy and Holiness, Clean and Unclean." In *Dictionary of the Old Testament: Pentateuch*, edited by T. Desmond Alexander and David W. Baker, 420–31. Downers Grove, IL: InterVarsity, 2003.

Haydock, Nocholas. *The Theology of the Levitical Priesthood*. Eugene, OR: Wipf & Stock, 2016.

Hays, J. Daniel. *The Message of the Prophets: A Survey of the Prophetic and Apocalyptic Books of the Old Testament*. Grand Rapids: Zondervan, 2010.

Hays, Richard B. *The Moral Vision of the New Testament: Community, Cross, New Creation, a Contemporary Introduction to New Testament Ethics*. San Francisco: HarperSanFrancisco, 1996.

Healy, Mary. *The Gospel of Mark*. Grand Rapids: Baker Academic, 2008.

Hedlund, Roger E. *The Mission of the Church in the World: A Biblical Theology*. Grand Rapids: Baker, 1991.

Hengel, Martin. *Acts and the History of Earliest Christianity*. London: SCM, 1979.

Hennessy, Anne. *The Galilee of Jesus*. Rome: Pontificia Universita Gregoriana, 1994.

Hertig, Paul. "The Galilee Theme in Matthew: Transforming Mission Through Marginality." *Missiology* 25 (1997) 155–63.

Hilary, Mbachu. *Inculturation Theology of the Jerusalem Council in Acts 15: An Inspiration for the Igbo Church Today*. Frankfurt am Main, Germany: Peter Lang, 1995.

Hirsch, Alan. *The Forgotten Ways: Reactivating Apostolic Movements*. Grand Rapids: Brazos, 2006.

Holladay, William Lee. *The Root šûbh in the Old Testament with Particular Reference to Its Usages in Covenantal Contexts*. Leiden: Brill, 1958.

Howard, David M., Jr. *Joshua*. Nashville: Broadman & Holman, 1998.

Immanuel, Babu. "Jesus' Cross, Conflicts and the New Testament." *Transformation* 23 (2006) 24–29.

International Missionary Council. *The Missionary Obligation of the Church*. London: Edinburgh House, 1952.

Jacob, Edmond. *Theology of the Old Testament*. Translated by Arthur W. Heathcote and Philip A. Allcock. London: Hodder & Stoughton, 1958.

Janzen, Waldemar. "Tabernacle." In *The New Interpreter's Dictionary of the Bible*, edited by Katharine Boob Sakenfeld, 5:447–58. Nashville: Abingdon, 2010.

Jeremias, Joachim. *Jesus' Promise to the Nations*. Naperville, IL: Alec R. Allenson, 1958.

———. *New Testament Theology: The Proclamation of Jesus*. New York: Scribner, 1971.

Johnson, Dennis E. "Jesus Against the Idols: The Use of Isaianic Servant Songs in the Missiology of Acts." *The Westminster Theological Journal* 52 (1990) 343–53.

Johnson, Luke Timothy. *The Acts of the Apostles*. Collegeville, MN: Liturgical, 1992.

Johnstone, William. *Exodus 1–19*. Macon, GA: Smyth & Helwys, 2014.

Jones, Judith Anne. "Twelve, the." In *The New Interpreter's Dictionary of the Bible*, edited by Katharine Doob Sakenfeld, 5:690. Nashville: Abingdon, 2007.

Jung, Musung. "Toward a theology of *pareo Dei*: Exploring a contextual theology of *missio Dei* for the missiological reconciliation of the Korean Protestant Church." PhD diss., Asbury Theological Seminary, 2012.

Kaiser, Walter C., Jr. *Mission in the Old Testament: Israel as a Light to the Nations*. Grand Rapids: Baker, 2000.

Kee, Howard Clark. "Early Christianity in the Galilee: Reassessing the Evidence from the Gospels." In *The Galilee in Late Antiquity*, edited by Lee I. Levine, 3–22. Cambridge, MA: Harvard University Press, 1992.

Keener, Craig S. *Acts*. 3 vols. Grand Rapids: Baker Academic, 2012–14.

———. *A Commentary on the Gospel of Matthew*. Grand Rapids: Eerdmans, 1999.

———. *The Gospel of John: A Commentary*. Vol. 2. Peabody, MA: Hendrickson, 2003.

———. *The Gospel of Matthew: A Socio-Rhetorical Commentary*. Grand Rapids; Cambridge: Eerdmans, 2009.

———. *Spirit Hermeneutics: Reading Scripture in Light of Pentecost*. Grand Rapids: Eerdmans, 2016.

Kim, Sinyil. "Korean Immigrants and Their Mission: Exploring the Missional Identity of Korean Immigrant Churches in North America." DMiss diss., Asbury Theological Seminary, 2008.

Kim, Tai-I. "The Biblical Foundations of Mission in the Abrahamic Covenant." DMiss diss., Reformed Theological Seminary, 1996.

Kingsbury, Jack D. "The Developing Conflict Between Jesus and the Jewish Leaders in Matthew's Gospel: A Literary-Critical Study." *Catholic Biblical Quarterly* 49 (1987) 57–73.

Klink, Edward W., III. *John: Zondervan Exegetical Commentary on the New Testament*. Grand Rapids: Zondervan, 2016.

Köstenberger, Andreas J. "The Challenge of a Systematized Biblical Theology of Mission: Missiological Insights from the Gospel of John." *Missiology: An International Review* 23 (1995) 445–64.

———. *Encountering John: The Gospel in Historical, Literary, and Theological Perspective*. Grand Rapids: Baker, 1999.

———. *John*. Grand Rapids: Baker Academic, 2004.

———. *The Missions of Jesus and the Disciples According to the Fourth Gospel.* Grand Rapids: Eerdmans, 1998.

———. *A Theology of John's Gospel and Letters.* Grand Rapids: Zondervan, 2009.

Köstenberger, Andreas J., and Peter T. O'Brien. *Salvation to the Ends of the Earth.* Leicester, England; Downers Grove, IL: Apollos; InterVarsity, 2001.

Küng, Hans. *The Church.* New York: Sheed and Ward, 1968.

Kupp, David D. *Matthew's Emmanuel: Divine Presence and God's People in the First Gospel.* Cambridge; New York: Cambridge University Press, 1996.

Kurz, William S. *Acts of the Apostles.* Grand Rapids: Baker Academic, 2013.

Laing, Mark. "Recovering Missional Ecclesiology in Theological Education." *International Review of Mission* 98 (2009) 11–24.

Lambert, David A. *How Repentance Became Biblical: Judaism, Christianity, and the Interpretation of Scripture.* New York: Oxford University Press, 2015.

Larkin, William J., Jr. *Acts.* Downers Grove, IL: InterVarsity, 1995.

———. "Mission in Acts." In *Mission in the New Testament: An Evangelical Approach,* edited by William Larkin Jr. and Joel F. Williams, 170–86. Maryknoll, NY: Orbis, 1998.

LaSor, William Sanford. "The Prophets During the Monarchy." In *Israel's Apostasy and Restoration: Essays in Honor of Roland K. Harrison,* edited by Avraham Gileadi, 59–70. Grand Rapids: Baker, 1988.

Lauterbach, Jacob Zallel. *Mekhilta De-Rabbi Ishmael.* Vol. 2. Philadelphia: The Jewish Publication Society, 2004.

Lee, Gil Pyo. "From Traditional to Missional Church: Describing a Contextual Model of Change for Ingrown Korean Diaspora Church in North America." DMiss diss., Asbury Theological Seminary, 2010.

Leffel, Gregory Paul. "Faith Seeking Action: Missio-Ecclesiology, Social Movements, and the Church as a Movement of the People of God." PhD diss., Asbury Theological Seminary, 2004.

Legrand, Lucien. *Unity and Plurality: Mission in the Bible.* Translated by Robert R. Barr. Orbis: 1990.

Levine, Baruch A. *Leviticus.* Philadelphia: The Jewish Publication Society, 1989.

Lindars, Barnabas. *New Testament Apologetic: The Doctrinal Significance of the Old Testament Quotations.* London: SCM, 1973.

Lister, John Ryan. "The Lord Your God is in Your Midst: The Presence of God and the Means and End of Redemptive History." PhD diss., Southern Baptist Theological Seminary, 2010.

Lohfink, Gerhard. *Does God Need the Church?: Toward a Theology of the People of God.* Collegeville, MN: Liturgical, 1999.

———. *Jesus and Community: The Social Dimension of Christian Faith.* Philadelphia: Fortress, 1982.

Longenecker, Richard N. "Luke." In *The Expositor's Bible Commentary,* edited by Tremper Longman III and David E. Garland, 10:663–1102. Grand Rapids: Zondervan, 2007.

Longman, Tremper, III, and Raymond B. Dillard. *An Introduction to the Old Testament.* 2nd ed. Grand Rapids: Zondervan, 2006.

Luz, Ulrich. *Matthew 21–28.* Minneapolis: Fortress, 2005.

March, W. Eugene. "Prophecy." In *Old Testament Form Criticism,* edited by John H. Hayes, 141–77. San Antonio, TX: Trinity University Press, 1974.

Marshall, I. Howard. *The Acts of the Apostles*. Grand Rapids: Eerdmans, 1980.

———. *New Testament Theology: Many Witnesses, One Gospel*. Downers Grove, IL: InterVarsity, 2004.

Martens, Elmer. *God's Design: A Focus on Old Testament Theology*. Grand Rapids: Baker, 1981.

Martin-Achard, Robert. *A Light to the Nations: A Study of the Old Testament Conception of Israel's Mission to the World*. Translated by John Penney Smith. London: Oliver and Boyd, 1962.

Matthew, Ed. "Yahweh and the Gods: A Theology of World Religions from the Pentateuch." In *Christianity and the Religions: A Biblical Theology of World Religions*, edited by Edward Rommen, 30–44. Pasadena, CA: William Carey Library, 1995.

Matthey, Jacques. "The Great Commission According to Matthew." *International Review of Mission* 69 (1980) 161–73.

McKnight, Scot. "Covenant and Spirit." In *The Holy Spirit and Christian Origins: Essays in Honor of James D. G. Dunn*, edited by Stephen C. Barton et al., 41–54. Grand Rapids: Eerdmans, 2004.

McMahan, Craig Thomas. "Meals as Type-Scenes in the Gospel of Luke." PhD Diss., The Southern Baptist Theological Seminary, 1987.

McQuilkin, J. Robertson. "The Role of the Holy Spirit in Mission." In *The Holy Spirit and Mission Dynamics*, edited by C. Douglas McConnell, 22–35. Pasadena, CA: William Carey Library, 1997.

Meier, John P. "Two Disputed Questions in Matt 28:16–20." *Journal of Biblical Literature* 96 (1977) 407–24.

Meyer, Ben F. *The Aims of Jesus*. London: SCM, 1979.

Michaels, J. Ramsey. *The Gospel of John*. Grand Rapids: Eerdmans, 2010.

Milgrom, Jacob. "Holy, Holiness, Old Testament." In *The New Interpreter's Dictionary of the Bible*, edited by Katharine Doob Sakenfeld, 2:850–58. Nashville: Abingdon, 2010.

———. *Leviticus: A Book of Ritual and Ethics*. Continental Commentaries. Minneapolis: Fortress, 2004.

Miller, David M. "Reading Law as Prophecy: Torah Ethics in Acts." In *Torah Ethics and Early Christian Identity*, edited by Susan J. Wendel and David M. Miller, 75–91. Grand Rapids: Eerdmans, 2016.

Minatrea, Milfred. *Shaped by God's Heart: The Passion and Practices of Missional Churches*. San Francisco: Jossey-Bass, 2004.

Minear, Paul S. *Images of the Church in the New Testament*. Philadelphia: Westminster, 1960.

Moltmann, Jürgen. *The Church in the Power of the Spirit: A Contribution to Messianic Ecclesiology*. New York: Harper & Row, 1977.

Morris, Leon. *The Gospel According to John*. Grand Rapids: Eerdmans, 1995.

Mosis, R. "Ex.19,5b–6a: Syntaktische Aufbau Und Lexikalische Semantik." *Biblische Zeitschrift NS* 22 (1978) 1–25.

Mowery, Robert L. "Lord, God, and Father: Theological Language in Luke-Acts." *Society of Biblical Literature Seminar Papers* 34 (1995) 82–101.

Muilenburg, James. "Abraham and the Nations: Blessing and World History." *Interpretation* 19 (1965) 387–98.

———. "Holiness." In *The Interpreter's Dictionary of the Bible*, edited by Katharine Doob Sakenfeld, 2:616–25. New York: Abingdon, 1962.

Mullins, Michael. *The Acts of the Apostles*. Blackrock, Dublin: Columba, 2013.

Munck, Johannes. *Paul and the Salvation of Mankind*. Translated by Frank Clarke. Richmond, VA: John Knox, 1959.

Newbigin, Lesslie. *The Gospel in a Pluralist Society*. Grand Rapids: Eerdmans, 1989.

———. *The Open Secret: An Introduction to the Theology of Mission*. Grand Rapids: Eerdmans, 1995.

———. *The Other Side of 1984: Questions for the Churches*. Geneva: World Council of Churches, 1984.

Nikolajsen, Jeppe Bach. "Missional Church: A Historical and Theological Analysis of an Ecclesiological Tradition." *International Review of Mission* 102 (2013) 249–61.

Niringiye, D. Zac. "To Proclaim the Good News of the Kingdom." In *Mission in the Twenty-First Century: Exploring the Five Marks of Global Mission*, edited by Andrew F. Walls and Cathy Ross, 11–24. Maryknoll, NY: Orbis, 2008.

Nissen, Johannes. *New Testament and Mission: Historical and Hermeneutical Perspectives*. 3rd ed. Frankfurt am Main, Germany: Peter Lang GmbH, 2004.

Nolland, John. *The Gospel of Matthew*. Grand Rapids; Bletchley, UK: Eerdmans; Paternoster, 2005.

Noth, Martin. *Exodus: A Commentary*. London: SCM, 1962.

Ogilvie, Lloyd John. *Acts*. Waco, TX: Word, 1983.

Okoye, James. *Israel and the Nations: A Mission Theology of the Old Testament*. Maryknoll, NY: Orbis, 2006.

Olson, Dennis T. *Numbers*. Louisville, KY: John Knox, 1996.

Osborne, Grant R. *Matthew*. Grand Rapids: Zondervan, 2010.

Oswalt, John N. *The Book of Isaiah, Chapters 1–39*. Grand Rapids: Eerdmans, 1986.

———. *The Book of Isaiah, Chapters 40–66*. Grand Rapids: Eerdmans, 1998.

———. *Called to be Holy*. Nappanee, IN: Evangel, 1999.

———. "The Mission of Israel to the Nations." In *Through No Fault of Their Own: The Fate of Those Who Have Never Heard*, edited by William V. Crockett and James G. Sigountos, 85–95. Grand Rapids: Baker, 1991.

Otto, Rudolf. *The Idea of the Holy: An Inquiry into the Non-Rational Factor in the Idea of the Divine and Its Relation to the Rational*. New York: Oxford University Press, 1950.

Pachuau, Lalsangkima. "Gospel and Culture." Lecture for Biblical Theology of Mission Course, Asbury Theological Seminary, Wilmore, Kentucky, March 2015.

———. "*Missio Dei*." In *Dictionary of Mission Theology: Evangelical Foundations*, edited by John Corrie et al., 232–34. Nottingham; Downers Grove, IL: InterVarsity, 2007.

Padilla, C. R. "Holistic Mission." In *Dictionary of Mission Theology: Evangelical Foundations*, edited by John Corrie et al., 157–62. Nottingham; Downers Grove, IL: InterVarsity, 2007.

Park, Joon-Sik. "Hospitality as Context for Evangelism." *Missiology* 30 (2002) 385–95.

Patterson, Richard Duane. "The Widow, the Orphan, and the Poor in the Old Testament and Extra-Biblical Literature." *Bibliotheca sacra* 130 (1973) 223–34.

Paul VI. *Decree on the Mission Activity of the Church: Ad Gentes*. Boston: Daughters of St. Paul, 1965.

Perrin, Norman. *Rediscovering the Teaching of Jesus*. New York: Harper & Row, 1967.

Peterson, David G. *The Acts of the Apostles*. Grand Rapids; Nottingham: Eerdmans; Apollos, 2009.

Peterson, David L. "Prophet, Prophecy." In *The New Interpreter's Dictionary of the Bible*, edited by Katharine Doob Sakenfeld, 4:622–48. Nashville: Abingdon, 2009.

Pettegrew, Larry Dean. *The New Covenant Ministry of the Holy Spirit*. Grand Rapids: Kregel, 2001.

Polhill, John B. *Acts*. Nashville: Broadman, 1992.

Purkiser, W. T. *Exploring Christian Holiness*. Vol. 1. *The Biblical Foundations*. Kansas City, MO: Beacon Hill Press of Kansas City, 1983

Rapske, Brian. "Opposition to the Plan of God and Persecution." In *Witness to the Gospel: The Theology of Acts*, edited by I. Howard Marshall and David Peterson, 235–56. Grand Rapids; Cambridge: Eerdmans, 1998.

Redford, Shawn B. *Missiological Hermeneutics: Biblical Interpretation for the Global Church*. Eugene, OR: Pickwick, 2012.

Rendtorff, Rolf. *The Covenant Formula: An Exegetical and Theological Investigation*. Edinburgh: T. & T. Clark, 1998.

Rightmire, R. David. "Apostle." In *Evangelical Dictionary of Biblical Theology*, edited by Walter A. Elwell, 33–35. Grand Rapids: Baker, 1996.

Rodriguez, Angel Manuel. "Sanctuary Theology in the Book of Exodus." *Andrews University Seminary Studies* 24 (1986) 127–45.

Rooke, Deborah W. "Priests and Priesthood." In *The Oxford encyclopedia of the Bible and theology*, edited by Samuel E. Balentine, 2:191–201. Oxford: Oxford University Press, 2015.

Rosner, Brain S. "The Process of the Word." In *Witness to the Gospel: The Theology of Acts*, edited by I. Howard Marshall and David Peterson, 215–33. Grand Rapids; Cambridge: Eerdmans, 1998.

Rouse, Richard W., and Craig Van Gelder. *A Field Guide for the Missional Congregation: Embarking on a Journey of Transformation*. Minneapolis: Augsburg Fortress, 2008.

Routledge, Robin. *Old Testament Theology: A Thematic Approach*. Westmont, IL: InterVarsity, 2013.

Rowley, Harold H. *The Biblical Doctrine of Election*. Louisa Curtis Lectures: 1948, London: Lutterworth, 1950.

———. "Living Issues in Biblical Scholarship: The Antiquity of Israelite Monotheism." *The Expository Times* 61 (1950) 333–38.

Roxburgh, Alan J., and Fred Romanuk. *The Missional Leader: Equipping Your Church to Reach a Changing World*. San Francisco: Jossey-Bass, 2006.

Ryken, Philip Graham. *Exodus: Saved for God's Glory*. Wheaton, IL: Crossway, 2005.

Sarna, Nahum M. *Exploring Exodus: The Origins of Biblical Israel*. New York: Schocken, 1996.

Schillebeeckx, Edward. *Jesus: An Experiment in Christology*. London: Bloomsbury, 2014.

Schmitt, John. J. "Prophecy (Preexilic Hebrew)." In *The Anchor Bible Dictionary*, edited by David Noel Freedman, 5:482–89. New York: Doubleday, 1992.

Schnabel, Eckhard J. *Early Christian Mission*. Vol. 1. *Jesus and the Twelve*. Downers Grove, IL; Leicester, England: InterVarsity; Apollos, 2004

Schultz, Hermann. *Old Testament Theology: The Religion of Revelation in Its Pre-Christian Stage of Development*. Translated by J. A. Paterson Vol. 2. Edinburgh: T. & T. Clark, 1909.

Seccombe, David. "The New People of God." In *Witness to the Gospel: The Theology of Acts*, edited by I. Howard Marshall and David Peterson, 349–72. Grand Rapids; Cambridge: Eerdmans, 1998.

Segal, Alan F. "Matthew's Jewish Voice." In *Social History of the Matthean Community: Cross-Disciplinary Approaches*, edited by David L. Balch, 3–37. Minneapolis: Fortress, 1991.

Selman, M. J. "Law." In *Dictionary of the Old Testament: Pentateuch*, edited by T. Desmond Alexander and David W. Baker, 497–515. Downers Grove, IL: InterVarsity, 2003.

Senior, Donald. *Jesus: A Gospel Portrait*. Dayton, OH: Pflaum, 1975.

Senior, Donald, and Carroll Stuhlmueller. *The Biblical Foundations for Mission*. Maryknoll, NY: Orbis, 1983.

Shaull, Richard. "Toward the Conversion of the Church." *Theology Today* 3 (1947) 502–11.

Shelton, James B. "Epistemology and Authority in the Acts of the Apostles: An Analysis and Test Case Study of Acts 15:1–29." *Spirit and Church* 2 (2000) 231–47.

Shenk, Wilbert R. "Recasting Theology of Mission: Impulses from the Non-Western World." In *Landmark Essays in Mission and World Christianity*, edited by Robert L. Gallagher and Paul Hertig, 117–32. Maryknoll, NY: Orbis, 2009.

Shoemaker, Samuel M. *The Conversion of the Church*. New York: Fleming H. Revell, 1932.

Shore, Mary Hinkle. "Preaching Mission: Call and Promise in Matthew 28:16–20." *Word and World* 26 (2006) 322–28.

Siker, Judy Yates. "Holiness." In *The Oxford Encyclopedia of the Bible and Theology*, edited by Samuel E. Balentine, 1, 477–80. New York: Oxford University Press, 2015.

Smith, Gary V. *Isaiah 40–66: An Exegetical and Theological Exposition of Holy Scripture*. Nashville: B&H Academic, 2009.

Smith, Robert H. *Matthew*. Minneapolis: Augsburg, 1989.

Snaith, Norman H. *The Distinctive Ideas of the Old Testament*. London: Epworth, 1944.

Snodgrass, Klyne R. "Matthew and the Law." In *Treasures New and Old: Recent Contributions to Matthean Studies*, edited by David R. Bauer and Mark A. Powell, 99–127. Atlanta: Scholars, 1996.

Snyder, Howard A. "Mission in the Context of Covenant." Paper presented at a missiology seminar of E Stanley Jones School of World Mission & Evangelism, Asbury Theological Seminary, Wilmore, Kentucky, December 12, 2018.

———. *Radical Renewal: The Problem of Wineskins Today*. Houston, Texas: Touch, 1996.

———. *Yes in Christ: Wesleyan Reflections on Gospel, Mission and Culture*. Toronto: Clements Academic, 2010.

Snyder, Howard A., and Joel Scandrett. *Salvation Means Creation Healed: The Ecology of Sin and Grace*. Eugene, OR: Cascade, 2011.

Soares-Prabhu, George M. "The Church as Mission: A Reflection on Mt. 5:13–16." *Jeevadhara* 34 (1994) 271–81.

———. "The Church as Mission." In *The Dharma of Jesus*, edited by Francis X. D'Sa, 259–67. Maryknoll, NY: Orbis, 2003.

Soulen, Richard N. *Handbook of Biblical Criticism*. 2nd ed. Atlanta: John Knox, 1981.

Stein, Robert H. *Luke*. Nashville: Broadman, 1992.

———. *Mark*. Grand Rapids: Baker Academic, 2008.

Stephen, Neill. *A History of Christian Missions*. 2nd ed. London: Penguin, 1986.

Stob, Henry. "Lo, I Am with You Always." *Reformed Journal* 3 (1953) 15–16.

Stott, John R. W. *The Spirit, the Church, and the World: The Message of Acts*. Downers Grove, IL: InterVarsity, 1990.

Strauss, Mark L. *Mark*. Grand Rapids: Zondervan, 2014.

Strong, David K. "The Jerusalem Council: Some Implications for Contextualization." In *Mission in Acts: Ancient Narratives in Contemporary Context*, edited by Robert L. Gallagher and Paul Hertig, 196–208. Maryknoll, NY: Orbis, 2004.

Strong, David K., and Cynthia A. Strong. "The Globalizing Hermeneutic of the Jerusalem Council." In *Globalizing Theology: Belief and Practice in an Era of World Christianity*, edited by Craig Ott and Harold A. Netland, 127–39. Grand Rapids: Baker Academic, 2006.

Stuart, Douglas. *Exodus*. Nashville: Broadman & Holman, 2006.

Stubbs, David L. *Numbers*. London: SCM, 2009.

Talbert, Charles H. *Matthew*. Grand Rapids: Baker Academic, 2010.

———. *Reading Acts: A Literary and Theological Commentary on the Acts of the Apostles*. New York: Crossroad, 1997.

Tennent, Timothy C. *Invitation to World Missions: A Trinitarian Missiology for the Twenty-First Century*. Grand Rapids: Kregel, 2010.

Terrien, Samuel. *The Elusive Presence*. San Francisco: Harper & Row, 1978.

Thompson, Alan J. *The Acts of the Risen Lord Jesus: Luke's Account of God's Unfolding Plan*. Nottingham; Downers Grove, IL: Apollos; InterVarsity, 2011.

Thompson, J. A. *1, 2 Chronicles*. Nashville: Broadman & Holman, 1994.

Thompson, Richard P. *Acts: A Commentary in the Wesleyan Tradition*. Kansas City, MO: Beacon Hill Press of Kansas City, 2015.

———. "Gathered at the Table: Holiness and Ecclesiology in the Gospel of Luke." In *Holiness and Ecclesiology in the New Testament*, edited by Kent E. Brower and Andy Johnson, 76–94. Grand Rapids: Eerdmans, 2007.

Tizon, Al. *Transformation After Lausanne: Radical Evangelical Mission in Global-Local Perspective*. Eugene, OR: Wipf & Stock, 2008.

Towner, Philip H. "Mission Practice and Theology under Construction (Acts 18–20)." In *Witness to the Gospel: The Theology of Acts*, edited by I. Howard Marshall and David Peterson, 417–36. Grand Rapids; Cambridge: Eerdmans, 1998.

Trites, Allison A., and William J. Larkin, Jr. *The Gospel of Luke and Acts*. Carol Stream, IL: Tyndale, 2005.

Tuell, Steven S. *First and Second Chronicles*. Louisville, KY: John Knox, 2001.

Turner, David L. *Matthew*. Grand Rapids: Baker Academic, 2007.

Twelftree, Graham H. *People of the Spirit: Exploring Luke's View of the Church*. Grand Rapids: Baker Academic, 2009.

Van Engen, Charles E. "The Glocal Church: Locality and Catholicity in a Globalizing World." In *Globalizing Theology: Belief and Practice in an Era of World Christianity*, edited by Craig Ott and Harold A. Netland, 157–79. Grand Rapids: Baker Academic, 2006.

———. *God's Missionary People: Rethinking the Purpose of the Local Church*. Grand Rapids: Baker, 1991.

———. "Peter's Conversion." In *Mission in Acts: Ancient Narratives in Contemporary Context*, edited by Robert L. Gallagher and Paul Hertig, 133–43. Maryknoll, NY: Orbis, 2004.

———. "The Relation of Bible and Mission." In *The Good News of the Kingdom: Mission Theology for the Third Millennium*, edited by Charles E. Van Engen et al., 27–36. Maryknoll, NY: Orbis, 1993.

Van Gelder, Craig. *The Ministry of the Missional Church: A Community Led by the Spirit*. Grand Rapids: Baker, 2007.

Van Gelder, Craig, and Dwight J. Zscheile. *The Missional Church in Perspective: Mapping Trends and Shaping the Conversation*. Grand Rapids: Baker Academic, 2011.

VanderKam, James C. "Covenant and Pentecost." *Calvin Theological Journal* 37 (2002) 239–54.

Vanhoye, Albert. *Old Testament Priests and the New Priest: According to the New Testament*. Translated by J. Bernard Orchard, OSB. Petersham, MA: St. Bede's, 1986.

Vaux, Roland de. *Ancient Israel: Its Life and Institutions*. New York: McGraw-Hill, 1961.

Verkuyl, Johannes. *Contemporary Missiology: An Introduction*. Grand Rapids: Eerdmans, 1978.

Vicedom, Georg F. *The Mission of God: An Introduction to a Theology of Mission*. Saint Louis: Concordia, 1965.

Vogels, Walter. *God's Universal Covenant: A Biblical Study*. 2nd ed. Ottawa, ON: University of Ottawa Press, 1986.

von Rad, Gerhard. *Old Testament Theology*. Vol. 1. New York: Harper and Row, 1962.

Wagner, C. Peter. *Acts of the Holy Spirit*. Ventura, California: Regal, 2000.

Walls, Andrew F. *The Missionary Movement in Christian History: Studies in the Transmission of Faith*. Maryknoll, NY; Edinburgh: Orbis; T. & T. Clark, 1996.

Waltke, Bruce K. "The Kingdom of God in the Old Testament: Definitions and Story." In *The Kingdom of God*, edited by Christopher W. Morgan and Robert A. Peterson, 49–71. Wheaton, IL: Crossway, 2012.

Watts, James W. "The Legal Characterization of God in the Pentateuch." *Hebrew Union College Annual* 67 (1996) 1–14.

———. "The Phenomenon of Conditionality within Unconditional Covenant." In *Israel's Apostasy and Restoration: Essays in Honor of Roland K. Harrison*, edited by Avraham Gileadi, 123–39. Grand Rapids: Baker, 1988.

Wells, Jo Bailey. *God's Holy People: A Theme in Biblical Theology*. Sheffield: Sheffield Academic, 2000.

Whitacre, Rodney A. *John*. Downers Grove, IL: InterVarsity, 1999.

Wikenhauser, A. *Die Apostelgeschichte Und Ihr Geshictswert*. Münster, Germany: Aschendorff, 1921. Quoted in Harry R. Boer, *Pentecost and Missions* (Grand Rapids: Eerdmans, 1961), 119.

Wilkins, Michael J. *Matthew*. Grand Rapids: Zondervan, 2004.

Willimon, William H. *Acts*. Atlanta: John Knox, 1988.

Wilson, S. G. *Luke and the Law*. Cambridge: Cambridge University Press, 1983.

Witherington, Ben, III. *Matthew*. Macon, GA: Smyth & Helwys, 2006.

———. *New Testament History: A Narrative Account*. Grand Rapids: Baker Academic, 2003.

Wright, Christopher J. H. *God's People in God's Land: Family, Land, and Property in the Old Testament*. Carlisle, England: Paternoster, 1997.

———. *Knowing Jesus through the Old Testament*. Downers Grove, IL: InterVasity, 2014.

———. *The Mission of God: Unlocking the Bible's Grand Narrative.* Downers Grove, IL: IVP Academic, 2006.

———. *The Mission of God's People: A Biblical Theology of the Church's Mission.* Grand Rapids: Zondervan, 2010.

———. *Old Testament Ethics for the People of God.* Downers Grove, IL: InterVarsity, 2004.

Wright, G. Ernest. *The Old Testament Against Its Environment.* London: SCM, 1950.

Wright, N. T. *Jesus and the Victory of God.* London: SPCK, 1996.

———. *Resurrection of the Son of God.* Minneapolis: Fortress, 2003.

———. *Simply Good News: Why the Gospel is News and What Makes it Good.* New York: HarperOne, 2015.

———. *Surprised by Hope: Rethinking Heaven, the Resurrection, and the Mission of the Church.* New York: HarperOne, 2008.

Wyckoff, John W. *Pneuma and Logos: The Role of the Spirit in Biblical Hermeneutics.* Eugene, OR: Wipf & Stock, 2010.

Yao, Santos. "Table Fellowship in the New Testament: Towards a Missionary Praxis for Evangelizing the Nations." PhD diss., Fuller Theological Seminary, 1996.

Scripture Index

Genesis

1–11	17, 17n71
1–3	17
2:15	17n67
3:8	32n60
6–8	17
9	17
9:8–17	16, 18, 47n129
9:9–10	16
9:17	16
10	17
11	17
12–50	62
12	17, 17n71
12:1–3	17, 18, 22, 48
12:3	17, 18, 26
17:7–8	101n62
17:9–14	187
22:18	26

Exodus

2:24	22
3	37
3:6	23
3:15–17	47
5:23	47
6:4	47
6:7	101n62
6:8	47
15:11	38
15:13	38
18:8–11	23n15
19	50
19:3–6	50
19:4–6a	25
19:4	24, 45n119, 49, 63
19:4b	51
19:5–6	26, 28, 29, 49
19:5–6a	26
19:5	29, 45n119, 46, 92
19:5a	45, 46
19:6	29
19:9	63
19:22	32n64
23:9–18	68n208
24:3–8	30
24:7	68n208
25:8	65
29:20	30
29:42–43	65
32–34	48, 68, 70
32	68
33	64, 68, 69
33:4	70
33:5	68
33:7–9	70
33:15–16	69
34	68, 69
34:1–27	70
34:10–28	48
39:45	40
40:36–37	66

Leviticus

8:23–24	30
10:3	32n64
11	40
11:44–45	40n99
19	58, 59

Leviticus *(continued)*

19:1–2	58
19:2	40n99
19:2b	39, 42
19:18	116n123
20:24b–26	169
20:26	40n99
21:8	40n99
25:23	60
26:11–12	66, 101n62

Number

10	71
10:11–36	71
11:1—21:35	72n223
11	71, 72
11:1	71
11:2	71
11:4–6	71
11:18–23	71
11:31–32	71
11:33–35	71
25	72n223

Deuteronomy

4:6–8	55
6:4	130
6:5	46
7:6	27n30
10:14	60
10:14–15	27n30
10:17–19	116n123
14:2	27n30
15:4	161
26:18	27n30

Joshua

1:9	46
6:17–19	73
7	73
7:10–11	73
8:30–35	73

Judge

1:1—2:5	73
2:10	73
2:11–12	73
3:1–6	34n68
3:1–4	74
21:25b	74

1 Samuel

8:7	75
12:17	75
12:24	75

1 Kings

8:10-11	67n205

2 Chronicles

15:8–15	149

Psalms

10:11	68n209
24:1	60
29:3	130
34:23	130
86:15	130
94:6–7	68n209
112:7	46
135:4	27n30

Isaiah

1:2–15	82
1:2–20	82
1:16–17	82
1:21–31	82
1:25	82
7–39	83
9:1	121n144
9:8–21	34n68
26:3	46
40-66	83
40–55	91n13
42:1–4	89n8, 90

43	101, 101n63, 102
43:10	101, 102
43:12	101, 102
44:8	102
47:10	68n209
49:1–6	89n8, 90n8
49:5	90
49:6	90
50:4–9	89n8
52:13—53:12	89n8
53	91
61:1–3	91n13
61:1–2	91, 91n13

Jermiah

31:31–34	101, 149, 150n10
31:33	101, 101n62

Ezekiel

9:9	68n209
10	42n111
36:24–28	149
36:26–27	150n10
37:14	150n10
42:13	32n64
43:19	32n64

Daniel

7:14	128n175

Hosea

4:1–3	82
6:6	119n136

Amos

4:6–11	76
9	194
9:11–12	196

Jonah

4	174

Malachi

3:17	27

Matthew

1–2	109
1:23	109
3:3	104n70
3:14–15	104
3:19	104n70
4:15	121, 121n144
4:17–22	98
4:18–22	124
4:18	120
4:21	120
5	207
5:11–12	120n140
5:13–16	103, 105, 106
5:16	106
5:17–20	107
5:21–48	112, 112n114
5:44–45a	108n92
5:44	137
8:5–13	121, 122
8:10	96, 121
8:11–12	96, 122, 123
9:10	117n128
9:13	119n136
10:5–6	94, 95
11:19	117, 117n128
11:20–24	104n75, 108n92
12:1–14	113
12:7	119n136
12:15–21	90
13:44–46	120n140
14:22–32	133
15:1–20	119n134
15:21–28	121
15:24	94, 95
15:28	122
16:5–12	147
16:24	120n140
18:20	133, 154
19:28	98
22:35–40	116n123, 137
23:1–39	108n92
23:13–36	119

Matthew (continued)

23:23	119
26:28	140n207, 140n210
26:69–75	125n163, 156n31
28	140
28:16–20	91, 120
28:17	133
28:18	128, 128n175
28:18–20	128, 129, 139
28:19	128
28:19–20	133
28:20	108, 133, 134, 147, 154, 177, 177n99

Mark

1:14–20	98
1:15	92, 104n75
2:15–17	117n128
3:1–6	113, 119
3:14	110
7:1–23	119
7:24–30	121, 122
7:29–30	122
9:33–37	147
10:45	140n207
12:28–34	101n62, 116n123
14:24	140n207
14:66–72	126n169, 156n31
15:11–15	108n92
16:7	126n169

Luke

3:9	104n70
4:1	101n61
4:16–21	91
7:31–35	117n128
9:46–48	147
10:13–14	108n92
12:12	134
13:10–17	113
13:22–30	122, 123
13:29	123n156
15:10–11	124
15:27–28	124
22:19	137
22:30	98
22:37	91
22:42	137
23:34	137
24	101, 101n63, 126, 127
24:7	101n61
24:10–11	126
24:13–35	125, 126
24:21	125n163, 126
24:27	126
24:31	126
24:33–35	126
24:44–48	91
24:48	101, 128
24:49	154
24:54–62	156n31
25:25	126

John

1:1	109, 130
1:14	109
1:18	110, 130
3:16	140n207, 141
4:34	91
5:30	91
5:38	91
6:38–39	91
7:21–24	113
9:1–34	113
10:30	110
13:34–35	111, 138
14:9	110
14:15–16	147
14:16–17	134
14:26	219
15:12–14	138n203
15:17	138n203
15:26	154
16:7–15	154
16:12–15	194
17:1	111
18:15–27	156n31
19:1–16	108n92
20	129, 130

20:21	91, 128	4	157, 158, 159, 160, 166
20:25	128, 129		
20:28	129	4:1–22	157
21	125, 125n163, 126, 127	4:18	157
		4:19–20	157
21:1–19	125	4:23–31	155, 157, 163
21:3	125	4:24	157
21:4–6	125	4:24–28	158
21:15–17	126	4:29	158
21:19	126	4:29–30	158
		4:31	158
		4:32–37	160

Acts

		4:33	163
1	101n63	4:34	161
1–5	148	4:36–37	165
1:1–11	148	5:1–2	164
1:4	155	5:1–1	164
1:8	101, 127, 128, 134, 151, 152, 154, 155, 155n25, 191	5:3	164
		5:4	164
		5:9	164
		5:11	165
1:14	155	6:6	163n51
1:16	159	8:15	163n51
2–5	155, 160, 163, 164, 173	9–11	167
		9:1–19	167
2	101, 150, 157, 158, 159, 160, 162, 166	9:32—11:18	173
		10	167, 168, 174, 176, 177
2:1–13	155	10–11	148, 167, 168, 172, 173, 175, 176, 179, 181, 193, 194, 197, 200
2:1–4	155, 163		
2:4–6	151, 152, 154		
2:4	152, 170n71		
2:5–6	152	10:1–7	168
2:13	156	10:4	168
2:14–36	128, 131	10:11–13	168
2:14	157	10:13	168n63
2:23	156	10:16	169
2:32–36	131	10:17–18	169
2:36	131	10:19–21	169
2:38–39	155n25	10:19	168n63
2:38	156	10:23	169
2:42	163	10:28	168n65, 169, 170n72
2:43	163		
2:44–45	160	10:33	170n72
2:46	162, 163	10:34	169, 170n72
2:47	163, 164	10:34–43	170
		10:44	170
		10:45	170

Acts *(continued)*

10:46	163n51, 170, 170n71
11–14	177
11	167, 168, 171, 172
11:1–18	167, 179n107
11:1–3	171
11:11	174
11:15–17	177n99
11:17	170n71
11:18	163n51, 172, 174
11:20	177
11:21	177
11:22–26	175
11:26	178
13	167, 178
13:1–3	178
13:2–3	163n51
15	148, 174n92, 176, 177, 179, 179n107, 181, 181n115, 184, 186n145, 189, 190, 191, 192, 193, 197, 200
15:1	179, 180, 180n113, 180n115, 181, 181n115, 182, 183
15:3	175n92
15:5	179, 180, 180n113, 180n115, 181n115, 182, 195
15:7	194
15:7–11	185
15:7–9	193
15:8	193
15:9	193
15:10	193
15:11	185, 188, 193
15:12	193, 194
15:15–18	194
15:15	180, 196
15:19–21	184
15:19	184, 194
15:20–21	185
15:20	185, 185n138
15:22–30	184
15:22	190
15:25	190
15:29	185n138
15:30	190
15:32	190
15:41	190
16–20	190
16:5	190
20:36	163n51
21:17–26	188
21:20	163n51, 188
21:25	185n138

Romans

2:28–29	150n11
7:6	150n11
15:18–19	190

1 Corinthians

2:6–16	219
3:17	220
10:25–27	185n141

2 Corinthians

3	150n11

Galatians

2	181, 181n115
2:1–10	181
3:1—4:7	150n11

Ephesians

1:20–23	129n177

Philippians

2:6–11	129n177
3:3	150n11

Colossians

1:15–20　　　129n177
2:11　　　150n11

1 Thessalonians

4:8　　　150n11

1 Peter

3:18–22　　　129n177

Revelation

21:12–14　　　98

www.ingramcontent.com/pod-product-compliance
Lightning Source LLC
Chambersburg PA
CBHW050848230426
43667CB00012B/2197